SLAVERY AND FREEDOM

SLAVERY

and FREEDOM

by Nicolai Berdyaev

Translated from the Russian by R. M. French

CHARLES SCRIBNER'S SONS ◆ New York

TRANSLATOR'S NOTE

I feel that a translation should not need notes, but nevertheless there are three words in this book to which I must draw attention.

GENIALITY, *on page 57*. From the Russian word for genius there is formed an adjective 'genialny' and then an abstract noun 'genialnost'. The corresponding sequence in English would be genius, genial and geniality. But the last two have acquired a quite different meaning. In spite of this I can think of nothing better than to put 'geniality' for 'genialnost', but in italics as some indication that it is not used in its ordinary sense.

NARODNITCHESTVO, *(pages 97, 168, 169)* means the movement in 19th century Russian life which was founded upon a sense of obligation to devote oneself to the general interests of the common folk—the 'narod'. Berdyaev's book '*The Origin of Russian Communism*' *(page 64 ff.)* contains an extended account of it. The *Narodnik* is a man who believed in narodnitchestvo and practised it. I see that narodnik has appeared in English as 'populist'. But what is a populist?

SOBORNOST, *(pages 68, 201)* is the despair of all translators from Russian. 'Altogetherness' would come near to its meaning. It is the dynamic life of the collective body.

♦ Contents

IN PLACE OF AN INTRODUCTION: CONCERNING INCONSISTENCIES IN MY THOUGHT

After I had begun to write this book I looked back over the past and became aware of the necessity of making clear, both to myself and to other people, the road along which my mind and spirit have travelled; and of understanding the inconsistency which has made its appearance in my thought in the course of time.

The subject of the book is slavery and liberation, and there are many passages in which it has a bearing upon social philosophy; but I have embodied in it my whole way of looking at life from a philosophical point of view; it has as its basis the philosophy of personalism. It is the outcome of a long philosophical journey in search of truth, of a long struggle on behalf of a transvaluation of values.

As a philosopher I have not only wished to gain knowledge of the world; in my case the desire to know the world has always been accompanied by the desire to alter it. Not only in thought but in feeling also, I have always denied that the things which the world presents to us are stable and final reality.

To what extent is the thought of this book true to my whole thought as expressed in my earlier writings? In what sense can there be development in the thought of a thinker? And is this development a continuous process or are there interruptions in it—does it move forward through crises and self-contradictions? In what sense does development exist in my thought and in what way have the changes in it come about?

There are philosophers who achieve a system from the outset and remain faithful to it all their lives. There are philosophers who in their philosophy shew signs of spiritual struggle, and in their thought various stages can be discovered. In stormy periods of history, times of spiritual break-up, the philosopher who does not remain an armchair philosopher, a bookish person, cannot refrain from taking part in the spiritual conflict.

I was never a philosopher of the academic type and it has never been my wish that philosophy should be abstract and remote from life. Although I have always read a great deal, books have not been the source of my thought. Indeed I never could understand a book of any sort otherwise than by bringing it into connection with the experience through which I myself was living. What is more, I think that authentic philosophy has always been a conflict. The philosophies of Plato, Plotinus, Descartes, Spinoza, Kant, Fichte, Hegel, were of that kind. My thought has always belonged to the existential type of philosophy. The inconsistencies and contradictions which are to be found in my thought are expressions of spiritual conflict, of contradictions which lie at the very heart of existence itself, and are not to be disguised by a façade of logical unity. True integrality of thought, which is bound up with integrality of personality, is an existential unity, not a logical. Existentiality indeed is a controversial conception. Personality is changelessness in change. That is one of the essential definitions of personality. Changes arise in one and the same subject. If one subject is replaced by another, there is then no change in the proper sense of the word.

Change destroys personality when it is transformed into treason. The philosopher is guilty of treason if the basic themes of his philosophical thinking are altered, the fundamental *motifs* of his thought, the groundwork of his scale of values. One can change one's view about where and how freedom of the spirit is realized. But if love of freedom is replaced by love of servitude and violence, then treason is the result. The change in one's views may be actual, but it may also be in appearance only as the result of seeing them in a false perspective. I think that man is after all an inconsistent and polarized being. The thought of a philosopher also is inconsistent and polarized, if it is not drawn entirely from life and unless it preserves its connection with life, which is its primary concern. Philosophical thought is a complex product of the mind, and even in the most logical and highly finished systems of philosophy it may be discovered that inconsistent elements have been included. Nor is this a bad thing, it is all to the good. A final monism in thought is not to be realized, and if it were realized, it would be a bad thing. I feel little confidence that systems of philosophy are either possible or to be desired. But even if a system of philosophy has been brought into actual being, it is never final and rounded off. The fundamental inconsistency in Hegel's philosophy lay in the fact that in it the dynamic and dialectic of thought take the form of a completed system, that is to say, it would seem to put an end to dialectic development.

The end of the dynamic of the spirit and its ever newly arising contradictions can only be the end of the world. Until the world comes to an end contradictions cannot be abolished. For that reason thought inevitably depends upon an eschatological perspective. An eschatological perspective throws a reflected light upon thought and gives rise to contradiction and paradox within the life of the world.

So far as my own position is concerned, I should like to define the basic themes, the fundamental problem, and the scale of values in my whole life and thought. Only so can the inward connection of thought be understood, and fidelity to the unchanging in the midst of changes. The fundamental contradiction in my thinking about social life is bound up with the juxtaposition in me of two elements—an aristocratic interpretation of personality, freedom and creativeness, and a socialistic demand for the assertion of the dignity of every man, of even the most insignificant of men, and for a guarantee of his rights in life. This is the clash of a passionate love of the world above, of a love of the highest, with pity for this lower world, the world of suffering. This contradiction is age-long. I stand at the same time near to Nietzsche and to Leo Tolstoy. I value Karl Marx very highly but I also value J. de Maistre and K. Leontiev. I feel affinity with and love for J. Boehme, but I feel an affinity also with Kant. When a levelling tyranny offends against my understanding of the dignity of personality, my love of freedom and creativeness, I rebel against it and I am ready to express my revolt in the extremest form. But when the defenders of social inequality shamelessly defend their own privileges, when capitalism oppresses the labouring masses, and turns a man into a thing, then also I rebel. In both cases I reject the foundations of the contemporary world.

It is possible to make clear the inward springs of a complex philosophical general outlook upon life, only by turning to the philosopher's primary feeling about the world, to his elemental view of the world. At the base of philosophical knowledge lies concrete experience, it cannot be determined by an abstract series of conceptions, by discursive thought which is only an instrument. If I turn to my knowledge of myself, which is one of the principal sources of philosophical knowledge, I discover in myself something elemental and primitive: a reaction against world data; a refusal to accept any sort of objectivity such as the slavery of man; and the opposition of the freedom of the spirit to the compulsion of the world, to violence, and to compliancy. I speak of this not as of an autobiographical fact, but as a fact of philosophical knowledge, a fact which I have encountered on the path of philosophical experience.

Thus the inward motive forces of philosophy are determined elementally: the primacy of freedom over existence, of spirit over nature, subject over object, personality over the universal, creativeness over evolution, dualism over monism, love over law. The acknowledgement of the supremacy of personality involves metaphysical inequality, distinction, dissent from fusion, the affirmation of quality against the power of quantity. But this metaphysical qualitative inequality certainly does not involve social and class inequality. Freedom which has no knowledge of compassion, becomes demoniacal. Man ought not only to ascend but also to descend.

As the result of a long spiritual and intellectual journey I have arrived at a particularly keen awareness of the fact that every human personality, the personality of the least significant of men, bearing as it does within itself the image of the highest existence, cannot be a means to any end whatever. It has in itself an existential centre and has a right not only to life, a right which is denied by contemporary civilization, but also a right to possess the universal content of life. This is a truth of the Gospel, although it is not brought sufficiently into the open. Qualitatively distinct and unequal personalities are not only in a profound sense equal before God, but they are equal before society, to which no right belongs to discriminate among personalities on the basis of privilege, i.e. on the ground of differences in social position. The meaning of a social levelling in the direction of a classless structure of society ought to be based simply upon the evident personal inequality of people, upon qualititive differences, not of social position but of their own natures.

And so I arrive at anti-hierarchical personalism. Personality cannot be a part of any kind of hierarchical whole. It is a microcosm in a potential condition. Thus, in my consciousness two principles were united, two principles which are both in the world and in myself, and may be found in a state of antagonism and strife; the principle of personality and freedom and the principle of compassion, sympathy and justice. The principle of equality in itself has no independent significance; it is subordinate to freedom and the dignity of personality. I have never seen any difficulty in sacrificing the social traditions, prejudices and interests of the gentlefolk society from which I sprang. It was from freedom that I made my start upon my journey. Neither have I ever felt myself in the slightest degree bound by the artificial, crystallized and ossified ideas and feelings of the Russian intelligentsia. I did not feel that I belonged to that world nor indeed to any world. In addition to this I have felt repelled by the bourgeoisie, I have had no love for the state, and combined with this were anarchist tendencies, though of a particular sort. One should not start from love of the world; one must start from the antithesis between freedom of the spirit and the world; but to start from freedom of the spirit does not mean to start from vacuity, from nothing. There is a spiritual content of the world of ideas about which something must be said in order to understand the path of the philosopher; and first of all about the world of philosophical ideas.

It is impossible to understand the primary foundation of my philosophical outlook and especially the idea which occupies the central place for me, the idea of objectivization set over against existence and freedom, if one takes the point of view of Platonism or of the philosophy of Hegel and Schelling. Plato and Plotinus, Hegel and Schelling have had an enormous significance for Russian religious philosophy. But my sources were different. My thought is more easily understood by reference to Kant and Schopenhauer than to Hegel and Schelling, and in actual fact Kant and Schopenhauer were of great importance to me at the very outset of my journey. I am not a philosopher of the schools and I do not and I did not belong to any school. Schopenhauer was the first philosopher whom I took in deeply. I read philosophical books while still a boy. Although in my earlier years I stood near to Kantianism, yet I never accepted the philosophy of Kant or of Schopenhauer in any sense as a whole. I even contested Kant's position. But there are certain determining ideas which in one form or another have been present throughout the whole extent of my philosophical journey. I feel a special affinity with the dualism of Kant, with his distinction between the realm of freedom and the realm of nature, with his doctrine of freedom as of a character which is apprehended by the mind, with the Kantian doctrine of the will, with his view of the world of phenomena as distinct from the real world which he not very happily called 'the world of things in themselves'. I find myself close also to Schopenhauer's distinction of will and 'representation', to his doctrine of the objectivization of the will in the natural world, which creates an unreal world, and to Schopenhauer's irrationalism. The differences go further. Kant obscured the path of knowledge of the authentic world of existence as distinct from the world of phenomena, for the category of spirit is almost entirely lacking in his philosophy. Schopenhauer's anti-personalism is also alien and hostile to me. But what is entirely alien to me is the monism, the evolutionism and optimism of Fichte, Schelling and Hegel, their understanding of the objectivization of the spirit, of the universal ego, of reason in the world and the historical process, and especially Hegel's doctrine of the self-revelation of the spirit and its development towards freedom in the world process, of the emergence of God. Kant's dualism and Schopenhauer's pessimism are nearer to the truth. So much must be said about purely philosophical ideas.

It is perhaps still more important to understand the source to which I owe my first impulses in relation to the social reality around me and in forming my moral estimates of the surrounding world. In this respect, during the very early years of adolescence, while still almost a boy, I derived a great deal from Leo Tolstoy. I learned very much from him. My quite early conviction that falsehood and injustice lie at the very roots of civilization, that there is original sin in history, that the whole of the society around me is built up on falsehood and injustice, is due to Tolstoy. I was never an adept of Tolstoy's doctrine, nor did I love the followers of Tolstoy over much. But Tolstoy's revolt against the false standards of greatness and the false sanctities of history, against the falsity of all social position and the social relations of mankind, penetrated my very being. Even now after the long way I have travelled I recognize in myself these original appraisements of historical and social reality, this freedom from clinging social traditions, from the moral prejudices of well-meaning people, this revulsion from violence both of the right and of the left. I realize that this is a disposition to spiritual revolution in me which may give rise to various reactions to my environment.

Later on in my student years, in my relation to the social reality I came under the influence of Marx and my attitude to social problems became very concrete. I have never felt myself able to be a partisan of any 'orthodoxy' and I have always fought against 'orthodoxy'. I have never been an orthodox Marxist. I have never been a materialist and even in my Marxist period I was an idealist in philosophy. I tried to combine my idealism in philosophy with Marxism in social questions. I based my socialism upon an idealist foundation, although I acknowledged the truth of many propositions in the materialist interpretation of history. The low type of culture among the greater part of the revolutionary Marxists was a torment to me. I felt no kinship with that *milieu*. I felt this particularly acutely in the years of my exile in the north. There were two sides to my attitude to Marxism.

I could never accept Marxism in its totality. And in the disputes with Marxists of the more totalitarian sort which I carried on in Marxist circles in my youth I see at the present time a *motif* which is very much alive and very vigorous in our own day. I see this *motif* in the controversies which have centred around André Gide and his two books on the U.S.S.R. I remember very well the disputes that I had with the comrade of my youthful days in Marxist circles, A. V. Lunacharsky. I did not quarrel with him when he became people's Kommissar for Education, as I tried never to meet him. In all these disputes—and I was a bitter controversialist—I maintained the existence of truth and goodness as idealist values which are independent of the class struggle, of social conditions and the rest; and I did not acquiesce in the final subjection of philosophy and ethics to the revolutionary class struggle. I believed in the existence of truth and justice as determining my revolutionary attitude to social reality, and not as determined by it. Lunacharsky asserted that such a defence of disinterested truth, of the independence of the intellect and the right of personal judgment, contradicted Marxism, which subordinates the interpretation of truth and justice to the revolutionary class

[13]

struggle. Plekhanov also used to tell me that it was impossible to remain a Marxist while holding my independent idealistic philosophy.

Our contemporary *intellectuels* who appreciate the social truth of communism are faced by the same problem. Gide was refused the right to say the truth as he had seen it about Soviet Russia, because truth cannot reveal itself to the individual man and he has no right to insist upon his own truth. Truth is what promotes the revolutionary proletarian struggle and serves the cause of the triumph of the proletariat. A truth which is bound up with the most indisputable facts becomes a falsehood if it injures the cause of the victory of the proletarian revolution, while falsehood becomes a necessary dialectic moment of the proletarian struggle. I always thought and I continue to think, that truth does not serve anybody or anything; they serve it. One ought to take one's stand in defence of truth, say what is right even if this is detrimental and harmful to the conflict. Today the change of attitude towards truth has gone very far. Communists and fascists alike assert that only communities know the truth and that it reveals itself only in a collective conflict. Personality cannot know truth and cannot take its stand upon it against the community. The centre of consciousness is shifted. It is transferred to communities. I used to watch this at its very conception during the Marxist years of my youth. I rebelled against this side of Marxism in the name of personalism, although I continued to regard the social demands of Marxism as just.

In the spiritual struggle through which I passed in those years my contact with Ibsen and Nietzsche was of great importance. Here *motifs* of another kind were acting than those connected with Marx and Kant. At the beginning Ibsen had an even greater significance for me than Nietzsche. Even now I cannot read through Ibsen's plays without profound emotion. Many moral values of mine were much akin to Ibsen, to his sharp opposition of personality to the community. Still earlier I had seen in Dostoyevsky, whom I had loved from childhood, the depth of the problem of personality, and of personal destiny. I saw no consciousness of this problem in Marxism and in the attitude of the left Russian intelligentsia. I read Nietzsche when he had not yet become popular in Russian cultured circles. Nietzsche was akin to one of the poles of my nature, as Tolstoy was

[14]

akin to the other. There was a time when Nietzsche conquered Tolstoy and Marx in me, but that never happened completely and finally. Nietzsche's transvaluation of values, his revulsion from rationalism and moralism entered profoundly into my spiritual conflict, and became, so to speak, an underground active force. But in regard to the problem of truth, I was aware of the same clash with Nietzsche as with Marx. In any case my personalism was all the while increasing in force and definiteness and with it was bound up my relation to Christianity.

In human life spiritual reactions play an immense part. It is with difficulty that man applies himself as a whole at one and the same time. It is not within his power to bring the principles within him into a complete and harmonious unity, principles which may appear to be opposed to each other and mutually exclusive. For me this was always a clash between love and freedom, the clash of independence and the creative vocation of personality with the social process which crushes personality and regards it as a means to an end. In my case the first strong reaction against social conditions took place when at the very beginning of my life I rebelled against 'gentle' society and went over to the camp of the revolutionary intelligentsia. But I saw with grief that in that camp also there was no reverence for the dignity of personality, and the liberation of the people was too often associated with the enslavement of man and his conscience. At a very early stage I saw the results of this process. The revolutionaries had no love for freedom of the spirit; they denied the rights of human creativeness. I experienced an inward psychological and moral reaction against the first small revolution. It was a reaction not against the elements of political and social liberation which were included in that revolution, but against its mask of spirituality, and against its moral results for man which seemed to me to be unattractive. I knew this *milieu* fairly well. I recognized that criticism of the traditional spiritual type of the left revolutionary intelligentsia was my task. Moreover I felt a greater revulsion from the left radical intelligentsia than from the intelligentsia which was revolutionary in the proper sense and with which I had kept some personal links.

In the year 1907 I wrote an article in which I predicted the inevitable victory of the bolshevists in the revolutionary movement. At that time my deep penetration into Dostoyevsky's *Legend of the Grand Inquisitor* exerted an enormous influence in the spiritual conflict which was taking place in me. It might be said that taking my stand as a Christian I accepted the picture of Christ in the *Legend of the Grand Inquisitor*; I turned to Him, and in my Christianity I was opposed to everything which could be ascribed to the spirit of the *Grand Inquisitor*. But I saw this spirit of the *Grand Inquisitor* displayed both from the right and from the left, in authoritarian religion and statecraft as well as in authoritarian revolutionary socialism. The problem of man, the problem of freedom, the problem of creativeness came to be the fundamental problems of my philosophy. My book, *The Meaning of Creativeness,* was 'assault and battery' and in it my independent philosophical outlook upon life found its expression.

I must also note the importance of my meeting with the writings of Jakob Boehme. Something of him was grafted into me. In the main I stood outside the existing religious-philosophical and social-political camps. Inwardly I felt that the prevailing tendencies of the beginning of the twentieth century were alien to me. I went through a spiritual reaction against the political, literary and Orthodox circles of the time. There was no direction in which I could bring the whole of me completely to bear and I felt rather lonely. The *motif* of loneliness has always been basic with me. But owing to the activity and combativeness of my character, I took my part from time to time in a good deal that was going on; and this was torture to me for it led to disillusion.

I went through a stormy inward reaction also against the second, the great Russian revolution. I considered the revolution inevitable and just; but its spiritual aspect was uncongenial to me from the very beginning. Its ignoble aspect, its encroachment upon freedom of the spirit was a contradiction of my aristocratic interpretation of personality and my cult of spiritual freedom. My refusal to accept the Bolshevik revolution was not so much on social grounds as on spiritual. I expressed this too passionately and often unfairly. I saw all the while the same triumph of the *Grand Inquisitor*. At the same time I did not believe in the possibility of any sort of restoration and I certainly did not want it. I was banished from Soviet Russia simply and solely because of my reaction in defence of freedom of the spirit.

But in Western Europe I again passed through a psychological reaction and that a two-fold one—reaction against the Russian *émigrés* and reaction against the bourgeois capitalist society of Europe. Among the Russian *émigrés* I saw the same revulsion from freedom, the same denial of it as in communist Russia. This was explicable, but very much less justifiable than in the communist revolution. No revolutions ever have loved freedom; the mission of a revolution is something different from that. In revolutions new social strata are thrown up to the surface, strata which had not before been permitted any activity and which had been oppressed, and in the fight for their new position in society they cannot display a love of freedom: they cannot be over careful in their attitude to spiritual values. Less understandable and less justifiable was such a lack of love for freedom and spiritual creativeness in those who regard themselves as the cultured stratum of society and as guardians of spiritual culture. In Western Europe indeed I saw clearly to what an extent the anti-communist front is controlled by bourgeois capitalist interests. The circle of my thought on social philosophy was completely closed. I returned to the verity of the socialism which I had professed in my youth, but now on the ground of ideas acquired in the course of my life. I call this personalist socialism, and it is radically distinct from the prevailing metaphysical socialism which is based upon the supremacy of society over personality. Personalist socialism starts from the supremacy of personality over society. It is simply the social projection of personalism, in which my belief has grown ever more and more firm.

Ten years and more ago I finally got rid of the last traces of historical romanticism which is linked up with an æstheticizing attitude towards religion and politics, with the idealization of historical grandeur and power. This historical romanticism never went very deep in me, it was never originally mine. I felt once more the primary truth of Tolstoy's attitude to the false romanticism of historical values. The value of man, of human personality, is higher than the historical values of the mighty state and of nationality, of a flourishing civilization, etc., etc. Like Hertzen, like Leontiev among us, like Nietzsche, and like Léon Bloy in the West, I often feel the approach of the sway of the second-rate and common. The bourgeois system of life is not only a capitalist but also a socialist civilization. But the usual romantic argument about the sway of the second-rate appears to me now to be false. I have grasped the very heart of the truth that every objectivization of the spirit in the world is the realm of the second-rate. You cannot defend social injustice on the ground that social justice will be administered by second-rate people. This is Leontiev's argument. You cannot refuse to solve the problem of daily bread for the labouring masses on the ground that when this problem was not solved and while the masses were oppressed culture was very beautiful. Especially is this impossible for Christians. The idealization of the organic in history is just as repellent to me. Already in *The Meaning of Creativeness* I criticized the organic point of view. The idealization of the cultured *élite* also appears to me to be false. The self-content and self-exaltation of the cultured *élite* is egoism, and the fastidious isolation of the self is a lack of consciousness of one's vocation to service. I believe in a real aristocracy of personality, in the existence of men of genius and of great men who always recognize the duty of service, and feel the necessity not only to rise but also to descend. But I do not believe in the aristocracy of a group, in an aristocracy which is founded upon social assortment. There is nothing more repellent than contempt for the mass of the people among those who regard themselves as the *élite*. The *élite* may even show themselves 'colourless' in the metaphysical sense of the word and it is specially necessary to say this about the bourgeois *élite*. It is necessary to make clear that the Christian idea of the Kingdom of God and the Christian eschatological consciousness, have no connection with the idolizing of historical sanctities, such as the conservative tradition of authoritarianism, monarchy, nationalism, family property, as well as of revolutionary democratic socialist sanctities. It does not suffice to assert the truth of an apophatic negative theology. One must also assert the truth of an apophatic negative sociology. Kataphatic sociology—and still more if it is founded in religion—is a source of slavery to man.

This book is dedicated to the fight against the slavery of man. The philosophy of this book is deliberately personal. In it I write, about man, the world and God, only such things as I have seen and lived through. In it a concrete man philosophizes and not a world intelligence or a world spirit. To explain the intellectual path upon which I have moved it is necessary also to say that the world presents itself to me as eternally new. I apprehend it, as it were, in my primary intuition, even though it were a truth which has long been known to me. Those who looked to find a practical programme in it, and a concrete solution of social problems, would not understand my book aright. This is a philosophical book and it presupposes spiritual reform.

Paris, 1939.

PART I

1. PERSONALITY

'Sagt nicht Ich, aber that Ich'
NIETZSCHE, *Also sprach Zarathustra.*

'Sollt Ihr schaffende sein'
NIETZSCHE, *Also sprach Zarathustra.*

Man is a riddle in the world, and it may be, the greatest riddle. Man is a riddle not because he is an animal, not because he is a social being, not as a part of nature and society. It is as a person that he is a riddle—just that precisely; it is because he possesses personality. The entire world is nothing in comparison with human personality, with the unique person of a man, with his unique fate. Man lives in an agony, and he wants to know who he is, where he comes from and whither he is going. Already in Greece man desired to know himself and in that he saw the reding of the riddle of existence and the fountain spring of philosophical knowledge. It is possible for man to get knowledge of himself from above or from below, either from his own light, the divine principle which is within him, or from his own darkness, the elemental subconscious demonic principle within him. And he can do this because he is a twofold and contradictory being. He is a being who is polarized in the highest degree, God-like and beast-like, exalted and base, free and enslaved, apt both for rising and for falling, capable of great love and sacrifice, capable also of great cruelty and unlimited egoism. Dostoyevsky, Kirkegaard and Nietzsche recognized the tragic principle in man and the inconsistency of his nature with peculiar distinctness. Before that Pascal had expressed better than anyone this two-sidedness of man. Others have looked at man from below and revealed the base elemental principles in him, the impress of his Fall. As a fallen being, determined by elemental forces, he appeared to be actuated solely by economic interests, subconscious sensual impulses, and anxiety. But a sense of need in suffering and martyrdom in the case of Dostoyevsky, horror and penitence in the case of Kirkegaard, and, with Nietzsche, the will to power and cruelty, also bear witness to the fact that man is a fallen being, but that he suffers as the result of this Fall and that he desires to get the better of it. It is precisely the consciousness of personality in man which speaks of his higher nature and higher vocation. If man were not a person, albeit a personality which has not yet emerged into full view, or which has been crushed, albeit one struck down by disease, albeit a personality which exists only as potential or possible, then he would be like other things in the world and there would be nothing unusual about him. But personality in man is evidence of this, that the world is not self sufficient, that it can be overcome and surmounted. Personality is like nothing else in the world, there is nothing with which it can be compared, nothing which can be placed on a level with it. When a person enters the world, a unique and unrepeatable personality, then the world process is broken into and compelled to change its course, in spite of the fact that outwardly there is no sign of this. Personality finds no place in the continuous complex process of world life, it cannot be a moment or an element in the evolution of the world. The existence of personality presupposes interruption; it is inexplicable by any sort of un-interruption; it is inexplicable by any sort of uninterrupted continuity.

Man, the only man known to biology and sociology, man as a natural being and a social being, is the offspring of the world and of the processes which take place in the world. But personality, man as a person, is not a child of the world, he is of another origin. And this it is that makes man a riddle. Personality is a break through, a break-ing in upon this world; it is the introduction of something new. Personality is not nature, it does not belong to the objective hierarchy of nature, as a subordinate part of it. And, therefore, as we shall see, hierarchical personalism is false. Man is a personality not by nature but by spirit. By nature he is only an individual. Personality is not a monad entering into a hierarchy of monads and subordinate to it. Personality is a microcosm, a complete universe. It is personality alone that can bring together a universal content and be a potential universe in an individual form. That universal content is not to be attained by any other reality in the world of nature or of history. Such other realities are always characterized as parts. Personality is not a part and cannot be a part in relation to any kind of whole, not even to an immense whole, or to the entire world. This is the essential principle of personality, and its mystery. To whatever extent empirical man enters as a part into any sort of natural or social whole, it is not as a personality that he does so, and his personality is left outside this subordination of the part to the whole. According to Leibnitz, and Renouvier as well, the monad is simple substance entering into a complex organization. The monad is closed, shut up, it has neither windows nor doors. For personality, however, infinity opens out, it enters into infinity, and admits infinity into itself; in its self-revelation it is directed towards an infinite content.

And at the same time personality presupposes form and limit; it does not mingle with its environment nor is it dissolved in the world around it. Personality is the universal in an individually unrepeatable form. It is a union of the universal-infinite and the individual-particular. It is in this apparent contradiction that personality exists. The personal in man is just that in him which he does not have in common with others, but in that which is not shared with others is included the potentiality of the universal. The understanding of human personality as a microcosm is set in antithesis to the organic-hierarchical interpretation of him, which transforms man into a subordinate part of a whole, into a common, a universal.

But personality is not a part of the universe, the universe is a part of personality, it is its quality. Such is the paradox of personalism. One must not think of personality as a substance, that would be a naturalistic idea of personality. Personality cannot be recognized as an object, as one of the objects in a line with other objects in the world, like a part of the world. That is the way in which the anthropological sciences, biology, psychology, or sociology would regard man. In that way man is looked at partially: but there is in that case no mystery of man, as personality, as an existential centre of the world. Personality is recognized only as a subject, in infinite subjectivity, in which is hidden the secret of existence.

Personality is the unchanging in change, unity in the manifold. It strikes us unpleasantly, alike if there is the unchanging in man and not change, and if there is change and not the unchanging; if there is unity and not the manifold, or the manifold and not unity. Both in the one case and in the other the essential qualitativeness of personality is disclosed. Personality is not a congealed condition, it breaks up,

[22]

it develops, it is enriched; but it is the development of one and the same abiding subject. That is its very name. The very change itself takes place for the preservation of this unchanging abiding thing, as Poulain correctly says.

Personality is not in any case a ready made datum, it is the posing of a question, it is the ideal of a man. Perfectly accomplished unity and wholeness of personality is the ideal of man. Personality is self-constructive, Not a single man can say of himself that he is completely a person. Personality is an axiological category, a category of value. Here we meet the fundamental paradox in the existence of personality. Personality must construct itself, enrich itself, fill itself with universal content, achieve unity in wholeness in the whole extent of its life. But for this, it must already exist. There must originally exist that subject which is called upon to construct itself. Personality is at the beginning of the road and it is only at the end of the road. Personality is not made up of parts, it is not an aggregate, not a composition, it is a primary whole. The growth of personality, the realization of personality certainly does not mean the formation of a whole out of its parts. It means rather the creative acts of personality, as a whole thing, which is not brought out of anything and not put together from anything. The form of personality is integral, it is present as a whole in all the acts of personality, personality has a unique, an unrepeatable form, *Gestalt*. What is known as *Gestalt* psychology, which regards form as the primary qualitative value, is more acceptable to personalism than other systems of psychology.

The very break up of the form of personality does not indicate its final disappearance. Personality is indestructible. Personality creates itself and exists by its own destiny finding the source of its strength ina n existence which surpasses it. Personality is potentially the universal, but quite certainly a distinct, unrepeatable, irreplaceable being with a unique form. Personality is the exception, not the rule. The secret of the existence of personality lies in its absolute irreplaceability, its happening but once, its uniqueness, its incomparableness. Everything individual is irreplaceable.

There is a baseness in the replacing of an individual creature which you have loved, permanently recognizing in it the form of personality, by another being. This irreplaceableness exists not only in reference to people, but also in reference to animals. One personality may have traits of resemblance to other personalities, which allow a comparison to be made. But these marks of similarity do not touch that essence of personality, which makes it personality, not personality in general, but this personality.

In every human personality there is the common, the universal, not the inward universal as the creative acquisition of a qualitative content of life, but an outward, adherent universal. But personality, this concrete personality, exists by its non-common expression, not by the fact that it has two eyes, like all other people, and not by the common expression of those eyes. In human personality there is much that is generic, belonging to the human race, much which belongs to history, tradition, society, class, family, much that is hereditary and imitative, much that is 'common'. But it is precisely this which is not 'personal' in personality. That which is 'personal' is original, connected with the primary fountain head, authentic. Personality must perform its self-existent, original, creative acts, and this alone makes it personality and constitutes its unique value.

Personality must be the exception, no law at all is applicable to it. Everything generic and hereditary is only material for the creative activity of personality. The whole burden which is laid upon man by nature and society, by history and the demands of civilization, confronts us in the form of difficulties which demand resistance and creative transformation into the personal, uniquely the personal. The typical members of a group, a class, or a profession may be clear individualities but not clear personalities. Personality in man is the triumph over the determination of the social group. Personality is not a substance but an act, a creative act. Every act is a creative act: a non-creative act is passivity. Personality is activity, opposition, victory over the dragging burden of the world, the triumph of freedom over the world's slavery. The fear of exertion is harmful to the realization of personality. Personality is effort and conflict, the conquest of self and of the world, victory over slavery, it is emancipation.

Personality is rational being, but it is not determined by reason and it cannot be defined as the vehicle of reason. Reason in itself is not personal, but universal, common, impersonal reason. The moral and rational nature of man with Kant is an impersonal common nature. The Greek understanding of man as a rational being, does not fit in with personalist philosophy. Personality is not only rational being, but also free being. Personality is my whole thinking, my whole willing, my whole feeling, my whole creative activity. The reason of Greek philosophy, the reason of German idealism is impersonal reason, universal reason. But there exist also my personal reason and especially my personal will. Personalism cannot be founded upon idealism, Platonic or German, and cannot be based on naturalism, on evolutionary philosophy or on vital philosophy, which dissolves personality in the impersonal, cosmic, vital process. Scheler has correctly stated the difference between personality and organism, between spiritual being and vital being.

Personality is not a biological or a psychological category, but an ethical and spiritual. Personality cannot be identified with the soul. Personality has an elemental-unconscious foundation. Man in his sub-conscious is submerged in the blustering ocean of elemental life and is but partially rationalized. It is necessary to distinguish in man, the profound and the superficial ego. Too often, to other people, society and civilization man presents his superficial ego, which is capable of various sorts of external communication, but it not capable of communion. Tolstoy understood this admirably. He always depicts the double life of man, the outwardly conditional, unreal life, replete with falsehood, which he brings into relation with society, the state and civilization, and his inner real life in which man confronts primary reality, and the deeps of life. When Prince Andrew is gazing at the starry heavens, that is more real life than when he is engaged in conversation in a Petersburg drawing-room. The superficial ego in man which is much socialized, rationalized and civilized, is not the personality in man. It may be even a distortion of the form of man and a thing which conceals his personality. The personality of man may be crushed, man may assume many disguises, and his form may not be capable of being grasped. Man often plays a part in life, and he may play a part which is not his. Dichotomy of personality is especially striking in primitive man and in the psychologically unstable and unsound. In semi-normal civilized man it assumes

[25]

another character, the duality acquires the normative character of adaptation to the conditions of civilization, and gives rise to the necessity of falsehood as a means of self-defence. Social training and the civilizing of barbarous man may be a beneficial process, but it does not mean the formation of personality. The completely socialized and civilized man may be entirely impersonal; he may be a slave and not notice that he is.

Personality is not a part of society, as it is not part of a race. The problem of man, that is to say, the problem of personality, is more primary than the problem of society. All the sociological doctrines about man are erroneous, they know only the superficial, objectified stratum in man. Looking at things from the sociological point of view it is only externally that personality is seen as a subordinate part of society; and a very small part at that, compared with the massiveness of society. But only an existential philosophy, and not a sociological philosophy, any more than a biological philosophy can construct the true doctrine of man as personality.

Personality is a subject, and not an object among other objects, and it has its roots in the inward scheme of existence, that is in the spiritual world, the world of freedom. Society on the other hand is an object. From the existential point of view society is a part of personality, it is its social side, just as the cosmos is a part of personality, its cosmic side. Personality is not an object among other objects and not a thing among other things. It is a subject among subjects and the turning of it into an object or a thing means death. The object is always evil, only the subject can be good. It might be said that society and nature provide the material for the formation of personality. But personality is emancipation from dependence upon nature, from dependence upon society and the state. It opposes all determination from without, it is determination from within. And even within, the determination is self-determination, not even God can do it. The relation between personality and God is not a causal relation, it lies outside the realm of determination, it is within the realm of freedom, God is not an object to personality. He is a subject with whom existential relations exist. Personality is the absolute existential centre. Personality determines itself from within, outside the whole object world, and only determination from within and arising out of freedom, is personality. Everything defined from without, everything determined, everything that is based upon the power of the object world is not personal, it is the impersonal in man. Everything determined in the human ego is past and has become impersonal.

But personality is the coming into being of the future, it consists of creative acts. Objectivization is impersonality, the ejection of man into the world of determinism. The existence of personality presupposes freedom. The mystery of freedom is the mystery of personality. And this freedom is not freedom of the will in the elementary sense, freedom of choice, which presupposes rationalization. The worth of man is the personality within him. Human worth consists solely in personality. Human worth is liberation from slavery, liberation also from the servile understanding of religious life and of the relation between man and God. God is the guarantee of the freedom of personality from the enslaving power of nature and society, of the Kingdom of Caesar and of the object world. This takes place in the realm of the spirit and not in the realm of the object world. And no categories of the object world can be transferred to these inward existential relations. Nothing in the object world is an authentic existential centre.

Personality as an existential centre, presupposes capacity to feel suffering and joy. Nothing in the object world, nation or state or society, or social institution, or church, possesses this capacity. They speak of the sufferings of the masses of the people in an allegorical sense. No communities in the object world can be recognized as personality. Collective realities are real values, but not real personalities, their existentiality refers to the realities of personalities. One can allow the existence of collective souls, but not of collective personalities. The conception of collective or 'symphonic' personality is a disputable conception. To this we shall return again later on.

It is true that we hypostatize everything we love, and everything we pity, inanimate things and abstract ideas. But this is a mythopœic process, without which there is no intensity of life, but it does not mean a real bestowal of personality. Personality is not only capable of experiencing suffering, but in a certain sense personality is suffering. The struggle to achieve personality and its consolidation are a painful process. The self-realization of personality presupposes resistance, it demands a conflict with the enslaving power of the world, a refusal to conform to the world. Refusal of personality, acquiescence in dissolution in the surrounding world can lessen the suffering, and man easily goes that way. Acquiescence in slavery diminishes suffering, refusal increases it. Pain in the human world is the birth of personality, its fight for its own nature. Already in the animal world individuality suffers. Freedom gives rise to suffering. One can lessen it if one refuses freedom. The worth of man, that is to say personality, and again that is to say freedom, presupposes acquiescence in pain, and the capacity to bear pain. The degradation of my people or my faith causes pain in me, but not in the people and not in the religious community, which do not possess an existential centre, and consequently are devoid of capacity to feel pain. Capacity to experience pain is inherent in every living creature, above all in man, but it is in animals also, and perhaps in another way in plants as well, but not in collective realities nor in ideal values. This question is of first importance, it is by it that the ethics of personalism are defined. Man, human personality is the supreme value, not the community, not collective realities which belong to the object world, such as society, nation, state, civilization, church. That is the personalist scale of values. We shall repeat it over and over again.

Personality is connected with memory and certitude; it is linked with the whole of a man's fate, and with his whole life history. And, therefore, the existence of personality is difficult and painful. In Christianity there has always been a twofold attitude to man. On the one hand Christianity has, as it were, degraded man by regarding him as a sinful and fallen being who is called to humility and obedience. And it is this they can never forgive Christianity. But on the other hand Christianity extraordinarily exalts man in that it regards him as made in the image and likeness of God, recognizes a spiritual principle in him, which raises him above the natural and social world, it recognizes in him a spiritual freedom which is independent of the Kingdom of Caesar, and it believes that God Himself became man and by this exalted man to heaven. And only on this Christian basis can a doctrine of personality be constructed and the personalist transvaluation of values be worked out. Personalist philosophy must recognize that spirit does not generalize but individualizes, that it creates, not a world of ideal values, suprahuman and common, but a world of personalities with their qualitative content, that it forms personalities. The triumph of the spiritual principle means, not the subordination of man to the universe, but the revelation of the universe in personality. If one imagined oneself endowed with the highest universal qualities of mind, genius, beauty, goodness, holiness, but with the removal of the existential centre, with the transference of the centre of gravity of the ego to the universal qualitative principles, that would be just as if the ego had endowed another being with those qualities, just as if the ego had seen another as such. The unity of the subject and its life history disappears, memory does not preserve personality. Herein lies the falsity of the idealist philosophy of values and of ideal existence.

Man is a being who surmounts and transcends himself. The realization of personality in man is this continuous transcending of self. Man desires to go out from the closed circle of subjectivity and this movement always takes place in two different and even opposite directions. Emergence from subjectivity proceeds by way of objectivization. This is the way which leads out into society with its forms of universal obligation, it is the way of science with its laws of universal obligation. On this path there takes place the alienation of human nature, its ejection into the object world: personality does not find itself. The other path is emergence from subjectivity through the process of transcendence. This is a passing over into the trans-subjective and not to the objective. This path lies in the deeps of existence, on this path there take place the existential meeting with God, with other people, with the interior existence of the world. It is the path not of objective communication but of existential communion. Personality reaches full realization of itself only on this path.

It is extraordinarily important to grasp this, in order to understand the relation between personality and the suprapersonal values, about which I have already spoken above. The relation of personality to suprapersonal values may be achieved either in the realm of objectivization, and this easily gives rise to the slavery of man, or in the existential realm, in a process of transcension, in which case life with freedom is born. Objectivization is never transcension. It is an error to think that transcension comes to pass in that. In objectivization man finds himself in the power of determination, in the realm of the impersonal: in transcension man finds himself in the realm of freedom, and the meeting of man with that which excels him has a personal character, the suprapersonal does not crush personality. This is a fundamental distinction. It is characteristic of personality that it cannot be self-suppressing and self-sufficient. Some other is necessary for its existence, something higher, on a level, or lower; without this the consciousness of difference is impossible. But I repeat what I have already said, the relation of personality to an other, even to the very highest, never means the relation of a part to the whole. Personality remains integral, it enters into nothing, even in its relation to the highest other. The relation of a part to the whole is a mathematical relation, just as the relation of an organ to an organism is a biological relation.

This relation of a part to a whole belongs to the world of objectivization in which man is turned into a part and an organ. But the existential relation of personality to an other, and that the very highest, has nothing in common with such a relation. Transcension does not mean that personality is subordinated to any whole whatever, enters as an integral part into any collective reality whatever, or is related to the highest other, to the highest being, as to a master. Transcension is an active dynamic process, it is the immanent experience of a man in which he lives through catastrophes, is carried across abysses, experiences interruptions in his existence, but is interiorized not exteriorized. Only a false objectivization of transcension, the ejection of man into the external, creates the illusion of the transcendent which crushes personality, dominates over it. Transcension in the existential sense is freedom and presupposes freedom, it is the liberation of man from captivity to himself. But freedom in this connection is not an easy thing, it is a difficult thing, it proceeds through tragic contradiction.

The problem of personality is a problem of an entirely different order from the ordinary problem of the relation of soul and body. Personality is certainly not the soul as distinct from the body, which

[30]

links man with the life of nature. Personality is the entire image of man in which the spiritual principle has the mastery over all the powers of man's soul and body. The unity of personality is created by the spirit. But the body belongs to the image of man. The old dualism of soul and body, which comes from Descartes, is absolutely false and out of date. Such a dualism does not exist. The life of the soul permeates the whole life of the body, just as the bodily life has its effect upon the life of the soul. There is a vital unity of soul and body in man. Dualism exists, not between soul and body, but between spirit and nature, between freedom and necessity. Personality is the victory of the spirit over nature, of freedom over necessity.

The form of the human body is already a victory of the spirit over natural chaos. Carus, a psychologist and anthropologist of the romantic period, was more in the right than many doctrines of the schools which are commonly considered scientific. He says that the soul is found not in the brain but in the form. Klages follows him. The form of the body is certainly not matter, it is certainly not a phenomenon of the physical world. The form of the body is not only of the soul, it is spiritual, The face of man is the summit of the cosmic process, the greatest of its offspring, but it cannot be the offspring of cosmic forces only, it presupposes the action of a spiritual force, which raises it above the sphere of the forces of nature. The face of man is the most amazing thing in the life of the world; another world shines out through it. It is the entrance of personality into the world process, with its uniqueness, its singleness, its unrepeatability. Through the face we apprehend, not the bodily life of a man, but the life of his soul. And we know the life of his soul better than his bodily life. The form of the body belongs to the spirit-soul. Here is personality in its entirety.

The form of the body was neglected in the consciousness of the people of the nineteenth century. There was a physiology of the body, but not a form of the body, they wished to let the form remain concealed. In this the Christian ascetic attitude to the body appeared all over again. But it was very inconsistent, since the functions of the body were by no means denied. But at that time, the functions of the body being physiological and bound up with the conception of man as a creature who belonged to the animal biological world, the form of the body was linked on to aesthetics. Greece was aware of the form of the body as an aesthetic phenomenon, and this awareness ran through the whole of its culture. In these days a partial return to the Greek attitude to the body is taking place, and the form of the body is coming into its rights. This presupposes a modification of Christian consciousness and the overcoming of abstract spirituality, which places spirit and body in opposition and sees in the body a principle which is hostile to the spirit. The spirit includes the body also in itself, it spiritualizes the body, and communicates another quality to it. They are ceasing to consider the body as a material physical phenomenon.

But this implies also the overcoming of a mechanistic outlook upon life in general, of an outlook which deprives the body of its soul and is hostile to the form of the body. To materialism the form of the body is unintelligible and inexplicable. The spirit communicates form to the soul and to the body, and brings them into a unity; it does not crush nor destroy them. This means also that spirit gives form to personality, to its entirety, into which the body enters, into which there enters the face of man. Personality—the spirit-soul-body entity, rises above the determinism of the natural world. It is subordinate to no mechanism whatever. The form of man, which is apprehended by the senses, does not depend upon matter, it means victory over matter, it acts against its depersonalizing determination. Personalism must recognize the dignity of the human body, the inadmissibility of treating it wrongly, and the right the body has to a truly human existence. And, therefore, even the problem of daily bread becomes a spiritual problem. The rights of the human body are bound up with the value of personality for this reason that the most shocking encroachments upon personality are in the first place encroachments upon the body. It is first of all the human body that they starve, beat and kill, and through the body this process spreads to the whole man, The spirit in itself you can neither beat nor kill.

In Greek philosophy there was no very clear idea of personality: glimmers of it appear in the Stoics. This created great difficulties for the Fathers of the Church in the exposition of dogma. They were obliged to make the very subtle distinction between ὑπόστασις and φύσις. In God there is one nature and three hypostases; in Christ one person and two natures. The thought of the Fathers of the Church moved in the categories and conceptions of Greek thought. But all the same the necessity had arisen to give expression to something entirely new, to a new spiritual experience, one unknown to Plato, Aristotle and Plotinus. From the point of view of the world history of thought, as concerned with the problem of personality, an immense importance attaches to the doctrine of the hypostases of the Holy Trinity. It might be said that the awareness of God as personality, preceded the awareness of man as personality. It is for this reason wholly incomprehensible that, for example, Karsavin denies the existence of human personality and acknowledges only the existence of divine personality (hypostasis). He constructs a doctrine of symphonic personality in which the divine triunity is realized. The doctrine of symphonic personality is profoundly opposed to personalism and provides a metaphysical ground for the enslavement of man. This question cannot be decided by a dialectic of conceptions, it is decided by spiritual and moral experience. Karsavin cannot reconcile personality with an all embracing unity. This only bears witness to the fact that personalism cannot be founded upon a monistic metaphysic. The Greek word ὑπόστασις in the sense of *substratum*, and the Latin word 'persona' meaning *a mask*, in connection with playing a part in the theatre, very incompletely express personality in the sense given to it by Christianity and the new philosophy. The word 'persona' was greatly transformed in the course of centuries and lost its theatrical meaning. The word 'persona' was received through the scholastics from Boetius who had already defined personality as reasoning individual being. The problem of personality was a difficult one for scholastic philosophy. Thomism connected individuality with matter: matter, not form, gives individuality, form is universal. But the Thomist philosophy already makes the important distinction between personality and the individual. To Leibnitz the essential reality of personality consists in consciousness of self, that is to say the form of personality is connected with consciousness. Kant introduces an important change in the understanding of personality; he passes over from the intellectual to

[33]

the ethical conception of it. Personality is connected with freedom from the determinism of nature, it is independent of the mechanism of nature. For this reason personality is not a phenomenon among phenomena. Personality is an end in itself, not a means to an end; it exists through itself. Nevertheless Kant's doctrine of personality is not true personalism because the value of personality is defined by its moral and rational nature, which comes into the category of the universal.

In Max Stirner, in spite of the falsity of his philosophy, true personalism is to be found, but in a distorted form. In him a dialectic of the self-affirmation of the ego comes to light. The 'unique one' is not personality because personality disappears in the infinity of self-affirmation, in unwillingness to know an other, and to achieve transcendence to the utmost. But in the 'unique one' there is a modicum of truth, for personality is a universe, a microcosm, and in a certain sense the whole world is its property and belongs to it; personality is not partial nor a particular nor subordinate to the whole and the common.

Scheler defines personality as unity of experience, and as the existential unity of a variety of actions. Here we have an important linking up of personality with action. But in opposition to Scheler it must be admitted that personality presupposes the existence of other personalities and of going out to meet them. Nyesmyelov has some remarkable thoughts about man. For him there is only one contradiction in the world, and only one riddle, and they are bound up with human personality. In personality the form of unconditioned being is reflected, and at the same time personality is set in the conditions of limited being. It is a contradiction between what human personality ought to be, and the conditions of its existence on earth. Nyesmyelov expresses the contradiction of human existence thus: man is a thing of the physical world who bears within himself the image of God. But personality in man is not a thing of the physical world. Vitalist philosophy which plays no small part in contemporary thought and which has its own doctrine of man, is not favourable to the principle of personality; it is anti-personalist. As I have said above, vital philosophy leads to the dissolution of human personality in the cosmic and social process. Anti-personalist dionysism, naturalistic pantheist mysticism, theosophy, anthroposophy, communism, fascism, as well as liberalism, are bound up with the capitalist structure of society.

In order to understand what personality is, it is very important to establish the difference between personality and the individual. The French Thomists very justly insist upon this distinction, though they take their stand upon different philosophical ground from mine. The individual is a category of naturalism, biology, and sociology. The individual is indivisible in relation to some whole; he is an atom. He not only can be a member of a species or community, as well as of the cosmos as a whole, but he is invariably thought of as part of a whole, and outside that whole he cannot be called an individual.

The individual is characterized alike, on the one hand as a subordinate part of the whole and on the other as a part which is self-affirming as an ego. Therefore, individualism, which is derived from the word individual, certainly does not signify independence in relation to the whole, that is to the cosmic biological and social process. It signifies only the isolation of the subordinate part in its feeble revolt against the whole. The individual is closely linked with the material world, he is brought to birth by the generic process. The individual is born of a father and a mother, he has a biological origin, which is determined by family heredity and also by social heredity. There is no individual without the family and no family without the individual. The individual is found entirely within categories which distinguish what belongs to the species from what is of the individual.

The individual carries on a struggle for existence in the family, the biological and the social processes. Man certainly is an individual, but he is not only an individual. The individual is bound up with the material world, and is nourished by it; but he is not universal, as such, he has not a universal content. Man is a microcosm, and a universe; but not in virtue of his being an individual. Man is also personality, the idea of man and his vocation in the world are bound up with his personality. And here everything is changed. Personality is not a naturalistic but a spiritual category. Personality is not the indivisible or the atom in relation to any whole whatever, cosmic, family, or social. Personality is the freedom and independence of man in relation to nature, to society and to the state; but not only is

[35]

it not egoistic self-affirmation, it is the very opposite. Personalism does not mean, as individualism does, an egocentric isolation. Personality in man is his independence in relation to the material world, which is the material for the work of the spirit. And at the same time personality is a universe, it is filled with universal content. Personality is not born of the family and cosmic process, not born of a father and mother, it emanates from God, it makes its appearance from another world. It bears witness to the fact that man is the point of intersection of two worlds, that in him there takes place the conflict between spirit and nature, freedom and necessity, independence and dependence.

Espinas says that the real individual is a cell. But personality most certainly is not a cell and does not enter into any organism as a part into a whole. It is the primary whole and unity, it is characterized by its relation to an other and to others, to the world, to society, to people, as a relation of creativeness, freedom and love, and not of determination. Personality lies outside the co-relation of individually-particular and that which is common to the species, outside the co-relation of parts and whole, of organs and organism. Personality is not the living individual. Personality in man is not determined by heredity, biological and social; it is freedom in man, it is the possibility of victory over the world of determination. Everything that is personal in man is set in opposition to any kind of automatism, that automatism which plays such a part in human life, automatism both psychical and social. There are not two separate men, but one and the same man is both an individual and a personality. That is not two different beings, but two kinds of qualitativeness, two different forces in man. Péguy says that the individual is every man's own bourgeois which he is called upon to conquer. Man, as an individual, endures the experience of isolation, egocentrically engulfed in himself, and called upon to wage a tormenting struggle for life, as he defends himself against the dangers that lie in wait for him. He finds his way out of difficulties through conformism, through adaptation. Man as a person, the same man, gains the mastery of the egocentric self-confinement, discloses a universe in himself, but insists upon his independence and dignity in relation to the surrounding world.

But it must always be remembered that our language often gets confused. We constantly make use of words which do not bear the meaning which we assign to them. That which is individual, individuality, denotes the unique within its kind, the original, distinguished from any other and from the rest. In this sense the individual is inherent in every person.

Personality has a higher degree of individuality than the individual. The individual also often denotes the irrational, in opposition to that which is common, to the universally binding, to the rational and normative. In this sense personality is irrational; and the individual much more subject to binding law, since it is more determined.

It is interesting, in the history of the discovery of the meaning of personality, to notice that among the romantics individuality is distinguished from personality in our sense of the word. Among the romantics themselves individuality was clearly presented, but personality was often very weakly expressed. The character of individuality is rather vital than spiritual and does not as yet indicate the victory of spirit and freedom. We see a reflection of a profound disintegration, of a dissociation of personality in the contemporary novel, for instance in Proust and among us, Andrei Byely. Inward unity and integrality are inherent in personality; whereas the individual may be torn to pieces by the forces of the world. A person cannot be completely a citizen of the world and of the state, he is a citizen of the Kingdom of God. For this reason personality is a revolutionary element in a profound sense of the word. This is bound up with the fact that man is a being who belongs not to one world, but to two. Personalism is a dualistic not a monistic philosophy.

The existence of personality presupposes the existence of suprapersonal values. There is no human personality if there is no existence which stands higher than it, if there is no higher world to which it ought to rise. There is no personality if there are no suprapersonal values, and there is no personality if it is nothing but a means to which suprapersonal values are the end. The relation of personality to the universal is certainly not a relation to the species and the common. Here we approach the most difficult problem of personalist philosophy, and the difficulty is connected with habits of thought which arise from a false way of stating the problem of nominalism and realism. What is the relation of personality to communities and to the world of objects? It is true that *universalia* are not *ante rem* (platonic realism, which is the same as idealism) and not *post rem* (empirical nominalism) but *in rebus*. For the problem which concerns us now this means that the universal is to be found in what is individual, i.e. in personality, not as derived from quantitative experience, but as a primary quality. The universal does not lie in an ideal suprapersonal sphere, but in personality, which belongs to the existential plane. The universal and the so-called suprapersonal values, belong not to the world of objects, but to the world of subjects. The objectivization of universal values indeed gives rise to the slavery of man. It is necessary, therefore, to say, for example, that the cosmos, mankind, society, are in personality and not the other way round. Man, i.e. individual, or according to other terminology, singular, existential, humanity is only the value of all-human unity in the human world, the quality of human brotherhood, which is not a reality that stands above man.

The universal is not the common; it is not abstract, but concrete, i.e. it is plenitude. The universal is all the less common in that it is not independent being, it is to be found in single beings, *in rebus*, according to the old terminology. The individual is by no means a part of the universal. The opposition of universal and singular is incorrect. Personality is certainly not partial, nor particular as opposed to universal. It can be said with more truth that personality is a universal. The very singleness of the individual is permeated not by that which is individual, but by that which is universal. All the old terminology is very confused and is bound up with an objectivized philosophy of concepts, not with existential philosophy. Leibnitz already attempted to get over the dispute between realists and nominalists. The universal, embodied in the individual, overcomes the antithesis between the universal and the individual. The universal is an essay, an attempt, on the part of the subject, not a reality in the object. An objective world of ideas does not exist. But that certainly does not mean that the universal, that universal ideas and values, are only subjective in the old sense of the word. The objectifying and hypostatization of universal ideas is a false way to take in order to overcome subjectivity. It is not transcension in the authentic sense of the word. Insuperable contradictions are connected with an understanding of God, with an idea of God, which is formulated by way of objectivization.

In the same way it would be untrue to say that God is universal, that God is singular, individual. The distinction between universal and singular lies in the realm of objectivization. But God is not to be found in that realm. He is in the existential realm, in the attempted experience of transcension. The relation between man and God is not a causal relation, it is not the relation between the particular and the common, nor between means and end, nor between slave and master. It does not resemble anything at all which can be taken from the object world of the natural and the social; it is a relation which has no analogy with anything in that world. God does not exist as an objective reality found to be necessary by me, as the objectivization of a universal idea. He exists as an existential contact and meeting, as the process of transcension, and in that meeting God is personality. Therefore, the question of the relation between personality and suprapersonal values is decided in an entirely different way.

It cannot be said that the suprapersonal is higher than man. God is the end, but personality is not a means to that end. Man as personality cannot be a means to God as Personality. The theological doctrine that God created man for His own glory and praise is degrading to man, and degrading to God also. It is a striking fact that any doctrine which is degrading to man also degrades God. The relation of personality to personality, even the most exalted personality of God, cannot be a relation of means and end, all personality is an end in itself. The relation of means and end exists only in the world of objectivization, i.e. the world of the ejection of existence into the external. Personality cannot ascend, cannot realize itself, and realize the fullness of its life, unless suprapersonal values exist, unless God exists, unless there is a divine level of life. The human idea in this connection—that human personality is the highest finality, that there is no God and that man himself is God, is trivial; it does not exalt man, it degrades him; it is a nightmare. But human personality is not a means to any suprapersonal value as its end, it is not an instrument of the divine power, When suprapersonal values turn human personality into a means to an end, it shows that man has fallen into

[39]

idolatry. Personality is a paradox to rational thought; paradoxically it juxtaposes the personal and the suprapersonal, the finite and the infinite, the abiding and the changing, freedom and fate.

Personality is not part of the world, it is a correlative of the world, and a correlative of God also. Personality allows only of correlation, meeting, communion. And God as personality does not desire a man over whom He can rule, and who ought to praise Him, but man as personality who answers His call and with whom communion of love is possible. Every personality has its own world. Human personality is the potential all, all world thought, all world history. Everything that has happened in the world has touched my personality. But this personality is only partially made actual, very much of it remains in a somnolent, hidden, condition. In the deeps which are hidden from my consciousness I am submerged in the ocean of world life. And in making actual the universal content, in disclosing it in myself, through knowledge and love, intellectually and emotionally, I am never turned into a means which has that universal content as its end. And there exists a complex and contradictory relation between my consciousness and my personality, my individuality. Personality builds up its consciousness out of the depths as a defensive base, or as a frontier line which prevents mingling and dissolution; but it is possible for consciousness to prevent the filling of my personality with universal content, and hinder communion with the cosmic whole. And at the same time there is in consciousness the supra-individual; consciousness never can be circumscribed by that which is individual. Consciousness arises in the relation between the ego and the non-ego, it denotes a going out from the ego, but at the same time it may be a hindrance to the going out of the I to the Thou as inward communion. It objectifies and may prevent the process of transcending. Consciousness is 'unhappy consciousness'. Consciousness is subject to law, which takes cognizance of the common but not of the individual. For this reason it is easy to fall a prey to illusion, through not having a true understanding of the relation between the personal and the suprapersonal. The very structure of consciousness readily produces slavery. But it is always necessary to keep in view the double rôle of consciousness, it both closes and opens out.

Hierarchical personalism, which is defended by many philosophers

(Leibnitz, Stern, Lossky, and in part Scheler), contains an inner contradiction which makes it anti-personalism. According to this theory, the world whole, organized hierarchically, is made up of personalities of various hierarchical degrees, in which every personality is subordinate to a higher rank, and enters into it as a subordinate part or organ. Human personality belongs to only one hierarchical rank, into which personalities of lower degrees enter. But a nation, mankind, the cosmos, may also be regarded as personalities of higher rank. Communities and societies are recognized as personalities, every real unity can be viewed as a personality. But true and consistent personalism must regard that as contradicting the very nature of personality. The hierarchical conception is obliged to regard human personality as a part in relation to the hierarchical whole, it appears as a value only in relation to that whole and from that whole it derives its value. The hierarchical whole to which personality is subordinate is considered a greater value than personality, it is in that whole that we must look for universality, for unity, and for totality.

But authentic personalism cannot admit this. It cannot recognize a whole, a collective unity in which there is no absolute existential centre, no point of sensitiveness to joy and suffering, no personal destiny, as a personality. Outside personality there is no absolute unity and totality in the world, to which personality would be subordinate: outside personality everything is partial, even the world itself is partial. Everything objectivized, everything which is an object can be partial only. Such is the whole objectivized world, and the whole of objectivized society with its objectivized bodies. This objectivized world is distinguished by a solidity which is able to threaten to crush personality, but it is not distinguished by wholeness nor by totality. An existential centre, and a suffering destiny are to be found in subjectivity, not in objectivity. But all the higher hierarchical ranks to which they subordinate personality belong to the world of objectivization. Objectivization is always antipersonalistic, hostile to personality and signifies the estrangement of personality. And everything which is existential in the objectivized ranks of the world, in the nation, in mankind, in the cosmos, etc. belongs to the inward being of personality and is not subordinate to any hierarchical centre. The cosmos, mankind, nation, etc., are to be found in human personality as in an individualized universe or microcosm, and their falling away from it, their ejection into external reality among objects, is the result of the fall of man, of his subordination to impersonal reality, exteriorization, and alienation.

In the existential system the sun is to be found not in the centre of the cosmos but in the centre of human personality and it is exteriorized only in the fallen state of man. The realization of personality, the concentration and actualization of its strength, takes the sun into itself, it inwardly receives the whole cosmos, the whole of history, all mankind. Collective personalities and suprapersonal personalities in relation to human personality are mere illusions arising from exteriorization and objectivization. There are no objective personalities, there are only subjective personalities. And in a sense, a dog and a cat are more truly personalities, more truly heirs of eternal life, than a nation, or society, or the state, or the whole world. Such is anti-hierarchical personalism, which is also the only real and true personalism. There is no wholeness, no totality, no universality of any kind outside personality, it exists only within personality; outside that there is only the partial objectivized world. To this we shall constantly return.

Personalism transfers the centre of gravity of personality from the value of objective communities—society, nation, state, to the value of personality, But it understands personality in a sense which is profoundly antithetic to egoism. Egoism destroys personality. Egocentric self-containment and concentration upon the self, and the inability to issue forth from the self is original sin, which prevents the realization of the full life of personality and hinders its strength from becoming effective. A hysterical woman is a clear example of egoism in her craze for herself and her odd way of referring everything to herself. But she is in the highest degree antithetic to personality; personality is destroyed in her, although it may be the case that she is a distinct individuality. Personality presupposes a going out from self to an other and to others, it lacks air and is suffocated when left shut up in itself. Personalism cannot but have some sort of community in view.

At the same time this going out of the personality from itself to an other does not by any means denote exteriorization and objectivization. Personality is I and Thou, another I. But the Thou to whom the I goes out and with whom it enters into communion is not an object, it is another I, it is personality. With an object, indeed, no communion is possible, no state of community can be shared with it, there can be only mutual obligation. The personal needs an other, but that other is not external and alien: the relation of the personal to it is by no means exteriorization. Personality is to be found in a series of external relations with other people and in acts of communion with them. External relations mean objectivization, whereas communion is existential. External relations, being in the world of objectivization, are to be classed as determination and therefore do not liberate man from slavery. Communion on the other hand, being in the existential world, and having no cognizance of objects, belongs to the realm of freedom, and means liberation from slavery. Egoism denotes a double slavery of man—slavery to himself, his own hardened selfhood, and slavery to the world, which is transformed exclusively into an object which exercises constraint from without. The egocentric man is a slave, his attitude to everything which is non-I is a servile attitude. He is aware of non-I only, he has no knowledge of another I, he does not know a Thou, he knows nothing of the freedom of going out from the I. The egocentric man usually defines his relation to the world and to people in a way that is not personalistic, he very readily adopts the point of view of the objective scale of values. There is something lacking in the humanity of the egocentric man. He loves abstractions which nourish his egoism. He does not love living concrete people.

Any ideology you please, even the Christian, can be turned to the service of egoism. Personalist ethics signify just that going out from the 'common' which Kirkegaard and Shestov consider a break with ethics, which they identify with standards of universal obligation. The personalistic transvaluation of values regards as immoral everything which is defined exclusively by its relation to the 'common'—to society, the nation, the state, an abstract idea, abstract goodness, moral and logical law—and not to concrete man and his existence. Those who are no longer under the law of the 'common', it is they who are the really moral people; while those who are subject to the law of the 'common' and determined by the social routine of daily life, they are the immoral people. Such people as Kirkegaard, are the victims of the old antipersonalistic ethics and antipersonalist religion, the religion of the social routine. But the tragedy which such people have lived through has an immense importance in the transvaluation of values which is now in progress.

In order to understand personality it is most important always to remember that personality is defined above all not by its relation to society and the cosmos, not by its relation to the world which is enslaved by objectivization, but by its relation to God, and from this hidden and cherished inward relation it draws strength for its free relation to the world and to man. The egocentric individual imagines that he is free in his relation to the world, which for him is non-I. But in actual fact he is slavishly determined by the world of the non-I, which shuts him up in himself. Egoism is an aspect of determination by the world: the egocentric will is external suggestion, for the world is in an egocentric condition. Of the egoism of the I and the egoism of the non-I, the latter is always the more powerful. Human personality is a universe only on condition that it has no egocentric relation to the world. The universality of personality which absorbs into itself the object world which crushes everything, is not an egocentric affirmation of self, but a throwing open in love.

Humanism is a dialectic moment in the revelation of human personality, The error of humanism certainly did not lie in the fact that it laid too great an emphasis upon man, that it was responsible for a forward movement along the path towards divine humanity, as is frequently asserted in Russian religious thought, but in the fact that it did not give sufficient emphasis to man, that it did not carry its affirmation of man through to the end, that it could not guarantee the independence of man from the world and included within itself a danger of enslaving man to society and nature. The image of human personality is not only a human image, it is also the image of God. In that fact lie hidden all the enigmas and mysteries of man. It is the mystery of divine-humanity, which is a paradox that cannot be expressed in rational terms. Personality is only human personality when it is divine-human personality. The freedom and independence of human personality from the world of objects is its divine-humanity. This means that personality is not formulated by the world of objects but by subjectivity, in which is hidden the power of the image of God. Human personality is theandric existence. Theologians will reply in alarm that Jesus Christ alone was God-man, and that man is a created being and cannot be God-man. But this way of arguing remains within the confines of theological rationalism. Granted man is not God-man in the sense in which Christ is God-man, the Unique One; yet there is a divine element in man. There are, so to speak, two natures in him. There is within him the intersection of two worlds. He bears within himself the image which is both the image of man and the image of God and is the image of man in so far as the image of God is actualized.

This truth about man lies beyond the dogmatic formulas and is not completely covered by them. It is a truth of existential spiritual experience which can be expressed only in symbols, not in intellectual concepts. That man bears within himself the image of God and in virtue of that becomes man, is a symbol. One cannot work out an intellectual concept about it. Divine-humanity is a contradiction for the line of thought which inclines towards monism or dualism. Humanistic philosophy never rose to such a height as to understand the paradoxical truth about divine-humanity. Theological philosophy, however, has endeavoured to rationalize this truth. All theological doctrines of grace have been but the formulations of the truth about the divine-humanity of man, and about the inward action of the divine upon the human. But it is absolutely impossible to understand this mystery of divine-humanity in the light of the philosophy of identity, monism, immanentism. The expression of this mystery presupposes a dualistic moment, an experience of the process of transcendence, of falling into an abyss and of escaping from that abyss. The divine is that which transcends man, and the divine is mysteriously united with the human in the divine-human image. It is for this reason only that the appearance in the world of personality which is not a slave to the world is possible. Personality is humane and it surpasses the human, which is dependent upon the world. Man is a manifold being; he bears within him the image of the world, but he is not only the image of the world, he is also the image of God. Within him conflict between the world and God takes place. He is a being both dependent and free. The image of God is a symbolic expression and if it is turned into a concept it meets with insuperable difficulties. Man is a symbol, for in him is a sign of something different, and he is a sign of something different. With this alone the possibility of liberating man from slavery is connected. This is the religious foundation of the doctrine of personality—not the theological foundation but the religious, that is to say, the spiritually empirical, the existential. The truth about God-humanity is not a dogmatic formula, not a theological doctrine, but an empirical truth, the expression of spiritual experience.

This same truth of the twofold nature of man, twofold and at the same time integral, has its reflection in the relation of human personality to society and to history. But here it is turned upside down, as it were. Personality is independent of the determination of society, it has its own world, it is an exception, it is unique and unrepeatable. And at the same time personality is social, in it there are traces of the collective unconscious. It is man's way out from isolation. It belongs to history, it realizes itself in society and in history. Personality is communal; it presupposes communion with others, and community with others. The profound contradiction and difficulty of human life is due to this communality. Slavery is on the watch to waylay man on the path of his self realization and man must constantly return to his divine image.

Man is subjected to forcible socialization during the very time that his human personality must be in free communion, in free community, in communality which is based upon freedom and love. And the greatest danger to which a man is exposed on the paths of objectivization is the danger of mechanization, the danger of automatism. Everything mechanical, everything automatic in man is not personal, it is impersonal, it is antithetic to the image of personality. The image of God, and the image of mechanism and the automaton clash against each other, the choice is either God-man or automatic humanity, machine-humanity. Man's difficulty is rooted in the fact that there is no correlation and identity between the inward and the outward, no direct and adequate expression of the one in the other. This is indeed the problem of objectivization. When he objectivizes himself in the external man enslaves himself to the world of objects; and at the same time, man cannot but express himself in the external, cannot dispense with his body, cannot but enter actively into society and history.

Even the religious life of humanity is subject to this objectivization. In a certain sense it may be said that religion in general is social; that it is a social link. But this social character of religion distorts the spirit, subordinates the infinite to the finite, makes the relative absolute, and leads away from the sources of revelation, from living spiritual experience. In the interior world, personality discovers its image through the image of God, through the penetration of the human by the divine. In the exterior world the actualization of truth denotes the subordination of the world, of society, and of history to the image of personality, it signifies permeation by personality. And that is personalism. Inwardly personality is given strength and is liberated through divine-humanity. Outwardly the whole world, all society and all history are transfigured and liberated through humanity, through the supremacy of personality. Communality passes from within outward, and this movement is not objectivization, it does not subordinate personality to objectivity. Personality must be God-human, whereas society must be human. The objectivization of God-humanity in society and in the course of history is a source of falsehood and slavery. It has established a false objective hierarchism which contradicts the dignity and freedom of human personality. With it there is connected the setting up of false ideas of sacredness. We shall see this in all forms of human slavery.

Personality is linked with character. A strong personality is an expressed character. Character is the victory of the spiritual principle in man, but victory in a concretely individual form, which is bound up with the soul-body constitution of man. Character is the possession of power over oneself, it is the victory over slavery to oneself, a triumph which makes possible victory over slavery to the surrounding world also. Character is revealed above all in relation to environment. Temperament is a natural gift; character is conquest and attainment; it presupposes freedom. All classifications of character and temperament are, however, very approximate and artificial. The mystery of personality does not lend itself to classification. The character of personality, which always denotes independence, is its concentration and its freedom which has already found some expression. Personality, the character of personality, indicates that a man has made a choice, that he has established differences, that he is not indifferent, and that he makes distinctions. This freedom is not freedom of the will, like the freedom of indifference, it is not freedom of the will in the elementary sense; it is deeper, and is bound up with the existence of the man as an integrality. It is freedom of the spirit, of the creative spiritual energy.

The psychical life of man contains an active creative principle which synthetizes personality; it is the activity of the spirit in man, which penetrates not only the life of the soul but also the bodily life. The spirit creates the form of personality and the character of man. Without the synthetizing activity of the spirit, personality becomes dissociated; man falls into parts, the spirit loses its integrality, its capacity for active reactions. The freedom of personality is certainly not its right; that is a superficial view. Freedom of personality is a duty, it is a fulfilment of vocation, the realization of the divine idea of man, an answer to the divine call. Man ought to be free, he dare not be a slave, because he ought to be a man. Such is the will of God. Man likes being a slave and puts forward a claim to slavery as a right, a claim which changes its form from time to time. It is precisely slavery to which man lays claim as a right. Freedom ought not to be a declaration of the rights of man; it ought to be a declaration of man's obligations, of the duty of man to be a personality, to display the strength of the character of personality. One ought not to refuse personality. One can refuse life and sometimes one ought to refuse it, but not personality, not the dignity of man, not the freedom to which that dignity is linked.

Personality is bound up with the consciousness of vocation. Every man ought to be conscious of that vocation, which is independent of the extent of his gifts. It is a vocation in an individually unrepeatable form to give an answer to the call of God and to put one's gifts to creative use. Personality which is conscious of itself listens to the inward voice and obeys that only. It is not submissive to outward voices. The greatest among men have always listened exclusively to the inward voice and have refused to conform so far as the world is concerned. Personality is connected also with asceticism and presupposes asceticism, that is to say spiritual exercise, the concentration of inward strength, the making of choice, the refusal to acquiesce in a mingling with impersonal forces, both within man and in the surrounding world. This certainly ought not to mean the acceptance of all the traditional forms of asceticism which belong to historical Christianity, in which there was much which was by no means Christian and which was even injurious to personality. Asceticism in its essence should mean the active exposition and the preservation of the forms of personality, of its image, active resistance to the power of the world, which desires to tear personality to pieces and to enslave it. Asceticism is the conflict of personality with slavery and only in that sense is it permissible. When asceticism is changed into slavery, which has so frequently happened in its historical forms, it ought to be rejected and war ought to be declared against it, and that is a fight which makes a demand for the true asceticism. Asceticism is by no means submission and obedience. It is personality's refusal of submission and obedience, it is the fulfilment of its vocation, its answer to the call of God. Personality in its essence is not submissive and obedient. It is resistance, an unbroken creative act. The asceticism which is connected with personality is the heroic principle in man. Slavish asceticism is an abomination. Character presupposes an asceticism which is capable of choice and resistance. But character denotes refusal to acquiesce in slavery, and repudiation of the enslaving majesty of the world.

Personality is a union of the one and the many. The *Parmenides* of Plato is a very subtle dialectic for the solution of the problem of the one and the many. It is at the same time a dialectic of the concept of being. The absolute monism of the *Parmenides* itself could not solve the problem of the many. There is to be found in it the prototype of false ontologism, of slavery to the idea of absolute being, from which there is no way out. The problem of the one and the many tormented Greek thought. It occupies a central place in Plotinus. How is the transition from the one to the many to be made? How is the one accessible to the many? Is there an other which exists for the one? The one, as absolute, would seem not to permit the existence of an other. Here lies the falsity of the very idea of the absolute, an idea which denies relationship, and the going out of the self to an other, to the many. This problem is insoluble on rational grounds. It is bound up with paradox; and in its most profound form it is connected with the problem of personality.

The mystery of Christ does not lend itself to rationalization; it is the mystery of the paradoxical union of the one and the many. Christ represents the whole of humanity. He is the universal Man and at the same time a concrete individual Man, in space and time. The mystery of Christ throws a light upon the mystery of human personality. The individual is only particularized; he belongs to the world of the many. Personality on the other hand is connected with the One, with the image of the One, but in an individually particularized form. Precisely for this reason personality is not a part of the world of the many in which everything is particularized. Human thought and human imagination are inclined to hypostatization, to the personification of forces and qualities. With this is connected the process of creating myths in the life of peoples. Mythopœic hypostatization often becomes false, illusory, and rivets the chains of slavery upon man. The only true hypostatization is the hypostatization of a human being himself, the interpretation of him as personality.

The hypostatization of man, the endowment of him with the qualities of personality is the real myth about man, and it also requires imagination. In accord with this myth man is not a part, he is not particularized, because he is the image of the One and is a universe. This is the God-likeness of man; but the other side of this God-likeness is the man-likeness of God. This is true anthropomorphism, not false. For this reason alone a meeting of man and God is possible, a relation between man and God. The knowledge of God is hypostatization, the understanding of God as personality. And this too requires imagination. This also is a true hypostatization, it is the other half of the hypostatization of man. Man is personality because God is personality and *vice versa*. But personality presupposes the existence of its other. It has a relation not only to the One but also to the many. How can this be in the case of the personality of God? Personality is an existential centre and in it is a capacity to feel sorrow and joy. There is no such thing as personality if there is no capacity for suffering. The conventional theology of the text books denies the suffering of God. This appears to it to be a degradation of the majesty of God; in God there is no movement, God is *actus purus*.

But such an understanding of God is taken not so much from biblical revelation as from the philosophy of Aristotle. If God is Personality and not the Absolute, if He is not only *essentia* but also *existentia,* if there is revealed in Him a personal relation to the other, to the many, then suffering is inherent in Him, and there is a tragic principle in Him. Otherwise God is not personality, but an abstract idea or being such as is conceived by the Eleatic philosophers. The Son of God suffers not only as Man but also as God. There are not only human, but also divine passions. God shares in the sufferings of men. God yearns for His other, for responsive love. God is not an abstract idea, nor abstract existence, elaborated by the categories of abstract thought. God is a Being, a Personality. If the capacity for love is ascribed to God, then the capacity for suffering must also be ascribed to Him. In actual fact atheism has been directed against God as abstract existence, as an abstract idea, as an abstract being, and that fact has given it its measure of truth. No theodicy is possible in regard to such a God. God is to be apprehended only through the Son, Who is a God of love, of sacrifice and of suffering. And that is what personality is.

Personality is bound up with suffering and with tragic contradiction, because it is a union of the one and the many, the relation to the other tortures it. And this other is never a whole, is not an abstract unity into which personality must enter as a part. It is a relation of personality to personality and to personalities. If the monistic interpretation of being is true, if supremacy belongs to that sort of being, then there is no such thing as personality, and it is quite incomprehensible how the consciousness of it could have arisen. The awareness of personality rebels against ontological totalitarianism. We shall see this in the chapter on *The Slavery of Man to Being.* Personality is not being nor a part of being. Personality is spirit, it is freedom, it is action. God also is not being but spirit, freedom, action. Being is objectivization, whereas personality is a phenomenon which belongs to subjectivity. Abstract, rational-conceptual philosophy has always had a defective understanding of personality, and in speaking about it, has subordinated it to the impersonal common. The problem of personality was stated with great acuteness in the nineteenth century by such men as Dostoyevsky, Kirkegaard, Nietzsche and Ibsen, by people, that is, who rebelled against the power of the 'common', against the growing dominance of rational philosophy. Nietzsche, of course, who is so important in the problems that personalism has to face, arrived at a philosophy which destroys personality, but from the other end. We see that it is impossible to frame a single concept about personality; it is characterized by antithesis; it is a contradiction in the world.

Personality does not exist if the transcendent does not exist. Personality is confronted by the transcendent and in realizing itself it transcends. A condition of anguish and distress is deeply inherent in personality as such. Man feels himself to be a creature which is suspended over an abyss, and it is just in man as personality, as he is breaking away from the primitive trend to collective existence, that this feeling reaches a special degree of acuteness.

It is necessary to distinguish anguish (*Angst*) from fear (*Furcht*). Kirkegaard does this, although it is a relative distinction in the terminology of every language. Fear has causes, it is connected with danger, and with the every day world of common experience. Anguish, on the other hand, is experienced, not in the face of empirical danger, but in confronting the mystery of being and non-being, when face to face with the transcendent abyss, in the face of the unknown. Death arouses not only fear in the face of an event which constantly occurs in the empirical every day world, but also anguish in the face of the transcendent. Fear is connected with anxiety, with the dread of suffering and the blows of fate. Fear fails to keep the higher world in mind. It is concerned with a lower level, it is chained to the empirical. Anguish, however, is a condition which borders upon the transcendent. It is experienced when a man is confronted by eternity, when he is faced by destiny.

Man is a being who experiences not only fear and anguish but also yearning. Yearning lies nearer to anguish than to fear, but it has its own quality. Yearning is certainly not what is experienced in passing through danger; it has certainly no connection with anxiety, and indeed it lessens anxiety. Yearning is directed upwards and is a mark of man's higher nature. Man has to submit to abandonment, loneliness and the strangeness of the world. There is nothing that causes more acute suffering than the experience of this strangeness of everything. As it moves along the path of its development personality goes through this experience. There is something of the transcendent in yearning, and that in a twofold sense. Personality passes through the tests of experience as a transcendent thing and as strange to the world; and it has experience of the gulf which separates it from the higher world, from that other world which ought to be its own home. Keen yearning is possible in the very happiest moments of life. There is deeply inherent in man a yearning for the divine life, for purity, for paradise, and no happiest moment of this life answers to that yearning, The existence of personality cannot but be accompanied by yearning, because yearning denotes a break with the world setting into which a man is born and the impossibility of adaptation to it.

Personality in its infinite subjectivity is crushed between the objective and the transcendent, between the processes of objectivization and transcension. Personality cannot come to terms with the everyday world of objects into which it is precipitated. Personality is to be found in the break between the subjective and the objective. Personality can experience the exaltation of its subjectivity and at the same time not pass over in transcendence to another world. This is the romantic stage. Yearning always indicates something lacking and movement towards the fullness of life. There is a tormenting yearning of sex. Sex is yearning; and this yearning cannot be finally overcome in the everyday objective world, for in that world final wholeness is not attainable; that wholeness which the way out from the subjectivity of sex demands. The issue into objectivity denotes a weakening of consciousness of personality, and a subordination of it to the impersonal principle of generic life. What we call sin, guilt, repentance, are, not in the everyday sense of the words, but in the existential sense, only the outcome of transcendence, they are something which stands by and faces the transcendent in the impossibility of transcension.

Man experiences the greatest anguish of all when he is confronted by death. There is a yearning for death, a deathly yearning. Man is a being who lives through an agony, and an agony already during life itself. It is precisely for personality that death is tragic; for everything which is impersonal this tragedy does not exist. Everything mortal must in the nature of things die; but personality is immortal; it is the one and only thing that is immortal; it is created for eternity. And for personality death is the greatest paradox in its destiny. Personality cannot be transformed into a thing, and this turning of a man into a thing, which we call death, cannot be extended to include personality. Death is personality's experience of a break with its destiny, it is a sundering of communication with the world. Death does not put an end to the inward existence of personality, but it puts an end to the existence of the world, that 'other' of the personality to which it went out during its progress. There is no difference between my disappearing to the world, and the world's disappearing to me. The tragedy of death is above all the tragedy of separation. But the relation to death is twofold; it has also a positive meaning for personality. The fullness of the life of personality is not to be realized in this life, in this objectivized world, and in it the existence of personality is impaired and partial. The issuing forth of personality towards the fullness of eternity presupposes death, catastrophe, a leap over the abyss. Therefore yearning cannot be avoided in the existence of personality, and anguish cannot be avoided in the face of transcendent eternity.

The usual teaching about the immortality of the soul as defended by spiritualist, as opposed to materialist, metaphysics does not by any means understand the tragedy of death, nor does it see the actual problem of death. Immortality can only be integral; it can only be the immortality of a whole personality in which the spirit becomes the controlling power of the constitution of man as soul and body. The body belongs to the eternal form of personality, and the separation of the soul from the body at the dissolution of the bodily constitution of man, with the loss of the form of the body, cannot lead to the immortality of personality, that is to say of the whole man. Christianity is opposed to the spiritualist doctrine of the immortality of the soul; it believes in the resurrection of the whole man, the resurrection even of the body. Personality passes through a process of unshackling and of breaking apart, to complete restoration. There is no natural immortality of man; there is only the resurrection and

[54]

eternal life of personality through Christ, through the union of man with God. Outside that there is only the dissolution of man in impersonal Nature. Therefore, the life of personality is continually accompanied by anguish and yearning, but it is also accompanied by hope. When I connect the immortality of man with Christ I by no means wish to say that immortality exists only for those who consciously believe in Christ. The problem goes deeper than that. Christ exists for those also who do not believe in Him.

Personality is bound up with love. Personality is that which loves and which hates, which has experience of *eros* and *anti eros,* it is an agonizing being. There is no personality without passion, just as without passion there is no genius. Love is the path to the realization of personality and there are two types of love, there is a love which ascends and a love which descends, love which is *eros* and love which is *agape*. Both the love which ascends and the love which descends are inherent in personality. In the ascent and in the descent personality is realized. Plato's teaching was only about the love which ascends, which is also *eros*. The Platonic *eros,* born of riches and poverty, is the ascent from the manifold world of the senses to the single world of ideas. *Eros* is not love for a concrete living creature, a mixed creature (a medley of the world of ideas and the world of sense), it is the love of beauty, of the supreme good, of divine perfection. Erotic love is the attraction of the heights, a movement upwards, an ascent, it is the fulfilment of an imperfect being, the enrichment of a poor one. This element is the determining factor in the love of a man and a woman, but it is mingled with other elements. Sex is imperfection and deficiency and it gives rise to a yearning for fulfilment, to a movement towards the completeness which is never attained.

The tragedy of love is connected with the conflict of love for a concrete being which belongs to the world of sense, and love for the beauty which belongs to the world of ideas. Not a single concrete being corresponds with the beauty of the world of ideas in the Platonic sense. Therefore, love as *eros,* love as ascent, love as rapture, must be united with love as descent, love as pity and sympathy. Love as *eros* exists in every love which is selective. It is in the love of a friend, in the love of one's native land, even in the love of the ideal values of philosophy and art. It is in religious life too. Caritative love is descent; it does not seek on its own behalf nor for its own enrichment; it bestows, it makes sacrifice; it is plunged into the suffering world, into the world which agonizes in darkness. Love which is *eros* demands mutuality; love which is compassion has no need of mutuality; in that lies its strength and wealth. Love which is *eros* sees the image of an other, of the loved one in God, as God's idea of man, it sees the beauty of the loved one. Love which is compassion sees the other as abandoned by God, as submerged in the darkness of the world, in suffering, in ugliness.

Scheler has some interesting thoughts about the difference between Christian love and Platonic love, between love directed towards a concrete personality and love directed towards an idea. But Platonism entered deeply into Christianity. For Platonism and the Platonic *eros,* the problem of personality did not arise. Christianity states this problem, but Christian thought and Christian practice have obscured the problem of personality by an impersonal interpretation of love, both of erotic love and of caritative love. The impersonality of the Platonic *eros,* so to speak, passes over into the impersonal interpretation of Christian *caritas.* But the revelation of the essential nature of love must lead to an interpretation of it as a movement directed from personality to personality. The impersonal *eros* is directed to beauty and perfection instead of to a concrete being, an unrepeatable personality. Impersonal love which is *agape,* caritative love, is directed to an impersonal neighbour who is suffering and in need of help. This is the fraction of love in the impersonal upper and lower worlds, in the impersonal world of ideas and the impersonal world of suffering and darkness.

But love which rises above the world of the 'common', of the impersonal, is love which is directed to the image of personality, it is the assertion of this image for eternity, and the assertion for eternity of its communion with that image. And this is equally the case, both when this relation to the other personality is rapture and a movement upwards, and also when the relation is compassion and a movement downwards. The relation to the other man cannot be either exclusively erotic—ascending, or exclusively caritative—descending. A union of the one and the other is necessary. Exclusively erotic love

[56]

contains an element within it which is demoniacal and destructive. An exclusively caritative, descending love contains an element within it which is degrading to the dignity of the other man. In this lies the complexity of the problem of love in its relation to personality.

Christian love, which so easily assumes forms which are rhetorical and degrading to man, when it is turned into an ascetic exercise for the salvation of the soul, and into 'good works', into practical virtue; Christian love at its highest is spiritual, not vitalist. But it cannot be abstractedly spiritual, it is concretely spiritual, it belongs to both soul and spirit, it is bound up with the integrality of personality. A love which is *eros* cannot be directed to all men. You cannot compel yourself to it; it is a matter of choice. Whereas love which is compassion, love which descends can be directed towards the whole suffering world; and in that lies its transfiguring power.

To the problem of love and to the allurement of *eros* we shall return. But it is a very important point in the problem of personality that personality is something which is capable of loving, capable of rapture and compassion and sympathy.

The problem of personality is connected with the problem of *geniality*. *Geniality** is not to be identified with genius. *Geniality* is the whole nature of a man; it is its intuitively creative relation to life. Genius, on the other hand, is the union of this nature with a special gift. *Geniality* is potentially inherent in personality, although it is not genius, for personality is integrality and a creative attitude to life. The image of God in man belongs to *geniality*, but this *geniality* can be concealed, crushed, obscured. Neither the problem of *geniality* nor the problem of genius has any connection at all with a social objectivized hierarchism. The true, not socialized, hierarchism is not connected with social position, nor with social origin nor with wealth, but with a distinction of gifts or vocations, with personal qualities. This is a matter of the social projection of personality. This projection cannot be socially hierarchical. Genius is solitary; it does not belong to any social group whatever, or to any *élite* which has secured possession of privileges; there is a prophetic element in it.

The consciousness of personality in the face of the world is profoundly connected with the existence of evil. Personality becomes

* See note on p. 4.

strong in its resistance to the power of world evil which always has its social crystallization. Personality is choice and in this lies its likeness to genius which is the whole character and effort of the will as it completes its choice. But choice is conflict, it is resistance to the enslaving confusing power of the world. Personality is shaped by the clash with evil in itself and in its environment. One of the paradoxes of personality consists in this that a keen awareness of personality presupposes the existence of sin and guilt. Complete insensitiveness to sin, to guilt, and to evil, is commonly also insensitiveness to personality, it is the dissolution of personality in the common, cosmic and social. The connection of evil with personality, with sin and guilt, leads to the personification of evil, to the creation of the image of a personality as the universal incarnation of evil. But that kind of hypostatization of evil has as its reverse side a weakening of the sense of personal guilt and responsibility. In that lies the complexity of the problem. This same problem exists in the attitude to evil which is adopted by any individual man. No man can be an incarnation and personification of evil, the evil in him is always partial. For this reason, there cannot be a final judgment upon anybody. This lays down limits also to the very principle of punishment. A man may commit a crime, but the man as a whole personality cannot be a criminal; he must not be treated as an incarnation of crime; he remains a personality, in him is the image of God. And the personality which has committed a crime does not belong as a whole and finally to the state and society. A personality is a citizen of the Kingdom of God and not of the kingdom of Caesar; the judgment and condemnation of the kingdom of Caesar in relation to it are partial, nor are they final. For this reason personalism is decisively and radically opposed to the death penalty.

Personality in man cannot be socialized. The socialization of man is only partial and does not extend to the depth of personality, to its conscience, to its relation to the source of life. Socialization which is extended to the depth of existence, to spiritual life, is the triumph of *das Mann,* and of social routine. It is the tyranny of the average and common over the personally individual. Therefore, the principle of personality ought to stand as a principle of social organization, one which will not permit the socialization of the inward existence of man.

Personality cannot even be enlisted under the banner of the service of the 'common good'. The 'common good' has served to cover much tyranny and slavery. The service of the common good, that is of something which has no existence of its own, is but the service of the good of one's neighbour, of every concrete being, but helpless, curtailed and abstract. It only means that in the objectivized world man is classed under the heading of mathematical number.

The supremacy of personality is tragic to man, for man contains within him that also which is not personal, and this non-personal in man rebels against the fact that the realization of personality is possible only through contradiction and disruption. The source of slavery is objectivization. Objectivization is always the organization of dominance, which is a contradiction of the dignity of personality. It is precisely in the objectivization, the exteriorization, and the alienation of human nature that man falls under the sway of the will to power, of money, of the thirst for pleasure, glory, etc., which are destructive of personality. Personality realizes its existence and its destiny in the contradictions and the combinations of the finite and the infinite, of the relative and the absolute, of the one and the many, of freedom and necessity, of the inward and the outward. There is no unity and identity of the inward and the outward, of the subjective and the objective, but a tragic lack of correspondence, and a conflict. But unity and universality are attained not in infinite objectivity but in infinite subjectivity, in subjectivity which transcends itself.

2. MASTER, SLAVE AND FREE MAN

It is well to repeat constantly that man is a being who is full of con-tradictions and that he is in a state of conflict with himself. Man seeks freedom. There is within him an immense drive towards free-dom, and yet not only does he easily fall into slavery, but he even loves slavery. Man is a king and a slave. In the *Phänomenologie des Geistes,* Hegel gives expression to some remarkable thoughts on the subject of master and slave, about *Herrschaft* and *Knechtschaft.* He is not there discussing the social categories of master and slave, but something deeper. It is the problem of the structure of consciousness. There are three conditions of man, three structures of consciousness, and they may be distinguished under the names of 'master', 'slave' and 'free man'. Master and slave are correlatives. Neither of them can exist without the other. The free man, however, exists in himself; he has his own quality within him, without correlation to anything placed in antithesis to him. The master is an existing consciousness for himself, but that consciousness is derived through some other, it is through the slave that he exists for himself. If the consciousness of a master is consciousness of the existence of some other for him, then the consciousness of the slave is the existence of himself for the other. The consciousness of the free man, on the other hand, is consciousness of the existence of each one for himself, but with a free outgoing from himself to the other and to all. The boundary of a state of slavery is the absence of awareness of it.

The world of slavery is the world of spirit which is alienated from itself. Exteriorization is the source of slavery, whereas freedom is interiorization. Slavery always indicates alienation, the ejection of human nature into the external. Feuerbach and later on Marx recognized this source of the slavery of man; but they connected it with a materialistic philosophy, which is the legitimatization of the slavery of man. Alienation, exteriorization, the ejection of the spiritual nature of man into the external denote the slavery of man. The economic slavery of man undoubtedly signifies the alienation of human nature and the turning of a man into a thing. Marx was right in this. But for the liberation of man his spiritual nature must be restored to him; he must be aware of himself as a free and spiritual being. If on the other hand man remains a material and economic being and his spiritual nature is regarded as an illusion of consciousness, as the effect of a deceptive ideology, then man remains a slave and he is a slave by nature. In the objectivized world man can be only relatively not absolutely free, and his freedom presupposes conflict and resistance to necessity, which he ought to overcome. But freedom presupposes a spiritual principle in man which offers resistance to enslaving necessity. The freedom which is the result of necessity will not be real freedom, it is only an element in the dialectic of necessity. Hegel in actual fact knew nothing of real freedom.

Consciousness which exteriorizes and alienates is always slavish consciousness. God the Master, man the slave; the church the master, man the slave; the state the master, man the slave; society the master, man the slave; the family the master, man the slave; Nature the master, man the slave; object the master, man-subject the slave. The source of slavery is always objectivization, that is to say exteriorization, alienation. It is slavery in everything; in the acquisition of knowledge, in morals, in religion, in art, in political and social life. Putting an end to slavery is putting an end to objectivization; and putting an end to slavery does not mean that mastership will make its appearance, for mastership is the reverse side of slavery. Man must become not a master but a free man. Plato truly said that the tyrant is himself a slave. The enslaving of another is also the enslaving of oneself. Mastership and enslavement were originally connected with magic which has no knowledge of freedom. Primitive magic was the will to power. The master is nothing but the figure of a slave who leads the world into delusion. Prometheus was a free man and a liberator; whereas a dictator is a slave and an enslaver; the will to power is always a servile will. Christ was a free man, the freest of the sons of men. He was free from the world; He was bound only by love. Christ spoke as one having authority but He did not have the will to authority, and He was not a master. Caesar, the hero of imperialism, is a slave; he is the slave of the world, the slave of the will to power, the slave of the human masses, without whom he cannot realize his will to power. The master knows only the height to which his slaves raise him. Caesar knows only the height to which the masses raise him. But the slaves, and the masses, also overthrow all masters and all Caesars. Freedom is freedom not only from the masters but from the slaves also. The master is determined from without; the master is not a personality, just as the slave is not a personality. Only the free man is a personality and he is that even if the whole world should wish to enslave him.

The fall of man finds expression most of all in the fact that he is a tyrant. He is a tyrant, if not on a great scale, then on a small, if not in the state, if not in the pages of world history, then in his family, in his shop, in his office, in the bureaucratic establishment in which he occupies the very smallest position. Man has an unconquerable inclination to play a part and in that part to assign a special importance to himself, to play the tyrant over those around him. Man is a tyrant not only in hatred but also in love. A man in love becomes a dreadful tyrant. Jealousy is a manifestation of tyranny in a passive form. A jealous person is an enslaver who lives in a world of fiction and hallucination.

Man is a tyrant over himself also and perhaps most of all over himself. He tyrannizes over himself as a dichotomous creature which has lost its entirety. He tyrannizes over himself by a false consciousness of guilt. A true consciousness of guilt would set man free. He tyrannizes over himself by false beliefs, superstitions, myths. He tyrannizes over himself by every sort of fear that is possible. He tyrannizes over himself by envy, by self-love, by *ressentiment*. An unhealthy self-love is a most dreadful form of tyranny. Man tyrannizes over himself by the consciousness of his weakness and insignificance and by the thirst for power and greatness. By his enslaving will man enslaves not only another but himself. There exists an age long tendency to despotism, a thirst for power and mastership. The primary evil is the power of man over man, the lowering of the dignity of man, violence and domination. The exploitation of man by man, which Marx considers the primary evil, is a derivative evil; it is a phenomenon which becomes possible when man lords it over man. But a man gets into the position of master over some other man because in accordance with the structure of his consciousness he has become a slave to the will to mastership. The same power by which he enslaves another, enslaves himself also. A free man does not desire to lord it over anyone.

The 'unhappy consciousness', according to Hegel, is the consciousness of a being who is aware of another being who is opposed to him, and so of one who is aware of his own insignificance. When the essential being of a man is felt by another to be opposed to him, then he may suffer the vexation of a slavish consciousness of dependence. But in such a case he often wins back his losses, and compensates himself by the enslavement of others. The most terrible of all is the slave who has become a master. As a master, however, the least terrible is the aristocrat who is conscious of his nobility of origin and dignity, and is free from *ressentiment*. The dictator, a man of the will to power, never becomes such an aristocrat. The psychology of the dictator, who is essentially a *parvenu,* is a perversion of man. He is the slave of his own enslavements. He is, in the most profound sense, the antithesis of Prometheus the liberator. The leader of the crowd is in the same state of servitude as the crowd; he has no existence outside the crowd, outside slavery, over which he plays the master. He is entirely ejected into the external.

The will to power, to dominance, to mastership, is possession; it is not free will nor is it the will to freedom. The man who is possessed by the will to power is in the grip of fate and becomes a man of destiny. The Caesar-dictator, the hero of the imperialistic will, places himself at the disposal of fate. He cannot stop, he cannot set limits to himself; he goes on ever further and further towards perdition. He is a man whose fate has been decided. The will to power is insatiable. It does not witness to an abundance of strength which bestows itself upon men. The imperialistic will creates a fantastic ephemeral kingdom and gives rise to catastrophe and war. The imperialistic will is a demoniacal perversion of the true vocation of man. It contains a perversion of the universalism to which man is called. This universalism tries to realize itself through a false objectivization, through casting out human existence into the external, through the exteriorization which makes man a slave. Man is called to be lord of the earth and the world. Kingship is inherent in the idea of man. Man is called to expansion and to take possession of extended spaces; he is attracted to great adventure. But the Fall of man gives a false, an enslaving, direction to this universal will.

It was the lonely and unhappy Nietzsche who was the philosopher of the will to power. And how monstrously they have made use of Nietzsche, how they have vulgarized him. How they have made his thought the instrument of purposes which Nietzsche himself would have repudiated. Nietzsche addressed himself to the few; he was an aristocratic thinker; he despised the human masses, without whom the imperialistic will cannot be realized. He called the state the most cold-blooded of monsters and said that man only begins where the state ends. How in this case is empire to be organized, for empire is always the organization of the masses, of the average man? Nietzsche was a weak man who lacked strength of any sort—the very weakest of the men of this world. Nor did he possess the will to power; what he had was the idea of the will to power. He called upon men to be harsh, but it is doubtful whether he understood by harshness the violence of states and revolutions, and the harshness of the imperialistic will. The figure of Caesar Borgia was to him only a symbol of the inward tragedy of the spirit which he himself experienced. But the exaltation of the imperialistic will, the will to power, and to enslavement, in any case denotes a break with the ethics of the Gospel. And this break is taking place in the world. There was still nothing of it in the old humanism, nor did it exist in the French Revolution. The enslaving gesture of violence would like to be a gesture of strength, but it is in its very essence always a gesture of weakness. Caesar is the very weakest of men. Every man who inflicts punishment is a man who has wiped out the strength of the spirit, who has lost all consciousness of it. We come now to the very complex problem of violence.

That will to power, the imperialistic will is opposed to the dignity and freedom of man is absolutely clear. And indeed imperialistic philosophy has never said that it defends the freedom and dignity of man. It exalts the exercise of violence upon man, and makes it the mark of man's highest attainment. But the actual problem of force, and one's attitude towards it, are very complex and difficult. When men revolt against violence, they commonly have in view forms of violence which are crude and leap to the eyes. They beat men, put them in prison, kill them. But human life is full of unnoticed, more refined forms of violence. Psychological violence plays a still greater rôle in life than physical. Man is deprived of his freedom and is made a slave not only as the result of physical violence. The suggestion which reaches a man from his social environment and which he undergoes from childhood, may make a slave of him. A system of upbringing may completely deprive a man of his freedom and incapacitate him for freedom of judgment.

The weight and solidity of history use force on a man. It is possible to use force on a man by way of threat, by way of some mental contagion which has been turned into collective action. Enslavement is murder. Man always brings to bear upon man either a flow of life or a flow of death. And hate is always a stream of death brought to bear upon another, and doing violence to him. Hate always desires to take away freedom. But the astonishing thing is that love also can become deadly and send out the stream of death. Love enslaves no less than hate. Human life is permeated by underground streams, and man chances unseeingly upon an atmosphere which does violence to him and enslaves him. There is a psychological force of the individual person, and there is a psychological force of the community, of society. Crystallized, hardened public opinion becomes violence upon man. Man can be a slave to public opinion, a slave to custom, to morals, to judgments and opinions which are imposed by society. It is difficult to overestimate the violence which is perpetrated by the press in our time. The average man of our day holds the opinions and forms the judgments of the newspaper which he reads every morning: it exercises psychological compulsion upon him. And in view of the falsehood and venality of the press, the effects are very terrible as seen in the enslavement of man and his deprivation of freedom of conscience and judgment. And all the while how comparatively little this form of violence is noticed. It is noticed only in countries which live under dictatorship, where the falsification of men's opinions and judgments is an activity of the state.

There is a still more deep-seated form of violence, and that is the strong hand of the power of money. This is the hidden dictatorship in capitalist society. They do not use violence upon a man directly, in a noticeable fashion. The life of a man depends upon money, the most impersonal, the most unqualitative power in the world, and the most readily convertible into everything else alike. It is not directly, by way of physical violence, that a man is deprived of his freedom of conscience, freedom of thought, and freedom of judgment, but he is placed in a position of dependence materially, he finds himself under the threat of death by starvation and in this way he is deprived of his freedom. Money confers independence; the absence of it places a man in a position of dependence.

But even the man who possesses money finds himself in a state of servitude and is exposed to an unnoticed form of violence. In the Kingdom of Mammon, man is compelled to sell his labour and his

B.S.F.

labour is not free. Man has not known real freedom in labour. The labour of the artisan has been more free, relatively speaking, and so has intellectual labour, which by the way, has also been exposed to unnoticed violence. But the mass of human beings has served its time in toil which is servile, in forced labour, in the new slave labour of the capitalist world, and in bond-service after the pattern of the communist society. Man remains ever more and more a slave.

It is a very interesting fact that psychologically the easiest thing of all to accept as freedom is the absence of movement, the habitual condition. In movement there is already a certain exercise of force upon the surrounding world, upon material environment and upon other people. Movement is change, and it does not ask for the acquiescence of the world in this altered position, which is an effect of that change caused by the movement. Such an acceptance of rest as the absence of force; and of movement, change, as force, has conservative results in social life. Habitual, time-hardened slavery may not appear to be a form of violence, while a movement which is directed to the abolition of slavery may appear to be violence. The social reformation of society is accepted as violence by those to whom a certain habitual social order has presented itself as freedom, even though it may be terribly unjust and wrong. All reforms in the position of the working classes call forth from the side of the bourgeois classes, shouts about the violation of freedom and the use of force. Such are the paradoxes of freedom in social life. Slavery lies in wait for man on all sides. The fight for freedom presupposes resistance and without resistance its pathos is enfeebled. Freedom which has been established by an habitual way of living, passes over into an unnoticed enslavement of men; this is freedom which has become objectivized, whereas all the while freedom is the realm of the subject. Man is a slave because freedom is difficult, whereas slavery is easy.

In the servile world of objects, they regard violence as strength, as strength made manifest. The exaltation of violence always means the worship of power. But violence is not only not identical with power, it should never be connected with power. Power, in its most profound sense means the taking possession of that to which it is directed; not domination, in which externality is always maintained,

[66]

but a persuasive, inwardly subjugating union. Christ speaks with power. A tyrant never speaks with power. The man who exerts force is absolutely powerless over those upon whom he exerts it. They resort to force as a result of impotence, in consequence of the fact that they have no power whatever against those upon whom they exert violence.

The master has no power at all over his slave. He can put him on the rack, but this torture only means that he is confronted by an insuperable obstacle. And had the master had power, he would have ceased to be a master. The limit of powerlessness in relation to another man finds its expression in the murdering of him. Limitless power would be revealed if it were possible to raise a man from the dead. Power is the transfiguration, the enlightenment, the resuscitation of another. Violence, torture, and murder, on the other hand, are weakness. In the objectivized, assimilated, depersonalized, exteriorized world, that is not called power which is power in the existential sense of the word. This is expressed in the clash between power and value. The higher values in the world appear to be weaker than the lower, the higher values are crucified, the lower triumph. The policeman and the sergeant major, the banker and the lawyer, are stronger than the poet and the philosopher, the prophets and the saint. In the objectivized world, matter is stronger than God. The Son of God was crucified. Socrates was poisoned. The prophets were stoned. The initiators and creators of new thought and a new way of living have always been persecuted, and oppressed and often put to death. The average man of the social routine of daily life has triumphed. Only the master and the slave have triumphed, they could not endure free men. The higher value, that of human personality, they were unwilling to acknowledge, while the lower value, the state, with its violence and falsehood, with its espionage and cold-blooded murder, they regarded as the higher value, and servilely bow down before it.

In the objectivized world they love only the finite, they cannot bear the infinite. And this sway of the finite always shows itself as the slavery of man, whereas the hidden infinite would be liberation. They associated power with the bad means which were considered necessary for ends which were regarded as good. But the whole of life has been filled with these methods, and the purposes have never been attained, and man becomes a slave of the means which supposedly give him power. Man has sought power in false ways, in the ways of impotence, which are shown in acts of violence. Man has consummated acts of will which enslave, and he has not consummated acts of will which liberate. In the so-called great actors of history, the heroes of imperialistic will, it is murder that has always played an enormous part, and this has always been evidence of the metaphysical weakness of those 'strong' men, of a pathological will to power and might, and domination, accompanied by a mania for persecution. Spiritual weakness, powerlessness over the inner life of man, absence of strength which resuscitates to a new life, have led to this, that the tortures of hell have been readily admitted in the life to come, and executions, tortures, and cruel punishments in this life. Truth is crucified in the world, but real power is in truth—the truth of God.

The philosophical source from which the slavery of man derives is monism. The practical expression of monism is tyrannical. Personalism is most profoundly opposed to monism. Monism is the domination of the 'common', of the abstract universal, and the denial of personality and freedom. Personality and freedom are linked with pluralism or, more correctly, externally they take the form of pluralism, while inwardly they may signify concrete universalism. Conscience cannot have its centre in any sort of universal unity; it is not liable to alienation; it remains in the depth of personality. Conscience in the depth of personality does not by any means indicate the confinement of personality within itself; it does not denote egoism. On the contrary it presupposes an opening out inwardly, not in the external, and an inward fulfilling by the concrete universal content. But this concretely universal content of personality never means that it deposits its conscience and its consciousness with society, with the state, with the nation, or a class, or a party, or with the church as a social institution. There is only one acceptable, non-servile meaning of the word *sobornost*,* and that is the interpretation of it as the interior concrete universalism of

*See note on p. 4.

[68]

personality, and not the alienation of conscience in any kind of exterior collective body whatever. The free man is simply the man who does not allow the alienation, the ejection into the external of his conscience and his judgment. He who permits this is a slave. The master also permits it, but he is only another form of slave.

Terminologically it is inexact to speak of the autonomy of personality, or of the autonomy of consciousness, or of conscience. In Kant it means subjection to the persona¹ moral-intellectual law. In that case it is not man who is autonomous, but the moral-intellectual law. It is the autonomy of man, as personality, that must be called freedom. Men pitted either reason or nature against the authoritarian and hierarchical order in European history. Reason or nature rebelled against authority, but the freedom of man was not attained in this way. Man remains subjected to impersonal reason, to a sovereign society or simply to natural necessity. To the authoritarian consciousness or to the authoritarian order of life must be opposed, not reason, and not nature, and not a sovereign society, but spirit, that is to say, freedom, the spiritual principle in man, which organizes his personality and is independent of objectivized nature and the objectivized logical world. This presupposes a change of direction in the conflict against the slavery of man, that is to say it presupposes the personalistic transvaluation of values in the defence of which this book is written. The inward existential universalism of personality must be opposed to the outward objectivized universalism which is ever more and more creating new forms of slavery. Everything which is not personal, everything alienated into the sphere of the 'common', is the seduction and slavery of man. The free man is a self-governing being not a governed being; nor is it the self-government of a society and a people, but the self-government of a man who has become a personality. The self-government of a society, and of a people is still the government of slaves.

The change of direction in the fight for the freedom of man, for the manifestation of the free man, is above all a change in the structure of consciousness, a change in the scale of values. This process goes deep and its effects can but slowly become apparent. It is a profound interior revolution which is brought about in existential, not in historical, time. This change in the structure of consciousness is also

[69]

a change in the interpretation of the relation between immanence and transcendence. The immanent continuity which precipitates man into the continuous evolutionary process is the negation of personality, which presupposes interruption and transcension. Man is subordinated to the universal unity in relation to which God is fully immanent. But God is also completely transcendent in relation to this universal unity and to the process which takes place in it. And this transcendence of God, the freedom of God from world necessity, and from all objectivity, is the source of the freedom of man, it constitutes the very possibility of the existence of personality. But transcendence also can be understood in a servile way and may mean the degradation of man. Transcendence can be interpreted as objectivization and exteriorization, and relation to it not as an inward act of transcension in freedom, but as the relation of slave to master. The way of liberation lies on the other side of traditional immanence and transcendence. The process of transcension in freedom never means subjection to an alien will, which indeed is slavery, but subjection to the Truth which is at the same time also the Way and the Life.

Truth is always connected with freedom and is bestowed upon freedom only. Slavery is always the denial of truth, and the dread of truth. Love for the truth is triumph over enslaving fear. Primitive man who still lives on in contemporary man is under the sway of fear; he is a slave of the past, of what is customary, of the spirit of his ancestors. Myths can enslave. The free man does not live under the sway of myths. He is emancipated from that sway. But people of our contemporary civilization, at the highest point of civilization, are still under the power of myths, and, in particular, under the power of the myth of universal realities, of the realm of the 'common' to which man ought to be subjected. But universal common realities do not exist, they are phantoms and illusions created by objectivization. Universal values exist, for example, truths, but always in a concrete and individual form. Hypostatization of universal values is a false direction for consciousness to take. It is the old metaphysic and it cannot be justified. Outside personality no sort of universality exists. The universe is to be found in the personality of man, in the personality of God. The personification of principles is objectivization and in that process personality disappears.

Slavery is passivity. The victory over slavery is creative activity. Only in existential time is creative activity disclosed. Historical activity is objectivization, the projection of what has been accomplished in the core of personality. And historical time would make man its slave. The free man ought not to bend the knee either before history or before race or before revolution or before any objective unity which makes pretentions to universal significance. The master also bows the knee before history, before common unities, before false universals, as the slave does. Master and slave have a great deal more in common than they think. The free man cannot even desire to be a master. It would indicate the loss of freedom. In order to prepare the structure of consciousness which overcomes slavery and domination it is necessary to construct an apophatic sociology on the analogy of apophatic theology. Kataphatic sociology is to be found in the categories of slavery and domination. It has no issue in freedom. The usual sociological concepts are not applicable to thinking about society which is free from the categories of domination and slavery. Such thinking presupposes renunciation and a negative attitude in relation to everything upon which society in the kingdom of Caesar rests, that is to say in the objectivized world where man also becomes an object. A society of free men, a society of personalities, is not either a monarchy or a theocracy or an aristocracy or a democracy, nor is it authoritarian society nor a liberal society, nor a bourgeois society nor a socialist society: it is not fascism nor communism, nor even anarchism as far as objectivization exists in anarchism. This is pure apophatics as the knowledge of God is pure apophatics, free from concepts, free from all rationalization. For all this means that change in the structure of consciousness in which objectivization disappears, in which there is no antithesis between subject and object, no master, no slave. It is infinity, it is subjectivity filled with a universal content; it is the realm of pure existentiality. It would be a complete mistake to refer apophatic sociology to the other heavenly transcendent world, to the life 'beyond the grave' and to find peace and quiet in the thought that in this earthly immanent world, in the life before death, everything should be left in the old way. We shall see that this is an absolutely false understanding of eschatology, one which makes it an interpretation of the end without

[71]

any existential significance. In actual fact, change in the structure of consciousness, the putting an end to objectivization, the establishment of a society of free men, which are thinkable only for apophatic sociology, ought to take place already on this side of the grave.

Man lives not only in the cosmic time of the natural kaleidoscope of life and in the disrupted historical time which rushes towards the future; he lives also in existential time; he exists also outside the objectivity which he makes for himself. In the last part of this book we shall see that the 'end of the world' which in philosophical language denotes the end of objectivity, presupposes creative activity on the part of man and is accomplished not only 'on the other side' but also 'on this side'. This paradox of human destiny and the destiny of the world must be thought of paradoxically; one cannot think of it in rational categories. Master and slave, generally speaking, cannot think about this. Only free men can think of it. Master and slave will make superhuman efforts to prevent the end of objectivity, the 'end of the world', the coming of the Kingdom of God, the kingdom of freedom and free men. They will establish ever new forms of domination and slavery; they will fashion new disguises for new forms of objectivization in which the creative acts of man will meet with great failures; they will prolong the crimes of history. But free men should prepare their kingdom not only 'there' but also 'here' and above all prepare themselves, make themselves free, make themselves personalities. The free have a responsibility which lies upon them. Slaves cannot prepare a new kingdom, one to which in fact the very word 'kingdom' is not to be applied; the revolt of slaves always establishes new forms of slavery. Only free men can so grow as to achieve this. The master has one lot with the slave, and we must trace in what a number of varied and refined forms slavery lies in wait for man and seduces him.

PART II

1. BEING AND FREEDOM. THE SLAVERY OF MAN TO BEING

Metaphysics has always aspired to be ontology, a philosophy of being; this is a very ancient tradition in philosophy. Parmenides was the principal person to lay the foundation of it; he was an ontologist *par excellence*. There was never anything more abstract than the interpretation of being in Parmenides. Plato could not reconcile himself to such an abstractedness and tried to complicate and refine the problem of being. But the ontological tradition comes down from Plato also and in our time the representatives of ontological philosophy are Platonists. I have long had my doubts about the truth of ontologism in general and of Platonic ontology in particular, and I have already given expression to this in my book, *The Meaning of Creativeness,* in which I have affirmed the supremacy of freedom over being, although my terminology was not precise enough nor consistently worked out. Today, more than ever, ontologism is a mistaken philosophy. I regard existential philosophy as true, for I think there is another type of thought and a different interpretation of the ancient problem of the relation between *essentia* and *existentia*. True philosophy must reach out towards concrete reality, towards what actually exists, and there is such a tendency nowadays in philosophical thought. Besides in Plato himself there was eternal truth in spite of his abstract ontologism.

The problem of being is in the first place this:—to what extent is being a construction of thought, that is to say, objectivization effected by the subject, that is to say something secondary and not primary? Being is a concept, that is to say it is something which takes place as a result of objectivized thought; the imprint of abstraction lies upon it and, therefore, it enslaves man as every form of objectivization does. In the primary subjectivity of existence being was certainly not included. We have no experience of being as a primary datum. In the ontologies of Parmenides and the Platonists actually ideal being is a universal common. The individually unique is either derivative, subordinate or illusory. The ideal, that which belongs to ideas, is the actually real. Real things are universals. The manifold and individual world is a secondary world, a reflected world, not completely real. In it being is mingled with non-being. Such was the summit of Greek philosophic thought which is still prevalent in the new and even the newest ontological philosophy. But in fact the reverse is the case. It is precisely this empirical objectivized world which is the realm of the common, the realm of law, the realm of necessity, the realm of compulsion by universal principles, upon everything individual and personal. Whereas the other, the spiritual world is the realm of the individual, the unique, the personal, the realm of freedom. The 'common' which objectively compels is master only in this empirical world; there is nothing of it in the spiritual world. Spirit, in contradiction to widespread opinion, is opposed above all to the 'common'; it knows only the unique.

The problem of the one and the many must be posed in another way than in Plato and the Platonists. This objectivizing exteriorizing thought of man constructs being as 'common', as universal. Therefore, the personal, the singular is turned into the partial, the particular. But existential truth lies in the fact that the real thing exists singularly; the common is not real, and certainly not in the sense in which it is affirmed by the nominalists who represent only the opposite pole of objectivizing and abstracting thought. The Platonic realists (Frank and Lossky) say of the nominalists that they imagine that the reality of 'horse in general' means that 'horse in general' is grazing in some meadow. To this they reply that 'horse in general' exists as a unity made up of all separate horses. But in this case we still have the mistake of the old problems, the old way of stating problems which belongs to the controversies of the realists and nominalists. There remains the logical antithesis of the common and the unique and particular, of the universal and the individual; but this antithesis is brought into being by objectivizing thought. Within existence the one, the individual, is universal, concretely universal and no universal as common exists. 'Horse in general' and 'man in general' do not exist. There is no unity of all separate horses and men as 'common'. But in the separate horse and in the separate

[74]

man exists the universality (not the commonness) of equine and human existence. Unity in reality does not resemble unity in thought. We arrive at the universality of a separate man not by abstracting the properties common to us human beings but by submersion in his oneness. Using Kantian terminology it might be said that the realm of Nature is the realm of the common, whereas the realm of freedom is the realm of the unique and particular. But the realm of freedom is the realm of the spirit. A philosophy which lays the concept of being as its foundation stone, is naturalistic metaphysics. Being is nature (*ousia*), it belongs to the objectivized world which is brought into being by rationalization. To think of spirit as being means to think of it in the naturalistic way as nature, as an object. But spirit is not an object, it is not nature, it is not being in the sense of substance. Spirit is subject, it is an act, it is freedom. A primary act is not being, being is a congealed act. The mystics truly and profoundly taught that God is not being in the sense of substance, that the limiting concept of being is not applicable to God. God is; but He is not being in the sense of substance. In the words 'I am existing', the chief emphasis is upon 'I' and not upon 'existing'. The ego, personality, is more primary than 'being' which is the result of categorical thinking. *Personality is more primary than being.* This is the basis of personalism. Being is a product of abstract thought. And yet here is my favourite cat existing. Being has no existence. Cat (person) is the kernel of the phrase 'the cat exists'. In any case the concept of being cannot be laid as the foundation stone of philosophy because that concept is ambiguous. Being denotes both subject and predicate. Vladimir Solovyev proposes that we should use the term *sooshtchee*, the existent, to denote the subject of existence; but *sooshtchee*, the existent is connected with existence. The enchantment of ontology, the lure of being has become one of the sources of the slavery of man. Man has been accepted as the slave of being, which determines him entirely. He is not free in relation to being. His very freedom is born of being. Ontology can be an enslavement of man. The fundamental problem is the problem of the relation between being and freedom, between being and spirit.

One must choose between two philosophies, the philosophy which acknowledges the primacy of being over freedom and the philosophy

[75]

which recognizes the supremacy of freedom over being. This choice cannot be limited to the process of thinking alone. It is determined by the whole spirit, that is by the will also. Personalism must recognize the supremacy of freedom over being. The philosophy of the primacy of being is a philosophy of impersonalism; a system of ontology which acknowledges the absolute supremacy of being is a system of determinism. Every objectivized system of intellectualistic philosophy is a system of determinism. It derives freedom from being. Freedom appears as determined being; that is in the last resort freedom is the offspring of necessity. Being appears as ideal necessity; no break through is possible in it. Being is a continuous, compact absolute unity. But freedom cannot be derived from being; freedom is rooted in nothing, in baselessness, in non-being, if we use ontological terminology. Freedom is without foundation; it is not determined by being nor born of it. There is no compact uninterrupted being. There are breaks, fractions, abysses, paradoxes; there are transcensions. There exist, therefore, only freedom and personality. The supremacy of freedom over being is also the supremacy of spirit over being. Being is static, spirit is dynamic; spirit is not being.

One cannot by the means which intellectual processes provide think of spirit as of an object. Spirit is subject, subjectivity. It is freedom and creative act. Dynamic activity and creativeness oppose the intellectualistic conception of being. Impersonal· common reason conceives an impersonal common being, an object alienated from human existence. Intellectualistic philosophy always appears as anti-personalist and in addition as vitalist philosophy. The conception of personality, of freedom, is connected with the personal, the reason, with will and activity. Two points of view come into collision. (1) There is the unchanging; the eternal rational order of being. It expresses itself also in the social order which is not created by man and to which man must be subordinated. And (2) the foundations oj the life of the world and society which is staggered by the Fall, are not eternal and are not imposed from above; they change with human activity and creativeness. The first point of view enslaves man, the second liberates him. Ontologism is an impersonal conception, impersonal truth; no pre-arranged harmony of being exists, no whole unity like truth, goodness, righteousness.

[76]

The Greek point of view of the world was based upon an aesthetic contemplation of the whole. But in the world there is a conflict of polarized forces and, therefore, there is not only order but also disorder, not only harmony but also disharmony. Boehme understood this more profoundly than anyone. World order, world unity, world harmony are connected with the laws of logic, the laws of nature, the laws of the state, with the power of the 'common', with the power of necessity; this is objectivization and it is brought about by the Fall. In the other world, the world of spirituality, everything is free, everything is individual; there is no common, there is no necessity. The world is objectivized, that is to say, it is spirit estranged from itself. Going deeper it may be said being is alienation and objectivization, a change of freedom into necessity, the individual into the common, the personal into the impersonal. It is the triumph of reason which has lost its link with human existence. But the liberation of man signifies a return of the spirit to itself, namely to freedom. Even to Hegel spirit is existence which exists for itself; but Hegel did not understand that objectivization of the spirit is slavery. He did not understand personality; he did not understand freedom which is not consciously recognized necessity. In the understanding of objectivization Schopenhauer was more right than Hegel. But objectivization is not only the outcome of a certain direction of will; it is also the outcome of unquenchable desire in the objectivized world.

Platonism, as it passed through the new philosophy was changed essentially and this change was both for the worse and for the better. The Platonic ideas, *eidosi*, are species. The artistic genius of Plato gave them a unique life of their own. The new rationalistic philosophy finally turned the Greek 'common' ideas into concepts. In Hegel the world is a dialectic self-revelation of a concept, of a concept which, as it were, is subject to passions, but by this the character of the concept as specific is exposed, its dependence upon constructions of thought, upon a categorical process of thinking. Idealism (which is realism in the mediaeval sense) does not depend upon the subject as a concept. The merit of the new philosophy lay in this that it revealed the activity of the subject in the construction of the objective world. The service rendered by Kant was particularly great, He cleared the ground for an absolutely new way of philosophizing, although he

[77]

himself did not enter upon that way. Being as an object, the being of the universally 'common' is a construction of the subject in certain directions of its activity. Being is disclosed by the transference of existence, that is of the primary-real and concrete, out of the depth of the subject into the illusory depth of the exteriorized object. Then the common will appear as the higher and the individual as the lower; but within the subject in the depth of existence, the individual is the higher and the common is the lower. What is the most primary thing about the particular single horse? The idea of the horse, the common in it, or the individually-unrepeatable in it? This is an age-long problem. It is precisely the individually-unrepeatable in the single horse which is the most rich and full and the chief thing. Also what we call 'common' in the horse, its horseness, is only qualitativeness, the qualitativeness of the individually-unrepeatable and unique. In the same way the individually-unrepeatable unique man includes universal humanity in himself but does not enter into it as a subordinate part. In the same way everything which concretely exists is richer and more primary than abstract being. The abstract quality of being, the predicate of being, is only an inward integral part of the concretely existing unique. The 'common' belonging to being, the 'common' universal, the 'common' human, is to be found in concrete human personality and not the other way round. Abstract being is the product of constructing thought. It has no inward existence at all. Being does not exist. In mediaeval terminology *essentia* has no *existentia*. The real which we associate with being is only the inward property, the quality of concrete creatures and existences. It is in them, and not they in it. The worth of the concrete creature, of human personality, is certainly not determined by the ideal universal in it to which it is subordinate, but precisely by the concrete individually personal existence, the individual personal form of the disclosure of the universal from within. The concrete creature, human personality, is not subordinate to any 'being'; that subordination is the offspring of slavish consciousness. Slavery to being is indeed the primary slavery of man. It is wrong to suppose that the consciousness of man in its universally binding elements is not subjective but objective and universal, or—as Prince S. Trubetskoy says, is 'socialistic consciousness'. Objectivization and subordination to the universal as 'common' takes place in consciousness as exteriorization in relation to human personality. In actual fact consciousness is universalistic in its subjectivity, in its revelation, in its subjectivity of universal qualities, exteriorized but inward.

On the soil of Platonism there springs up a social philosophy which sees in necessary legal measures the ideal foundations of society. In this theory there is a false process in the classification of absolutes, and what amounts to deification of the laws of nature and the laws of society. This can be seen in the extreme universalism of Spann and in a milder form in Frank. The supremacy of being over freedom, the supremacy of being over spirit is always a philosophical presupposition. In this a partial acknowledgement of freedom denotes the derivation of it from necessity, from ideal necessity, of course, and subordination to it. But ideal necessity is in no degree less hostile to freedom than material necessity. German idealism was not the philosophy of freedom that it wished to be. Kant was nearer to freedom as the antithesis of determinism, since his philosophy was not monistic. Schelling endeavoured to state the problem of freedom, but the philosophy of identity was not favourable to this. Hegel's philosophy is absolutely hostile to freedom, and so is Fichte's, though only one half of it. Failure to understand freedom is also failure to understand personality. The currents of thought which take their rise in Platonism and German idealism cannot lead on to philosophies of freedom.

The tendencies of French philosophy in the nineteenth century, Renouvier, Maine de Biran, Revaisson, Boutroux and others, are more favourable to philosophies of freedom. But the problem must be taken deeper. A philosophy of freedom is not an ontological philosophy. Ontological philosophy in the last resort must arrive at a system of closed determinism. Being, as thought constructs it, being as object, being as concept, is the realm of determination, not material and physical but ideal determination. Ideal determination is most merciless and at the same time assigns to itself an exalted character as contrasted with material determination. Ideal determination exteriorizes, objectivizes universalism. But this universalism is a mortal foe of the freedom of man, a deadly enemy of personality. Personalism is also universalism. It is decisively distinguished from individualism. But it is not universalism exteriorized in the objective world, which transforms man into a subordinate part, but interiorized universalism, that of a subject, which is to be found in the heart of personality itself. Every system of hierarchical social universalism is a system of exteriorized universalism, transferred to the objective world and, therefore, enslaving man to itself. This is the fundamental antithesis. The being of ontology is a naturalistically conceived being, it is nature, it is substance, but not an entity, not personality, not spirit, not freedom. The hierarchical order of being from God down to a beetle is a crushing order of things and abstractions. It is crushing and enslaving and there is no room for personality in it either as an ideal order or as a real order. Personality is outside all being. It stands in opposition to being. Everything personal, truly existential and effectively real has no general expression; its principle is dissimilarity. Technization and mechanization make everything alike. This is one of the limits of impersonalizing objectivization. The abstract idea of being as the realm of unchanged order, of the abstract common, is always an enslavement of the free creative spirit of man. The spirit is not subject to the order of being; it intrudes upon it, interrupts it and may change it. With this freedom of spirit personal existence is connected; it requires the recognition of being as a secondary matter. The source of slavery is being as an object, being which is exteriorized in either a rational or a vitalistic form. Being as subject means something entirely different and ought to have another name. Being as subject is personal existence, freedom, spirit.

The acute experience of the problem of theodicy as we see, for instance, in Dostoyevsky and his dialectic about the single tear of a child and about the return of the admission ticket to world harmony, is a revolt against the idea of being as the realm of the universally 'common', as world harmony which crushes personal existence. In another form this was in Kirkegaard too. There is eternal truth in this revolt and the truth is this, that the particular single personality and its destiny are a higher value than the world order and the harmony of the whole, than abstract being, And this is a Christian truth. Christianity is by no means an ontology in the Greek sense of of the word. Christianity is personalism. Personality rebels against the world order, against being as the realm of the common, and in its revolt it is united with God as personality, and certainly not with the all-embracing unity, nor with abstract being. God is on the side of personality, not on the side of the world order and the all-inclusive oneness. The so-called ontological proof of the existence of God is only the play of abstract thought.

The idea of the all-inclusive oneness, the world harmony, is certainly not a Christian idea. Christianity addresses itself to persons dramatically in an anti-monistic way. God has created no sort of world order, and in His creation He is connected with no sort of being. God creates only creatures; He creates persons and He creates them as purposes which are made actual by freedom. We shall speak about this in the following chapter. Truth is not on the side of concepts, of metaphysics, not on the side of ontology which is concerned with being. Truth is on the side of spiritual knowledge which is concerned with concrete spiritual life and expresses itself in symbols, not in the concepts of metaphysics. Mysticism set out to be knowledge which did not consist of concepts, but it often showed a monistic tendency, which is hostile to personality. It may be permeated by false metaphysics. Truth is only in impersonalist dramatic mysticism and philosophy, and at its summit it must be a symbolism of life and the way of the spirit, and not a system of concepts and ideas reaching its climax in the idea of being. Man, upon his spiritual path and upon his journey in search of truth, is set not face to face with being, which is certainly not primary and means that rationalization has already taken place, but face to face with truth as the secret of existence and destiny. Man is searching not for being but for truth and the meaning of existence. And man is confronted not by abstract truth but by The Truth, as the way and the life. 'I am the Truth, the Way and the Life'. This means that truth is a concrete personality; it is its way and its life. Truth is in the highest degree dynamic. It is not given in a finished and a congealed form. Truth is not dogmatic. It is given only in the creative act. Truth is not being and being is not truth. Truth is life. It is the existence of the existing; only the existing exists. Being is only the congealed and indurated part of life, life which has been cast out into objectivity. The problem of being is indissolubly connected with the problem of God. Here another form of slavery lies in wait for man.

2. GOD AND FREEDOM. THE SLAVERY OF MAN TO GOD

There is an immense distinction to be drawn between God and the human idea of God, between God in His Essence and God as Object. Between God and man there stands human consciousness, the exteriorization and projection of the limited condition of that consciousness, there stands objectivization. An objectivized God has been the object of man's servile reverence but here there is a paradox in the fact that the objectivized God is a God alienated from man and lord over him. And at the same time God is created by the limitation of man and reflects that limitation. Man, so to speak, has fallen into slavery to his own exteriorization and objectivization. Feuerbach was right, although the question of God is by no means decided by this. Man creates God in his own image and likeness and puts into God not only the best in his own image but the worst also. Upon the God Who reveals Himself to human consciousness there lies the stamp of anthropomorphism and sociomorphism.

The sociomorphism of the human idea of God is especially important for our subject. Upon human ideas of God are reflected social relations with men, relations of the servile kind of which human history is full. The knowledge of God requires continual purifying, and purifying above all from servile sociomorphism. The relations between master and slave, taken from social life, have been transferred to the relations between God and man. When we spoke of God as the Master and man as the slave, we were thinking in sociomorphic terms. But in God and in His relation to man in the world there is nothing whatever like the social relations of man to man. The base human category of domination is not applicable to God. God is not a master and He does not dominate. No power is inherent in God. The will to power is not a property of His, He does not demand the slavish reverence of an unwilling man. God is freedom; He is the liberator and not the master. God bestows the feeling of freedom and not of subjection. God is Spirit and Spirit knows nothing of the relation of domination and slavery. God is not to be thought of on the analogy of what takes place in society or on the analogy of what takes place in nature. We cannot think in determinist terms in relation to God. He determines nothing. Nor can we think in terms of causality. He is not the cause of anything.

Here we stand face to face with Mystery and to this Mystery are applicable no analogies with necessity, with causality, with domination; with causality in natural phenomena, with domination in social phenomena. Analogy is only possible with the very life of the spirit. God is certainly not the cause of the world. He certainly does not act upon the human spirit as necessity. He certainly does not pass judgment as judgment is in the social life of man. He certainly is not a master, nor authority in the life of the world and of man. None of these sociomorphic and cosmomorphic categories are applicable to God. God is Mystery, a Mystery towards which man transcends and with which he enters into communion. A false servile understanding of God, a slavish kataphatistic knowledge of God are the last refuge of human idolatry. God has not made a slave of man. God is the liberator. Theology has made a slave of him. Theology and the seductions of theology have made a slave of him, and idolatry has been possible in relation to God; and the slavish social relations of man have been transferred to the relation of man to God. God understood as an object with all the properties of an objectivized world has become a source of slavery. God as object is only the highest natural force of determination made absolute or the highest power of domination made absolute. What is determinism in nature is domination in society.

But God as subject, as existing outside all objectivization, is love and freedom, not determinism and not domination. He himself is freedom and bestows freedom only. Duns Scotus was right in defending the freedom of God. But from the freedom of God he made false and servile deductions by regarding God as an unlimited sovereign. One must not work out any concept about God and least of all is the concept of being applicable. It always indicates determinism and in that case always, rationalization has already entered in. God can be thought of only symbolically. Apophatic, not kataphatic theology is right, but it is right only in part. It does not mean that God is unknowable, as, for example, with Spencer. Contacts with God and communion with him are possible, and dramatic struggle is possible. This contact is the communion and conflict of personalities between which there is neither determination nor causality nor domination nor subjection. The only true religious myth is contained not in the fact that God is master and aspires to domination, but in the fact that God yearns for His other, for responsive love and awaits the creative answer of man.

The patriarchal conception of God depends upon the social relationships that exist in the family and it reflects them. In the history of human knowledge of God the devil has not infrequently been taken for God. In slavish theological doctrines there is always exteriorization of spirit and this exteriorization of spirit always diverts men from inward spiritual experience to the sphere of abstract thought. The spirit is always subjectivity and in this subjectivity transcension takes place. The objectivizing direction of consciousness leads into another sphere. Objectivization is an apparent attainment of the transcendent. It is precisely the objectivized transcendent which remains in the immanence of consciousness. The objectivizing consciousness remains in a closed circle of immanence, however much it affirms the objectivity of the transcendent, and precisely for this reason that it does affirm the objectivity of the transcendent. This is the clearest confirmation of the paradox that the objective is subjective and the subjective objective, if we make use of that out-of-date terminology.

The conception of the Absolute is the extreme limit of the objectivizing of abstract thought. In the Absolute there are no signs whatever of existence, no signs of life. The Absolute belongs not so much to religious revelation as to religious philosophy and theology. It is a product of thought. The abstract Absolute shares the fate of abstract being which is in no way distinguished from non-being. You cannot pray to the Absolute. No dramatic meeting with it is possible. We call that the Absolute which has no relation to an other and has no need of an other. The Absolute is not a being, is not personality, which always presupposes a going out from itself and a meeting with an other. The God of revelation, the God of the Bible is not the Absolute. In Him there is dramatic life and movement, there is a relation to an other, to man, to the world. By the precepts of Aristotelian philosophy they have changed the God of the Bible into pure act, and excluded from Him all inward motion and every tragic principle. The Absolute cannot issue from itself and create the world. Movement and change cannot be attributed to It. The *Gottheit* of

[84]

Eckhart and the mystics is not the Absolute as the limit of abstraction. He is the limiting Mystery to which no categories are applicable. But it cannot be said of It, that It created the world and is to be found in correlation with it.

God is not the Absolute. God is relative to creation, to the world and to man, and with Him takes place the drama of freedom and love. But going deeper behind the limits of all thought, within the boundary of spiritual experience lies the incomprehensible divinity which philosophy imperfectly and rationally names the Absolute. When men have attempted to know God Himself as Absolute, the God Who reveals and not conceals Himself, then a monarchical understanding of God has been accepted, which is a source of theological seduction and slavery. Christianity is not the revelation of God as an absolute monarch. The Christian revelation of the Son of God Who sacrificed Himself, suffered and was crucified, saves us from that. God is not an absolute monarch. God is a God Who suffers with the world and with man. He is crucified Love; He is the Liberator. The Liberator appears not as a power but as Crucifixion. The Redeemer is the Liberator, and that not as settling accounts with God for crimes that have been committed. God reveals Himself as Humanity. Humanity is indeed the chief property of God, not almightiness, not omniscience and the rest, but humanity, freedom, love, sacrifice. It is necessary to free the idea of God from distorting degrading blasphemous sociomorphism. It is man, man most horribly dehumanized, who distorts his own image. But God is humane and demands humanity. Humanity is the image of God in man. Theology must be freed from a sociology which reflects the fall of the world and of man. Apophatic theology must go hand in hand with apophatic sociology. This means the purification of the knowledge of God from the ideas of bad earthly theocracy. It is precisely the absolutist monarchical understanding of God which has given rise to atheism as a righteous revolt. Atheism, not of the vulgar and malicious sort, but the lofty atheism of the martyr, was a dialectic moment in the knowledge of God. It had a positive mission. In it the idea of God was purified and divested of false sociomorphism, from human inhumanity, objectivized and transferred to the sphere of the transcendent. Feuerbach was right, not in his attitude to God,

[85]

but in his attitude to the idea of God. With this is connected the problem of theodicy, the most tormenting problem of the human consciousness and conscience. It is a problem of the slavery of man and of the whole creation.

One serious cause of atheism is connected with the tormenting experience of evil and the suffering of the world, which poses the problem of the justification of God. Marcion was profoundly shocked by the fact that the world is so full of evil and suffering, and yet it was created by a God to Whom is ascribed almighty power and supreme goodness. His solution was mistaken, but his problem was an everlasting one and was by no means solved by those who level accusations against him. But nobody, it would seem, has stated the problem of suffering as a problem of theodicy in an acuter form than Dostoyevsky, and no-one has disclosed the inward dialectic of this problem with so much power. The question here is, of course, not about an intellectual dialectic such as Hegel's, but about an existential dialectic, such as Kirkegaard's. Ivan Karamazov says that he does not accept God, nor does he accept God's world. No world harmony, no world order can be reconciled with unmerited suffering, even it it be of only one creature, with one tear of a tortured child. The entrance ticket to world harmony must be returned. The world ought not to have been made if there lies at the foundation of it unmerited suffering.

But the world is full of undeserved suffering, of tears, of unredeemed evil, and those who rebel against evil and suffering and wish to create a better world, a more righteous and a happier world are themselves the cause of innumerable sufferings. They create new forms of evil. Man in his revolt against suffering and injustice is easily permeated by Marat's love for humanity and exclaims 'freedom or death'. Belinsky extolled Dostoyevsky's dialectic in advance and Ivan Karamazov frequently repeats almost word for word Belinsky's letter to Botkin. In Belinsky there come into view all the contradictions of existential dialectic about human personality and world harmony. In him there was a revolt against the power of the common (the universal) over human personality, and the enslavement of human personality by a new common (universal), and in addition a readiness in the name of that new common (universal) to cut the throats of many thousands, hundreds of thousands of human personalities.

The problem which faces us is the problem of personality, the unrepeatable unique personality of an existential centre, which possesses a sensitiveness to sorrow and joy; of personality linked to its own particular destiny, to the world order, to world harmony. There is nothing more pitiable than the solution of this problem, which is also a problem of theodicy, as found in the major portion of theological doctrines. All these doctrines are founded more or less on the principle of the domination of the universal common over the individual singular. In the universal common, in the world order, in the world harmony, righteousness, reason, happiness, beauty triumph. Injustice, unreason, suffering, ugliness, on the other hand, exist only in parts which are unwilling to be subordinated to the whole. St. Augustine already gave voice to the ancient non-Christian point of view of the harmony of the whole, which justified evil on the ground that it is connected with parts. What value does the very idea of world order, world harmony possess, and could it ever in the least justify the unjust suffering of personality? The idea of the harmony of the whole in the world order, is also a source of slavery of man. It is the power of objectivization over human existence. The so-called world order and the so-called harmony of the world whole was never the creation of God. God is certainly not the constructor of the world order, or an administrator of the world whole. God is the meaning of human existence. But world order which crushes all parts and turns personality into a means to an end, is a product of objectivization, that is to say of the alienation and the exteriorization of human existence; but it is not the creation of God. The whole, the world order cannot justify anything. On the contrary it is in the position of being judged and requires justification.

The world order, the harmony of the whole, etc., can have no existential meaning. It is the realm of determination to which freedom is always in opposition. God is always in freedom, never in necessity, always in personality, never in the world whole. God acts, not upon the world order as though justifying the suffering of personality, but in the conflict, in the struggle of personality, in the conflict of freedom against that world order. God created concrete beings, personalities, creative existential centres, and not the world order, which is a mark of the fall of those creatures, and of their ejection into the sphere of the objectivized external. In reply to what is always said, we ought to say that the divine is disclosed in 'parts', never in the 'whole', in the individual and never in the common. It is not disclosed in the world order which has nothing in common with God, but in the revolt of suffering personalities against the world order, in the rebellion of freedom against necessity. God is in the child which has shed tears, and not in the world order by which those tears are said to be justified. The whole world order with the realm of the universal common, the impersonal, will come to an end and will be burnt. All concrete beings, human personalities above all, but also animals, plants and everything that has individual existence in Nature will inherit eternity, and all the kingdoms of this world, all the kingdoms of the 'common' which torment the individual personal will be burnt completely.

World harmony is a false and an enslaving idea. One must get free from it for the sake of the dignity of personality. World harmony is also disharmony and disorder. The realm of world reason is also the world of the irrational and senseless. It is a false aestheticism which sees a world harmony. This world harmony costs too much. Dostoyevsky everywhere hunts down this world harmony, and that is the most Christian thing about him. Rational theology establishes not only a false theodicy, which in actual fact justifies not God but godlessness; it also sets up a false doctrine of divine providence in the world. The world is not in such a state as justifies an optimistic doctrine of the action of divine providence in it. If everything is from God, and everything is directed by God towards happiness, if God acts in the plague and in cholera and in tortures, in wars and enslavements, alike, the consequence, when thought out, must be to lead to the denial of the existence of evil and injustice in the world. The providence of God in the world, which in any case we admit only as an inexplicable mystery, is rationalized by theological doctrines, and that is always an affront both to the honour of God and to the dignity of man. It makes God appear always as an autocratic monarch, making use of every part of the world, of every individuality, for the establishment of the common world order, for the administration of the whole to the glory of God. This is held to be a justification of every injustice, every evil, every sorrow, of the parts of the world.

But God is not world providence, that is to say not a ruler and sovereign of the universe, not *pantokrator*. God is freedom and meaning, love and sacrifice; He is struggle against the objectivized world order. A friend of mine told me in so many words that Leibnitz was the most terrible pessimist in the history of thought. Leibnitz thought this world is the best of all possible worlds. But if the best of all possible worlds is so horrible, how pessimistic such a doctrine is. Optimism about the world order is the servitude of man. Freedom from servitude is freedom from the crushing idea of world order which is the outcome of objectivization, that is to say, of the fall. The good news of the approach of the Kingdom of God is set in opposition to the world order. It means the end of the false harmony which is founded upon the realm of the common. The problem of theodicy is not solved by objectivizing thought in an objectivized world order. It is only solved on the existential plane where God reveals Himself as freedom, love and sacrifice, where He suffers for man and strives together with man against the falsity and wrong of the world, against the intolerable suffering of the world. There is no need to justify, we have no right to justify, all the unhappiness, all the suffering and evil in the world with the help of the idea of God as Providence and Sovereign of the Universe. This is a hard saying. One must turn to God for the struggle on behalf of freedom, on behalf of righteousness, on behalf of the enlightening and betterment of existence.

The orthodox of all confessions have always specially exposed and persecuted pantheistic tendencies. They have charged mystics with pantheism as the result of not understanding the paradoxical nature of the language the mystics use. As is well-known Roman Catholic theologians are particularly afraid of pantheism. The only thing they do not understand is that if pantheism is heresy, then this heresy is in the first place concerned with man and human freedom and not with God. When I say 'heresy' I am not speaking my own language. But the astonishing thing is that the most orthodox of dogmatic formulas and the most orthodox of theological doctrines themselves contain within them a pantheism which enslaves man. God is all in all. God holds everything in His hands and directs everything. Only God is real being; man and the world are nothing. Only God is free. Man does not possess real freedom. Only God creates; man is not capable of creation. Everything is of God. All this is constantly said by the orthodox. Extreme forms of abasing man, the acknowledgement of his nothingness, are just as much pantheism as the affirmation of the divinity of man, and the acknowledgement of him as an emanation of the divine. At the same time it is monism. In order to avoid both monism and pantheism it is necessary to recognize the independence of man, of freedom in him, which is uncreated, not determined by God, and to recognize his capacity for creativeness. But rationalizing orthodox theological systems fear this above everything.

The pantheistic current in the history of religious thought has been twofold. On the one side it means the emancipation of man from authoritarian oppression, from exteriorized transcendence, and from the interpretation of God as an object. But on the other side it means the enslaving of man, a denial of personality and freedom, and a recognition of the divine as the one and only effectual power. But this is connected with the contradictions which arise out of all thinking about God. This thought can be only symbolism, existential spiritual experience, but it cannot be objectivization. Objectivization either in the form of an extreme dualistic doctrine of transcendence or in the form of an extreme monistic doctrine of immanence, has in any case an enslaving character and contradicts the existential experience of the meeting of man and God. But the dualistic moment which must not be turned into dualistic objective ontology can by no means be escaped. Freedom and conflict require it. God is not the all inclusive unity, as Vladimir Solovyev taught and as many religious philosophers have taught. The idea of the all inclusive unity, which is tempting to philosophical reason, is an abstract idea of God. It is the outcome of objectivizing thought. In the all inclusive unity there is no existentiality. With the all inclusive unity there can be no meeting; there can be no dialogue; there can be no call, no answer, no wrestling. God, as the all inclusive unity, is a God of determinism;

He shuts out freedom. God is thought of as Nature, as all-embracing power, not as freedom, not as personality.

The very idea of unity is false and enslaving in its consequences. It is opposed to personalism. Only in the world of objectivization does unity present itself to us as the highest condition. This involves the thought that behind the world which is torn asunder and subject to chaotic disruption and at the same time compulsorily fettered and subject to necessity, there is a unity of moral world order. But this is only a projection of the fallen world seeking compensation; in actual fact, the existential higher world is not a world of unity but a world of creative freedom. It might be said that the Kingdom of God is by no means objective unity, which is a necessary thing only for the godless world, only for the realm of the godless. The Kingdom of God is above all personalistic. It is a personal and free kingdom, not a unity which stands above personal existence, but a union, a communion in love; and the Kingdom of God must be thought of apophatically, while unity means kataphatic thought. The idea of an all inclusive unity is only another form of the idea of the Absolute and is liable to the same criticism. The overcoming of the antithesis between the One and the many must not be thought of as the all inclusive unity. The mysterious union of the One and the many, the universal and the singular in the Person of Christ is certainly not expressible in the formula that Christ is the all inclusive unity. We have already said that in personality there is an instance of the universal but in a potential form. In the personality of Christ the universal was actualized. Here there is no abstraction from the existence of personality, no objectivization. Not only the word 'unity' but also the word 'all' badly express the mystery which faces us. 'All' in general has no real existence. 'All' does not exist outside abstract thought. There is no whole, no universal common. It is an illusory outcome of thought.

Church consciousness also must not be thought of as outside personality and above personality, as a whole. Thought about the church as an organism is a simple biological analogy which cannot be thought out to the end. Biological symbolism in Holy Scripture is as relative as juridical symbolism. This is a question of the limitations of language. The church certainly cannot be thought of as a suprapersonal whole, having its existential centre and centre of consciousness. This is the illusory objectivization of the existential community and communion in Christ. The existential centre of the church and its corporate consciousness is to be found in every personality in it, and in the personality of Christ, precisely in the Personality of Christ as God Man, but not in any community. not in any organism which is an incarnation of the all inclusive. The church does exist as a social institution, but in this aspect it belongs to the world of objectivization. To this are due all the inconsistencies in the existence of the church, which ought to set man free but often enslaves him. Religious slavery, slavery to God and slavery to the church, that is to a servile idea of God and a servile idea of the church, has been a most burdensome form of slavery for man and one of the sources of human slavery. It has been slavery to the object, to the common, to externality and to alienation. It is for this reason that the mystics have taught that man should cut himself off even from God. This is the path man has to tread.

The history of religions teaches us that the offering of sacrifice to the gods was a social act and indicated that man was still a slave. It is Christ Who gives the summons to set men free from this slavery, and in Christianity sacrifice has a different meaning. But in Christianity objectivized and socialized servile elements of worship have entered which are connected with the ancient terror. Even philosophers, in their teaching about God as the all inclusive unity, are not free from servile worship, although it seems to them that they are free from slavery. The ancient Roman conception of religion which was permeated with a utilitarian spirit passes into Christianity as a socialized religion. A slavish attitude to God has even entered into the interpretation of the infinity of God in which finite man loses himself; but the infinity of God is different from infinity in this world. The infinity of God denotes that living actual fullness for which man thirsts and is not in the least a power which quells and crushes finite man. The distinction of the slavery of man to nature and the cosmos, from his slavery to God as object is frequently something which cannot be grasped. 'Gott ist todt', says Zarathustra in Nietzsche, 'an seinem Mitleiden mit den Mensch ist Gott gestorben'.

3. NATURE AND FREEDOM

The Lure of the Cosmos and the Slavery of Man to Nature

The very fact of the existence of a slavery of man to being, and to God, may give rise to doubts and objections. But all will agree in this, that there exists a slavery of man to nature. The triumph over man's slavery to nature, to the natural elements, is indeed the basic theme of civilization. Man, collective man, wrestles against the primitive elements of nature which enslave him and threaten him, humanizes his natural environment, constructs for the struggle tools which stand between us and nature, and enters upon a new reality, that of the technique, civilization and reason upon which he makes his fate to depend. But he never attains to final emancipation from the power of nature, and periodically he demands a return to nature as a liberation from the technique and civilization which is stifling him. But I shall not concern myself with this comparatively elementary problem upon which an innumerable quantity of books have been written.

The very word 'nature' has a large number of meanings. To the mind of the nineteenth century, the word 'nature' came to mean first of all the field of mathematical natural science and of applied technical science. And this means that the cosmos in the ancient and mediaeval sense of the word had disappeared. This began with Descartes. This accounts for the anguish of Pascal in the face of immeasurable space, absolutely indifferent to man and his fate. Man ceased to feel himself an organic part of the hierarchical organism of the cosmos which had at one time given him the warm sensation of organic life. Man entered upon a conflict, at one stroke he both turned more to nature, and thrust himself further from its inner life. He began ever more and more to lose the rhythm of life in harmony with the rhythm of the life of nature. The old theological interpretation of what nature is was linked with the distinction between natural and supernatural, between nature and grace. From this point of view the difference between nature and culture is left entirely within the sphere of the natural.

I shall not use the word nature in the sense which placed it in antithesis to culture, civilization or the supernatural or to grace; nor in the old sense of the cosmos or the creation of God, nor exclusively in the sense of the world of matter in space, as distinguished from the soul. To me nature is above all the contradiction of freedom; the order of nature is to be distinguished from the order of freedom. In this connection Kant's thought keeps its permanent significance, although he himself did not make the necessary deductions from that thought. But if nature means the antithesis of freedom, it means by that very fact the antithesis of personality and the antithesis of spirit. Freedom denotes spirit, personality denotes spirit. The fundamental dualism is not the dualism of natural and supernatural, nor the dualism of material and psychical, nor the dualism of nature and civilization, but the dualism of nature and freedom, nature and spirit, nature and personality, the object world and the subject world. Nature in this sense is the world of objectivization, that is to say, of alienation, determinability, impersonality. By nature I do not here understand animals, etc., nor plants, nor minerals, nor stars, forests and seas, which all have an inner existence and belong to the existential and not the objectivized scheme of things.

The question of the communion of man with cosmic life lies outside this interpretation of nature as objectivization. The slavery of man to nature is slavery to that objectivization, to that alienation, to that determinability. Personality breaks in upon that cycle of natural determined life as a force which comes out of another order, out of the realm of freedom, out of the kingdom of spirit. There are in personality natural foundation principles which are linked with the cosmic cycle. But the personal in man is of a different extraction and of a different quality and it always denotes a break with natural necessity. Personality is the rebellion of man against slavery to nature. Empirically this revolt of man against slavery to nature meets with only partial success, he easily falls into slavery again and sometimes idealizes his servitude. He even sees in society, which is not nature, a reflected form of eternal nature, and sees in this naturalness, in this determinability, the ideal basis of society. Spirit itself and the spiritual life are interpreted in a naturalistic way as nature, and natural determination is introduced into spiritual life.

Nyesmyelov says that falling into sin consists in nothing but a superstitious magical attitude to material fruit (the apple), the feeding upon which should bestow knowledge. In this way men have subjected themselves to external nature. But this means that the Fall is no more than the repudiation of freedom. Man was turned into a part of nature. But as has been said more than once already, man, in virtue of his own image, man as personality is not a part of nature, he has within him the image of God. There is nature in man, but he is not nature. Man is a microcosm and therefore he is not part of the cosmos. In nature causal connections hold sway. But personality is a rupture of causal connections. The causal connections of nature are changed into connections of spirit which are full of meaning and purpose. A causal connection may be meaningless. We may note in passing that even the realm of nature does not denote the uniform and uninterrupted dominion of necessity and causation. There is interruption in nature, there is accident. The statistical interpretation of law limits the sway of determinism over nature. They have given up hypostatizing causality and law. The reign of law in nature is only the correlation of a given system of forces. Nature is an order of determinism but it is not a closed order. Forces of another order may break in upon it and change the effects of the incidence of law. Nature is an order which opens itself out receptively. But religious philosophy has frequently meant the legitimation of the consciousness of slavery to 'nature', although this nature might not have been understood in a material sense. Even spirit and God may be understood in a naturalistic way and in that case they bring man into servitude. The natural world, 'this world', and its massive environment, is certainly not identical with what we call the cosmos and cosmic life filled with existences. 'The world' is the servitude, the enchainment of existences, not only of men, but of animals and plants, even of minerals and stars. 'This world' ought to be destroyed by personality, it ought to be set free from its enslaved and enslaving condition. The enslavement, the enslaving state of the world, the determinism of nature are the outcome of objectivization. Everything is turned into object, but objects always indicate determination from without, alienation, ejection into the external, and impersonality.

The slavery of man to nature, as, of course, every other form of slavery, is slavery to the object world. Enslaved nature, as object, is nature which determines from without, it is nature which depersonalizes and oppresses inward existence. But nature, as subject, on the other hand, is the inward existence of the cosmos, its existentiality and consequently also its freedom. Subjectivity breaks through into objectivity, freedom into necessity, personality into the realm of the common. Then the process of liberation takes place. Matter always denotes dependence, and a state of determination from without. For this reason matter is always object. Matter as subject is no longer matter, it is already inward existence.

The slavery of man increases in proportion to the growth of materiality. Enslavement indeed is materialization. Matter crushes by its massive weight and in it there is nothing but what has the quality of being an object. Materiality is objectivization, it is making existence into a thing. On the other hand liberation is a return to inward existence, to subjectivity, to personality, to freedom, to spirit. Liberation is the imparting of spirit, as materiality is the making of slaves. But man's condition of slavery to the world of things, to material necessity, is a crude form of slavery and of all forms of servitude it is the most easily exposed. The more refined and less noticed forms of slavery to nature provide more interest. It is these that I call the lure of the cosmos and that lure may assume highly spiritualizing forms and be very far from the determinism of matter. Slavery to nature, as the lure of the cosmos, can be a spiritual phenomenon.

There are elementary forms of man's slavery to nature to which he gives no conscious assent. Of such a kind is the force which natural necessity exercises upon man, the natural necessity which is outside man and also within him. This is slavery to what are called 'laws' of nature, which man discovers and interprets by his scientific knowledge. Man wrestles with the violence of this natural necessity in the strength of his knowledge of it and perhaps only in this sphere can it be said that freedom is the result of necessity, that it is the consciousness and knowledge of necessity. The technical power of man over nature is due to this. In virtue of this technical power man is set free, he is partially set free from slavery to the elemental forces of nature, but he easily falls into servitude again to the very technical knowledge which he has created. Technical knowledge and the machine, have a cosmogonic character and denote the appearance, as it were, of a new nature, in the power of which man finds himself to be. In its struggle spirit creates the scientific knowledge of nature, creates technical science, and exteriorizes itself, objectifies itself and falls into servile dependence upon its own exteriorization and objectivization. This is the dialectic of the spirit, it is existential dialectic.

But there exist more subtle forms of the lure of the cosmos and slavery to it, to which man does give his assent, and which he is prepared to undergo with ecstasy. Man wrestles against nature, which is based upon determinism and the reign of law. But he has another attitude towards the cosmos, to that which presents itself to him as a world harmony, to the world whole, world unity, world order. In this he is willing to see a reflected image of the divine harmony and order, and the ideal basis of the world. The lure of the cosmos assumes a variety of forms. It may take the form of an erotic sexual lure (Rozanov, Lawrence) or of the mass of the nation (the mysticism of *narodnitchestvo*)* or of the earthly lure of the soil, and the lure of blood, race and family (the return to the land, racialism) or the lure of the collective-social (the mysticism of collectivism and communism). Dionysism in its various forms denotes the lure of the cosmos. It is a longing to be taken to the maternal bosom of the cosmos, a longing for mother earth, for fusion with the formless element, which emancipates from the pain and limitation of personal existence, or with the formless collectivism, national and social, which is by way of overcoming the separated individual existence. This always means the exteriorization of consciousness. In man, overwhelmed as he is by the conditioning character of civilization, by its enslaving standards and laws, there is periodically a thirst to return to primitive life, to cosmic life, to find not only communion but fusion with cosmic life, to enter into communion with its mystery, and to find joy and ecstasy in doing so.

The romantics always demanded a return to nature, and emancipation from the sway of reason and from the enslaving standards of civilization. The 'nature' of the romantics was never the 'nature' of the natural sciences and technical collaborative activity, it was not the 'nature' of necessity and the reign of law. To Rousseau nature means something entirely different from that and so it does to

* See note on p. 4.

Tolstoy. Nature is divine, it is beneficent, it brings healing to civilized man, sick and distracted as he is. These transports have an eternal significance and man will be seized by them periodically. But the attitude to cosmic nature here revealed is based upon an illusion of consciousness. Man desires to triumph over objectivization, to retrieve exteriorized, alienated nature, but he does not really and existentially attain to this. He looks to the freedom of the cosmos for salvation from the necessity of nature. Fusion with cosmic life presents itself to him as freedom to live, freedom to breathe. In wrestling with the necessity of nature man created civilization, the atmosphere of which is stifling, the standards of which do not give freedom of movement. In the very longing for communion with the inner life of the cosmos there lies much truth and right, but this truth and right are related to the cosmos in the existential sense, not to the objectivized cosmos, which is nature again with its determination.

The lure of the cosmos has usually meant fusion with the soul of the world. Belief in the existence of a soul of the world is a tenet of romanticism. It is commonly revived, however, in Platonist philosophy. But the existence of the cosmos as a world unity and harmony, the existence of a soul of the world, is an illusion of consciousness which is enslaved and injured by objectivization.

There is no hierarchical unity of the cosmos, in relation to which personality would be a part. You cannot lodge an appeal with nature as a whole on the ground of a complaint of disorder in its parts. The whole is to be found in spirit, not in nature. Appeal can be made to God alone, not to the soul of the world, nor to the cosmos as a whole. The idea of a world soul and a cosmic whole has no existential meaning. The natural sciences also have no concern with a world whole, or with a cosmic unity. It is precisely this partial character of nature which they take cognizance of, and they are not favourable to an optimistic view of the cosmos. Contemporary physics in the same way denies both the cosmos in the ancient sense of the word and the old deterministic materialism. That the world is partial, that the world as a whole and a unity does not exist, is entirely in accord with the revolution in contemporary physics. A whole, and a unity, can be sought only in spirit which is not alienated from itself and not objectivized. But in that case the whole and the unity acquire a different meaning, and do not imply the suppression of the 'partial', the multiple, the personal.

The teleological interpretation of the world process also contradicts the philosophy of personality and freedom. Not only determinism, the causal explanation of the phenomena of nature, but freedom also rebels against objective teleology. An objective teleology of the cosmic process runs counter to the freedom of man, to personality and creativeness, and in actual fact means an ideal spiritualized determinism. The objectivized world is certainly not purposive, or to speak more truly, its purposefulness is only partial, it is immanent in regard to processes taking place in certain parts of the world, but it does not exist in the clash and in the inter-action of those parts, it does not exist in the whole, for there is no whole. The infinity of the objectivized world cannot be the cosmic whole. Accident plays an immense part in world life and it does not simply indicate lack of knowledge. If a collision takes place between two planets and as a result there is cosmic destruction, that is to say a breach of cosmic harmony, that is something entirely unteleological, and even not necessary, in the sense that there exists no law under which that clash takes place. It is an accidental phenomenon. It is exactly as if a motor accident 'happens' to a man. It is an unhappy chance, there is no law for the accident. Everything occurs in accordance with the laws of mechanics, physics, chemistry, and physiology, but there is no law in virtue of which that man left his house at a certain hour and at such and such a moment walked into a car at the corner of the street. A miracle, for example, in no way indicates a breach of any laws of nature whatever, it is the appearance of meaning in human life, disclosed in the sphere of nature which is subject to partial and particular laws. It is a break through of spiritual force into the natural order, which in its isolation appears to be subject to the reign and incidence of law. There are no laws of the whole, no laws of the cosmos. And the law of universal gravitation is certainly not a cosmic law, it is partial and relates to the partial. Boutroux speaks with truth of the accidental laws of nature.

All this that I am saying does not by any means imply that in nature there is a mechanical complex and concatenation of elements taking place. The mechanical view of nature is good for nothing at all, and it may be regarded as completely refuted. It is the same false monism as the admission of the existence of a world soul and the presupposition of a world harmony which reflects the divine harmony. Natural philosophy always has a monistic tendency, it may be spiritualistic and idealistic, or it may be materialistic and mechanistic. But to admit the existence of a world soul, and world harmony is naturalism.

People fall into naturalism both when they affirm ideal principles of the cosmos, and when they propound a doctrine of a Sophia that penetrates and envelopes the whole cosmic life. Such a way of regarding the cosmos is an illusion of consciousness, which is due to failure to grasp the fact that the natural order is the product of objectivization, not an incarnation of spirit, but an alienation of spirit. The false hypostatization of cosmic principles, forces, energy and qualities is profoundly opposed to personalist philosophy, and enslaves human personality to the cosmic hierarchy. We see this in many theosophical and occult currents of thought.

One cannot look for the soul of the world, the inner life of the cosmos, in objectivized nature, because it is not the real world, but the world in a fallen state, an enslaved world, alienated, depersonalized. It is true that we break through into the inward cosmic life, into nature in the existential sense by the way of aesthetic contemplation, which is always a transfiguring creative activity, and by the way of love and compassion, but this always means that we are breaking through beyond the boundaries of objectivized nature and being set free from its necessity. What I call the lure of the cosmos is an ecstatic emergence beyond the boundaries of personal existence into the cosmic element, it is the hope of entering into communion with this primary element. All orgiastic cults have been founded upon this. But it has always been not so much an emergence from the closed existence of personality into a world of communion, as the depriving of personality of its very form, and its dissolution. This is the enslavement of man by the cosmos, which rests upon an illusion of communion with its inward infinite life. We find the lure of the cosmos depicted in that unfinished tragedy of genius, by Hölderlin, *The Death of Empedocles*.

Objectivized nature with its determinism has exacted vengeance for its apparent denial, and made man a slave, but psychologically this has been of another character than ordinary natural determination. The cosmic soul, the soul of the world, having no inward existence, becomes a power which envelopes man and engulfs his personality. Thus a return to pagan cosmocentricity has come about, the spirits and demons of nature have again arisen out of the hidden depths of the life of nature and taken possession of man. The demonolatry from which Christianity had liberated man has periodically seized upon him again. A pagan cosmocentricity sets itself up in the place of Christian anthropocentricity. But in the lure of the cosmos, as in almost all the lures to which man is exposed, a theme is presented which has a meaning and which demands a decision. His state of alienation from the inner life of nature is rightly a cause of great suffering to man; he cannot endure the crushing mechanism of nature, he desires in fact the return of the cosmos within him. The falling away of man from God has brought with it the falling away of the cosmos from man. And this is the Fall of the objectivized world. But man cannot turn the cosmos back to himself by means of the lure of the cosmos.

From slavery to the mechanism of nature he returns to slavery to the pandemonism of nature. We are present, as it were, at the liberation of the demons of nature which take possession of man. Fusion with cosmic life does not emancipate personality, it brings about its dissolution and annihilation. The form of slavery is changed. This has fateful results in social life, in the relations between personality and society. Society roots itself in the cosmos, and interprets itself as an organism which has a cosmic basis. Thus personality is inevitably subjected and enslaved to the organic and in the last resort to the cosmic whole; man becomes a mere organ, and all the freedoms of man, which are bound up with his spiritual independence of society and nature, are abolished.

Cosmism in social life has in fact a reactionary character, above all a spiritually reactionary character. It exalts the idea of organism and the organic. This is the illusorily cosmic, the mystically biological foundation of social philosophy. The cosmic nature of the peasantry is frequently emphasized in antithesis to the non-organic character of other classes, especially the intelligentsia and the workers. The active irruption of the masses of the people into history may be represented as a phenomenon of cosmic significance and in a certain sense this is true. But this irruption of the masses is connected precisely with the growth of the rôle played by technical skill at the expense of spiritual culture, and indicates a still greater breach with nature. Man moves in a vicious circle. To break out of this vicious circle is an act of the spirit, it is not subjection to the organic cosmic rhythm, which in objectivized nature does not in reality exist. To the power of the cosmic organic over the human spirit must be opposed not the mechanistic technical, not rationalization, but freedom of the spirit, the principle of personality, which depends neither upon organism nor upon mechanism. This is completely analogous to the fact that to objective teleology must be opposed not determinism but freedom. To the slavery of man to society one must oppose neither the reason of rationalism nor nature regarded as beneficent, but spirit, freedom of spirit, and personality in its spiritual quality, which is not dependent upon society and nature. This leads us to the question of the slavery of man to society.

4. SOCIETY AND FREEDOM

The Social Lure, and the Slavery of Man to Society

Of all the forms of slavery to which man is liable the greatest importance attaches to the slavery of man to society. Man has been a socialized creature all through the long millenia of civilized life. And the sociological doctrine of man would persuade us that it is precisely that socialization which has created man. Man lives, as it were, in a social hypnosis. And it is difficult for him to set his freedom in opposition to the despotic claims of society, because the social hypnosis, through the lips of sociologists of various schools of thought, convinces him that he has received his very freedom from society and from society alone. Society, so to speak, says to man: You are my creation; everything that is best in you has been put there by me, and therefore you belong to me and you ought to give your whole self back to me.

In his general outlook upon life, Hertzen was keenly aware of the claims of the community upon the individual, but he had some trenchant ideas which were prompted by his strong feeling for personality. His is the saying: 'the subjection of personality to society, to the people, to humanity or to an idea is an extension of the practice of human sacrifice'. And that is a solemn truth. If the distinction we have drawn between the individual and personality is accepted, then it can be said that only the individual is a part of society and subject to it; personality, on the other hand, is not a part of society; on the contrary, society is a part of personality. It follows from the fact that man is a microcosm and a microtheos, that society, like the state, is a constituent part of personality. The exteriorization of society, the objectivization of the relations to which society gives rise, enslaves man. In primitive society personality is entirely engulfed by the community. Lévy-Bruhl says with truth that in primitive consciousness, the consciousness of the individual depends upon the consciousness of the group. But that is not the final truth about man.

Society is a special reality, a degree of actuality. The 'I' with the 'you' is a different reality from the 'I' in the 'we'. But society is not an organism, it is not a being nor a personality. The reality of society consists in the personalities themselves; not in the simple interaction of personalities, but in the 'we', which is not an abstraction, and has a concrete existence. The reality of society is not a special 'I', it is 'we'. The communion of the 'I' with the others takes place in the 'we'. This 'we' is a qualitative content of the 'I', it is its social transcension. The 'I' holds communion not only with the 'you', communion of personality with personality, it holds communion also with the 'we', that is with society. But the 'I' enters into the 'we'—society, as a part into the whole, as an organ into the organism, only as an individual, as being a natural man. As a personality, the 'I' never enters into society as a part into the whole, as an organ into an organism. The 'we' is not a collective subject or substance. The 'we' has an existential significance, but it is not an existential centre. The existential centre is found in the 'I' and in its relation to the 'you' and the 'we'. It is precisely this relation of the 'I' not only to the 'you' but also to the 'we' which is the source of existential social reality. But the objectivization of human existence, the ejection of it into the external creates 'society', which lays claim to be a reality greater and more primary than man and than personality. Society is the objectivization of the 'we' which possesses no reality at all and no existence outside the relation to it of the 'I' and outside the relation between the 'I' and the 'you'. The 'we' in its existentiality is a community, a communion, a fellowship, but not society, Society is manifold unity (Frank). But this manifold unity may be the 'we' in the existential relations of the 'I' to the 'you' and the 'we'. Here there lies concealed the slavery of man to society.

That which constitutes the real in society is determined by this, that personality enters into relation not only with personality but also with a union of personalities in society. The enslaving power of society over human personality is the outcome of an illusion of objectivization. The real 'we', that is, the community of people, communion in freedom, in love and mercy, has never been able to enslave man, on the contrary it is the realization of the fullness of the life of personality, its transcension towards another. Simmel in his 'sociology' is more in the right than the supporters of the organic theory of society, when he sees in society an elemental crossing of the wills and aspirations of separate people. But with him, it is as if the 'we' did not possess any existential reality at all. He traces the processes of the socialization of man, but says nothing to explain where the socializing force comes from. The slavery of man to society finds expression in organic theories of society.

The organic interpretation of society is much broader than the doctrine of society as an organism in the proper sense of the word. The organic interpretation of society may be openly naturalistic and hostile to metaphysics, as for example in Spencer, Schäffle and others. In Russia Mikhaelovsky combatted these theories of the nineteenth century. He rightly saw in the doctrine of society as an organism a very grave danger to the individual. But the organic interpretation of society may be both organic and spiritual, it may see in society and in social communities an incarnation of spirit. This already had its beginning in German romanticism.

The interpretation of society and the social process in Hegel also may be regarded as organic. Among sociologists Spann is the principal representative of the organic interpretation of society on the basis of metaphysical universalism. Always and in all its forms the organic interpretation of society is antipersonalist, it inevitably recognizes the supremacy of society over personality and is compelled to see in personality an organ of the social organism. This is universalism, the outcome of objectivization, and ejected into the external. The universal is abstracted from personality and personality is subjected to it. The organic interpretation of society is always hierarchical. On this ground there can be only hierarchical personalism, which I consider to be erroneous and contradictory to the essence of personalism. Society is presented as though it were personality of a higher hierarchical degree than the personality of man. But this makes man a slave. The spiritualized interpretation of the organic nature of society idealizes the reign of law in the life of society and makes it the spiritual basis of society. The reign of law acquires, as it were, a normative character. The idea of the supremacy of society over personality is to be found in De Maistre and De Bonald, it has a reactionary counter-revolutionary origin. It was inherited by Comte also, whose influence is to be seen in Charles Maurras.

Sociologists who affirm the primacy of society over personality and teach a doctrine of the moulding of personality by society, are in fact reactionaries. This reactionary spirit is to be found even in Marx, although Marx did nor regard society as an organism. Reactionary conservative tendencies are always based upon the organic character of historical developments in the past, and at the same time necessity, the outcome of the massive solidity of history, is regarded as a good and as a spiritual value. The criterion of value is found not in personality but in the organism of society which stands on a higher level than personality. Conservatism is founded upon the idea that the individual man cannot put his interpretation of the good any higher than the interpretation which has been worked out by the experience of all preceding generations and which presents an organic tradition.

It would be entirely mistaken to suppose that the antithesis of this is individualism. Personalism sees the criterion of value in personality, in the depths of conscience, and supposes that here the distinction between good and evil is revealed more profoundly than in a collective tradition which is represented as organic. But the discriminating and appraising conscience which is revealed in the depth of personality always means, not the isolation and self-containment of personality but its opening out into universal content and its free communion with other personalities, not only the living but the dead also. To freedom belongs supremacy over tradition, but the possibility of free living lies in the fact that there has been truth in the tradition. In the life of society there does exist a link between the generations, a communion of the living and the dead, but this link between the generations is not outwardly imposed upon personality —it is not a hierarchical organic principle which stands on a higher level than it, it is a revelation of social universalism within personality, it is its extended immanent experience. Not for a moment does personality become a part of any organism whatever or of any hierarchical whole.

There is no organic principle, no integrality, no totalitarianism existing in society at all. Society is always partial and to claim an integral organic principle for the organization of society is to give a false character of sacredness to things that are relative. The organic in society is an illusion of objectivization. Not only is the totalitarian state an enslaving lie, but totalitarian society is an enslaving lie also. As nature is partial, so is society partial. It is not society that is an organism; it is man that is an organism. The idea of the integral man, not of the integral society, ought to be laid as the foundation-stone of the organization of society. The organic ideal of society is an enslaving lie. This is the social lure, and it is like the lure of the cosmos. Society is certainly not an organism; society is co-operation. The organic idea of society is an illusion of enslaving consciousness; it is a product of exteriorization. A society of free men, not of slaves, ought to be created not on the pattern of the cosmos but on the pattern of the spirit, that is to say, not on the model of hierarchism but on the model of personalism, not on the pattern of determination but on the pattern of freedom, not on the model of the domination of force and of the strong man, but on the model of solidarity and kindliness of heart. Such a society alone would not be servile, The source of human freedom cannot be in society; the source of human freedom is in the spirit. Everything which proceeds from society is enslaving; everything which issues from the spirit is liberating, The right and the true gradation is the primacy of personality over society, its primacy over the state; and behind this stands the primacy of spirit over the world. The organic interpretation of society, on the other hand, always involves the primacy of the cosmos over spirit, the naturalization of spirit, the giving of a false character of sacredness to necessity and enslavement. There is always this naturalism and cosmism in social philosophy. Personalist philosophy is a fight against the idealization of the organic.

The distinction which Tönnies makes between *Gemeinschaft* and *Gesellschaft* is well known. *Gemeinschaft* is a unity which is real and organic (for example, a family, a class, a village, a nation, a religious communion). *Gesellschaft* is a unity which is ideal and mechanical (for example, the state). There is warmth in *Gemeinschaft* and coolness in *Gesellschaft*. According to Tönnies, a *Gemeinschaft* has its origin in physical ties of blood. Tönnies' theory is naturalistic. *Gemeinschaft* has a character which is clearly naturalistic. But this distinction is very interesting in connection with the subject of the organic doctrine of sociey. In Tönnies everything which is organic has the character of *Gemeinschaft* and the naturalistic character of the organic is revealed. This is indeed the primary social reality. He refuses an organic character to society because it is an ideal organization; it is a fabrication. Tönnies' theory is more subtle than the usual organic theories of society, but all the same it is based upon idealization of the organic.

Within society there are organic formations, but society itself is not an organism. Within society there are organic formations and mechanical formations, but there is no place in it for a spiritual society which is neither an organic nor a mechanical formation. It would be possible to establish three types of human association— organic communities, mechanical societies, spiritual communities. Spiritual freedom as opposed to determination is the mark of a spiritual community. Family, blood *Gemeinschaft;* mechanical, atomistic society; spiritual, personalist community; the first two types belong to the objectivized world and are under the sway of determinism, though in different ways. The third type breaks through out of the world of determination into a different order. Thus, for example, the church is a spiritual community, but it is also a family organic *Gemeinschaft*-and an organized mechanical society.

In this consists the whole complexity of the problem of the church. Only a spiritual community liberates man. An organic family community and a mechanical organized society enslave man. Society is an organization and not an organism. But it assumes the form of an organism when necessary. Man himself in the actions of his objectivizing and hypostatizing consciousness, in those acts of his which impart a sacred character to things, creates his own enslavement. The 'organic' enslaves still more than the 'mechanical', the 'mechanical' at least makes no claim to sacredness.

Patriarchal society, which was the most organic of all, had its humanly good traits which were better than those of a mechanical bourgeois society. But in it man was still leading a half-vegetative existence and had not awakened from the sleep of organic slavery. In Germany the romantics and in Russia the slavophils very much misused the concept 'organic', and made it serve to cover everything which they liked and approved. The 'organic' was accepted as 'organic' after long centuries of veneration and transmission by tradition. But in reality it sometimes arose also as one of the consequences of human conflict and human organization, such as that which arises in conflict at the present time and is accused of being inorganic. It might be said that everything organic has an origin which is not organic. Behind everything which is now seen as organic, there stand in the depth of past centuries, bloody violence, rejection of the earlier organic and the most mechanical of organizations. It is necessary to emancipate oneself from romantic illusions about the 'organic'.

Revolutions destroy the inheritance of the organic process, but later on they create a new organic which they set in opposition to new revolutions. Human societies do not arise idyllically, they arise in passion, and in the bloody strife of polarized forces. There was a struggle between matriarchy and patriarchy. Bachofen gave expression to some profound thoughts on this subject. There was nothing sacred about the origin of human societies, and what was sacred in their history was only conditional symbolism. This is the realm of objectivization, it is the alienation of spirit, it is subjection to determinism. But the holy is to be found only in the spirit, in the realm of subjectivity, in the kingdom of freedom.

As Frank truly says, a social phenomenon is not capable of apprehension by the senses; it is hyperpsychical and its slow development is different from that of men. Men die, all the men die who constituted that society, but the society continues to exist. To Frank, as to a Platonist, the social phenomenon is an idea. It must be acknowledged that materialism in social philosophy is an absolute absurdity and it has never been thought out to the end. In a social phenomenon there are no characteristics whatever of a material phenomenon. But I should say that a social phenomenon is not an idea and not spirit, but an objectivization of an idea and of spirit. The objectivity of social phenomena which reaches beyond human existence is objectivization, alienation of human nature, as the result of which the relations of man to man within society present themselves as realities which exist outside people and on a higher level than people. Marx writes admirably on this subject in his doctrine of the fetishism of goods. In society man acts as a social being, that is to say, as a being in conjunction with other beings; but there is no society which exists as an organic reality to which supremacy over man would belong. The society does not consist of those people; it remains when they are already no more. It exists, however, in the linking chain of human memory, but not outside men. Society exists not only in the form of memory but also in the form of imitation. There exists among the people a 'common' which links them all together. But this 'common' is to be found in the relations of the people to each other, it does not lie outside the people and above them. And between the generations which are not alive in any given section of time there is their 'common' which links us together. But this 'common' is not determined by the fact that they belong to a social organism and constitute its parts, it is existential community which surmounts the breach in time and which is merely objectivized in society. It is not this 'common', but community of human existence which is the real. The past always continues to live and to act. This has a twofold significance—a positive and a negative.

In the Middle Ages mankind was regarded as a single mystical body. This was an analogy wth the interpretation of the church as the mystical Body of Christ. But mankind is not a mystical body, just as society is not an organism. Man is the organism and society is his organ; not the other way about. The contrary, however, appears to be the case owing to the fact that man exteriorizes his nature and is subject to the illusion of objectivization. It is a mistake to think that only 'objective' society exists, 'subjective' society exists also. The true communion, the community of the people is revealed only in subjectivity. This conception of subjectivity is certainly not individualism, as is commonly supposed. The reality of society discloses itself as a value in personal existence which can move in various directions as far as universality. Its hierarchical structure encourages the interpretation of society as an organism.

This hierarchical structure of society is to be noted in every society, it was in primitive society and it is revealing itself in communist society. But there is no direct correspondence between social hierarchism and spiritual, and all too often conflict and opposition occur between these hierarchies. Social hierarchism has at many times and in many forms been regarded with veneration; it has been looked upon as a sacred thing, but there has been nothing sacred in it in reality, and it has arisen out of a conflict of forces and interests which was by no means sacred. Social hierarchism has presented itself as an organism only on the strength of an attempt at analogy. In actual fact it has been organized in the same way as a society which is regarded as mechanical. The organic theory of society is a mere game in biological analogy. To make scientific laws absolute in adapting them to social life is a mere game in mechanical analogy. People hypostatize determinism and picture to themselves a force which despotically controls social life. Necessity and the reign of law they have endeavoured to spiritualize and in this way to justify social evil and injustice. But this does not correspond with realities and expresses merely the slavery of man. The necessity and the reign of law which belong to social life are merely its automatism, and automatism plays an immense part in social life.

The idea of the existence of eternal principles of life has a double significance. It has a positive significance when freedom, justice, the brotherhood of men, the supreme value of human personality as that which must not be turned into a means to an end, are acknowledged as eternal principles. And it has a negative significance when relative

[110]

historical social and political forms are regarded as eternal principles, when these relative forms are made absolute, when concrete historical institutions, represented as organic, are given the prestige and authority of sacred things, as for example, monarchy or some particular form of property. It can be expressed otherwise in this way, that the eternal principles of social life are values which can be realized in subjective spirit and not concrete forms which can be realized in the objectivization of history. The conservative tendency of the organic theory of society which defends the sacred character of concrete historical institutions cannot be recognized as Christian, not only because it contradicts Christian personalism, but also because it contradicts Christian eschatology. In the objectivized historical world there are no sacred things which might be transferred to eternal life; there is nothing worthy of eternal life, and for this reason there exists a moral obligation that the world should come to an end and be judged by a higher judgment. Organic theories of society are anti-eschatological; there is a false optimism, a reactionary optimism in them.

Memory of the past is spiritual; it conquers historical time. This however is not a conserving, but a creatively transfiguring memory. It wishes to carry forward into eternal life not that which is dead in the past but what is alive, not that which is static in the past but what is dynamic. This spiritual memory reminds man, engulfed in his historical time, that in the past there have been great creative movements of the spirit and that they ought to inherit eternity. It reminds him also of the fact that in the past there lived concrete beings, living personalities, with whom we ought in existential time to have a link no less than with those who are living now. Society is always a society not only of the living but also of the dead; and this memory of the dead which the usual theory of progress lacks, is by no means a conservatively static memory, it is a creative dynamic memory. The last word belongs not to death but to resurrection. But resurrection is not a restoration of the past in its evil and untruth, but transfiguration. We are linked with the creatively transfigured past, and it cannot be a burden of enslaving determination for us. We desire to enter with the past and with the departed people of the past into a new transfigured order, into the existential order. There is eternal truth in the criticism of the society of history by such men as Leo Tolstoy and Ibsen. Dr. Stockman was right in his revolt against society, against the tyranny of public opinion, against the lies, the shams, and the slavery by which society is held together. In that revolt there is always a voice from another world.

The autonomy of personality in relation to the surrounding world and to a society which has become habitually false is not a factual condition but the summit of qualitative achievement. Freedom of the spirit is not an abstract proclamation of rights but the highest condition of all, and one to which man ought to attain. Slaves ought to be set free by social action, but even so they might still remain slaves inwardly. The victory over slavery is a spiritual act. Social and spiritual liberation ought to go hand in hand. The genius never finds a place in society; he always rises above it and his creative acts come out of another order. In society, in every society there is an enslaving element which ought always to be overcome. Not only the genius, but every man ranks higher than society, higher than the state, and a purely human interest ranks higher than an interest of society or of the state. The order of the whole is necessary not for the sake of the whole and not because the whole is the highest value, but for the sake of personalities. This transvaluation of values is also an emancipating revolution which ought to be brought about in the world. And it is a revelation of the Christian truth about society. Society is held together by beliefs, not by force. When it begins to be held together solely by force it comes to an end and dies. But society is held together not only by true but also by false beliefs. Such are all beliefs about the supremacy of society and the state over man and over personality, with the claim that they are sacred things. A crisis in these beliefs signifies a crisis, a fracture, and even a catastrophe in the existence of society. Social myths and symbols always lie at the foundations of society, nations cannot exist without them. When conservative myths and symbols dissolve and die, societies also begin to decompose and die. Revolutions take place, and introduce new symbols and myths, for example the myth of the sovereignty of the people, the general will of which is impeccable (Rousseau), or the myth of the proletariat as the class Messiah, the liberator of mankind (Marx) or the myth of the state, or the myth of race, and the like.

Myths and symbols are adapted to the inarticulate majority of men. The insignificance and stupidity of the political ideas of the leaders of societies, are due to this adaptation to the average man. The real liberation is emancipation from all enslaving symbols and myths, and the transition to true human reality.

But what sort of a being is this concrete man, the real man? De Maistre says that he has no knowledge of man in general. He knows only a Frenchman, an Englishman, a German or a Russian. By this he means that a concrete man includes in himself distinguishing national traits from which he cannot be abstracted. Marx said there is no man in general, there is only a nobleman, a bourgeois, a peasant, tradesman, workman, that is to say, it is impossible to abstract the traits of his social class from the concrete man. One might go still further and say that there is no man in general, but there is an engineer, a doctor, a lawyer, a civil servant, a professor, a writer, and the rest; that is to say that into the concrete man there enter the traits of his professional calling. It is possible to go even further yet and to say that only this man here, with his own name and including the maximum quantity of national, social, professional and other traits is the concrete man. Such is one way to arrive at the concrete in which the maximum number of particular qualitative distinctions are assembled together.

But there is another way of reaching the concrete and by this method that man will be regarded as the most concrete who displays the greatest mastery over particularism and the greatest attainment of universality. The universal is not abstract but concrete and the most concrete is not the partial but the universal. The quantity of particular traits may be a sign of poverty, not of riches; that is to say a sign of abstraction. The man in whom the fact exclusively predominates that he is a Frenchman, an Englishman, a German or a Russian, or the fact that he is a nobleman or a bourgeois, a professor or a civil servant, is not by any means an abundant man, and he is not the concrete man *par excellence*. Concreteness is integrality and, therefore, it is not determined by the quantity of particular traits. The most concrete man is the universal man, who overcomes the exclusiveness, the isolation, the self-affirmation of national, social or professional traits. But into the universalism of the concrete man there enter also

B.S.F.

all the distinguishing traits which his exclusiveness presents. It is good to be a Russian, it is good to be a philosopher, but a separatist exclusiveness in the philosophical calling and specialized work is a very bad characteristic and a hindrance to the concreteness and integrality of a man. Universality is the attainment of fullness. The concrete man is a social man and you cannot abstract man from his sociality. But exclusive sociality in a man makes him an abstract being, just as, on the other hand, the complete abstraction of his sociality does. To regard man as exclusively a social being means slavery for man. The objectivization of human nature makes a man a creature composed of particular and partial properties, national, social, professional, which lay claim to wholeness. But this is just what a concrete man is not, concreteness is the actualization of universality. The concrete man cannot be the man who is most completely determined, it is the man who is most completely free. Man shows a disposition to exalt himself on the strength of the social group, party, or profession to which he belongs, but this is of course not a personal but an impersonal exaltation.

Man lives in an evil servile dependence upon society and he himself creates that dependence by hypostatizing society and creating myths about it. Social influences and suggestions distort religious beliefs, moral values and man's very grasp of truth. But there is a reality which lies deeper than that to which the name of society is given, the reality of the relations which exist among people within the society, the reality of the degrees of community among them. Knowledge depends to a very great extent upon the degrees of community existing among men. It is this that makes a sociology of knowledge necessary. I have already written about this more than once in other books. I now deal with it only so far as it is required by the subject matter of this book. In the process of cognition man acts not as an isolated being but as a social being. The apprehension of truth has a social character and, therefore, the process of cognition depends on the form taken by the communion which exists among men, upon the degree of their community. Logical universal validity in the apprehension of truth has a social character. It is a problem of communicability. But the dependence of the acquisition of knowledge upon the social relations of men is in a much deeper sense dependence upon the spiritual state of men. The social relations which men have with one another, have their effect upon the process of acquiring knowledge and indicate degrees in the spiritual isolation or spiritual community of men.

Determinism in the acquisition of knowledge, especially knowledge of a scientific kind, which leads into the realm of necessity and the reign of law, corresponds to a lower degree of spiritual community among people, with their lack of it in fact. Knowledge which is of general validity in this case establishes communication among people who are isolated in spirit; it corresponds to a world of dissension. Here the blame lies not in the cognition, which is a positive value, but in the spiritual condition of the world and of man, in the isolation and dissension of their very existence. The unifying logos is indeed revealed in the acquisition of knowledge. But it is revealed by degrees, in dependence upon the spiritual condition of men and their spiritual community. The social logos is the objectivized logos. The paradox lies in the fact that the universally binding character of cognition is to be found in its highest degree in mathematics and the physical sciences. Here cognition depends less upon spiritual conditions and the spiritual community which people share. It produces the same results for men of different religious beliefs, different nationalities and different classes. On the other hand, knowledge in the historical and social sciences and in sciences of the spirit and of values, that is to say in philosophy, has a lower degree of universally binding character just because it presupposes a greater spiritual community in which people share. Least of all universally binding are truths of a religious character, because they presuppose the maximum of spiritual community. Within the religious body these truths are accepted as the most universally binding, but outside it they appear as the least universally binding, as the least 'objective' and the most 'subjective'.

All this is evidence of the fact that the autonomy of the sphere of knowledge is relative and that it cannot be separated from the whole being of man, from his spiritual life, that is to say from the integral man. Cognition and the acquisition of knowledge depend upon this: what is man like and what sort of relations exist between man and man. And this dependence is at its greatest when the matter under consideration is profound knowledge of the spirit, of the meaning and value of human existence.

There are various degrees of objectivization. The most objectivized knowledge is mathematical. It is the most universally binding and it is the concern of the whole of civilized mankind. But it is the most remote of all from human existence, from knowledge of the meaning and value of human existence. The least objectivized and the least universally binding knowledge is the knowledge which is nearest to human existence. That which is objectivized and universally binding is the most 'objective' in the sense of verified truth. The least objectivized and the least universally binding belong to the realm of 'subjectivity', that is to say they are the least amenable to the test of truth. This rests upon a false identification of objectivity and truth. In actual fact the criterion of truth is found in the subject. and not in the object. The object is the creation of the subject. The idealistic theory of knowledge has often affirmed that the object exists for the sake of the subject; but this is an illusion. The object is created by objectivization which is brought about by the subject. The point is that the object and objectivization do not exist for the sake of the subject but that they enslave the subject. By objectivization the subject enslaves itself and creates the realm of determinism. The subject falls into the power of the exteriorization it has brought about. It is upon this that the slavery of man to society rests, slavery which is taken to be objective existence. If the identification of objectivity with truth is not true, the identification of it with reality is also untrue. It is expressly in subjectivity and not in objectivity that primary reality is found. Only a reflected, secondary, symbolized reality is to be found in objectivity. Man lives his life among symbolized realities. It is precisely the symbols and not the realities which enslave man. The slavery of man to society is above all slavery to social symbols. Society itself is a symbol and not a primary reality. The determinism of objectivized knowledge also is of a symbolic character.

Man cannot by his individual act destroy the world of objectivization, he can only attain to inward freedom from that world. But the destruction of the world of objectivization is a social act and a historical act. That means that with the attainment of the highest degree of spiritual community among men the world would be different and the knowledge of it would be different. Integral truth can only be known by integral spirit, and this truth cannot serve the organizations of the objectivized world. It might be said that the eschatological perspective has its own 'gnosiological' and sociological interpretation. The end of this world is nothing else than the final overcoming of objectivization, liberation from the power of the object world, emancipation also from the power of society as one of the forms of the object world. And this end is perhaps capable of being anticipated in our world, where movement towards the end is possible.

5. CIVILIZATION AND FREEDOM

The Slavery of Man to Civilization and the Lure of Cultural Values

Man is in a state of slavery not only to nature and society but also to civilization. I now use the word 'civilization' in the broad and widely diffused sense which connects it with the process of the socialization of man. I shall speak about cultural values later on.

Civilization is created by man in order to free himself from the power of the elemental forces of nature. Man has invented tools, which he has placed between himself and nature, and has gone on endlessly perfecting these tools. His intellect has been the greatest of man's implements and in the sphere of the intellect man has reached a very high degree of cultivation and inventiveness. But this has been accompanied by a weakening of the instincts, man's organism has begun to decline, for in the struggle organic implements have begun to be replaced by technical implements. At various epochs civilized man has been harassed by the thought that in getting away from nature he was losing his completeness and primary inherent strength, that he was becoming disintegrated. In addition to this man has raised the question of the value of civilization. Man has allied himself with man to wage the fight for life against the elemental forces of nature and for the organization of civilized society. But very soon man began to oppress man to this end, and the relation of master and slave came into being. Robinson Crusoe began to oppress Friday.

The development of civilization was accompanied by the oppression and exploitation of vast masses of mankind, of the labouring people; and this oppression was held to be justified by the objective values of civilization. Civilization, it would seem, could not come into being and could not develop otherwise than by way of terrible social inequality and oppression. It was conceived in sin. This is a very elementary question and it will not concern us at the moment. Such men as J. J. Rousseau and Leo Tolstoy have revolted against civilization and their revolt has brought to light a still deeper problem.

Doubt of the justification of civilization has been very characteristic of Russian thought and this not only in connection with the question of social inequality and exploitation. There is a poison in civilization; there is falsehood and wrong in it, and it makes man a slave: it hinders him from attaining to completeness and fullness of life. Civilization is not the final goal of human existence nor its highest value. Civilization promises to emancipate man and there can be no dispute that it provides the equipment for emancipation; but it is also the objectivization of human existence and, therefore, it brings enslavement with it. Man is made the slave of civilization. It is not only that it has been erected upon slavery and given rise to slavery in relation to itself. The problem is not by any means to be put like this, that it would be a good thing to set up in opposition to civilization some sort of healthy and happy barbarism, some kind of natural man, or savage who is good by nature. This is an absolutely naturalistic way of stating the problem, and it is so much out of date that it is not worth while to discuss it. It is impossible to place the evil and slavery of civilization in antithesis with the good and freedom of nature, and nature cannot pass judgment upon civilization. Only spirit can pass such judgment.

In opposition to civilized man with all his deficiencies there stands not the natural man but the spiritual man. Civilization has its place between the realm of nature and the realm of freedom, it is an intermediary realm. And the question is not one of passing from civilization to nature but of passing from civilization to freedom. The nature to which the romantics wanted to return, to which Rousseau appealed and to which Tolstoy appealed for salvation from the falsity of civilization, is not by any means nature as an objectivized realm of determinism and the reign of law. It is another transformed and transfigured nature which approaches very near to the realm of freedom. It is not an 'objective' nature but a 'subjective' nature. It is particularly clear that 'nature' in Tolstoy, which is divine, is not the nature of the merciless struggle for existence and of mutual destruction, of the domination of the weak by the strong, of mechanical necessity, and the like. It is a transformed and transfigured nature; it is the Divine itself. But Tolstoy fettered this nature to the soil and to the husbandman, to physical labour which makes use of simple tools, that is to say, he characterized it as simplification and a return to a primitive state. In fact he desired that material life should be made more simple in order that man might return to the spiritual life to which civilization was an obstacle.

The repudiation of civilization and its technique is never consistently carried through; there is always something left both of the civilization and of the technique, but in more simplified and elementary forms. It is a direct application of the will towards emancipation from the sway of the manifold world and towards union with the One, towards liberation within the One. It is the desire to pass over from disintegration to complete integrality. Behind the call of the 'natural', of the 'organic', there lies hidden the need to get free from the disuniting multiplicity of the world of civilization, and to pass over to the completeness and unity of the divine life. Man feels himself crushed by this intolerable multiplicity, disintegration, and relativeness and conventionality of the civilized world. He has fallen into the power of his own tools. Everyone knows how the overgrowth of the multiplicity of things in his everyday life embarrasses and enslaves a man and how difficult it is for him to free himself from the power of things. This is the endowment which a complex civilization has conferred upon man. Man is fettered by the standards and conventions of civilization. His whole existence is objectivized in civilization, that is to say it is ejected into the external, it is exteriorized. Man is crushed and enslaved not only by the world of nature but also by the world of civilization. Slavery to civilization is another side of slavery to society.

There is nothing more trivial and banal than the defence of the blessings of civilization by the ideology of the bourgeois classes.

These classes are fond of thinking of themselves as those who bear civilization forward and of contrasting themselves with the inward barbarian, by which they commonly mean the working class. They are afraid of the proletarian, because proletarian means a being from whom all the blessings of civilization and all the values of culture have been taken away, from whom, according to Marx's thinking, his human nature has been estranged. But who is to blame for the appearance of such an unhappy creature and for the increase in the number of such creatures? It is precisely those controlling classes who are to blame, who, in the defence of their interests declaim against the inward barbarian and shout about the threat to civilization. There is nothing more repellent than the bourgeois defence of civilization. The problem is much more complicated. There is a civilized barbarism which is much worse than primitive barbarism, barbarism at the back of which is to be sensed not 'nature' but the machine, and mechanism. Industrial technical civilization is showing itself an ever growing civilized barbarism, a decline in quality. But in this civilized barbarism there is no sort of return to 'nature'. In the man of civilization the beast and the savage are from time to time awakened, but in a form which is changed by civilization, that is to say in a deteriorated form. The civilizing of man is a process which does not go particularly deep and the trappings of civilization are very easily stripped from him. Meanwhile he continues to make use of all the equipment of civilization. In Carlyle there are some very profound ideas about clothes (*Sartor Resartus*). It is a problem of the relation between appearance and reality.

The relations between primitiveness and civilization are very complicated and entangled. Primitiveness continues to exist within civilization, but it is equipped by civilization and loses its pristine nature, its naïveté and its freshness. The properties of technical civilization are such that the barbarian can avail himself of it exactly in the same way as the man of the highest culture. With this is connected the problem of the active irruption of the vast masses of the people into history and into culture, which has always been aristocratic in principle. Ortega makes use of the expression 'the revolt of the masses'. An increase in numbers and the ascendency of the majority change the character of culture, spiritual life itself is re-born.

It is the purest prejudice to think that an increase of population is always a good thing. It is possible that exactly the reverse is the case.

It is also necessary to get rid of the misunderstanding which identifies the 'masses' with the working-class or with the 'people'. 'The masses' is a category of quantity and yet it is defined in terms of the highest qualities and values. The masses may have their origin in various classes. There are the bourgeois masses, and they are the most unattractive. The *petite bourgeoisie,* the inferior grades of officialdom, the proletarianized elements of all classes form the great masses from which the fascist gangs are recruited. The masses are to be defined not so much by social as by psychological traits. Over against the masses is to be set not some particular class, but personality. A lack of expressed personality, an absence of personal originality, a disposition to swim with the current of the quantitative force of any given moment, an extraordinary susceptibility to mental contagion, imitativeness, repeatability; these must be regarded as the principal traits which distinguish one who belongs to the masses. A man with such characteristics is a man of the masses, to whatever class he may belong. Le Bon observes with truth that the masses can be more magnanimous and self-sacrificing than the separate individual, just as they can also be more cruel and merciless. This fact comes to light in rebellions, in demonstrations, in revolutions and counter-revolutions and in religious movements. The masses are excitable but they are conservative rather than revolutionary.

The word 'people' does not mean the same thing as the word 'masses'. The people is to be defined qualitatively in terms of its labour, its religious beliefs, and the plastic forms of its existence. The irruption of the masses is the irruption of vast numbers of people in whom personality is not expressed, and with whom there is no qualitative definition but who possess great excitability and a psychological readiness for slavery. This creates a crisis in civilization. The masses appropriate to themselves the technical side of civilization and eagerly equip themselves with it, but it is with great difficulty that they assimilate spiritual culture. The masses had indeed in the past their own spiritual culture and it was based upon religious belief. The masses in the present transitional period, on the other hand, are devoid of all spiritual culture, they set store by nothing but the myths and symbols which are instilled into them by demagogues—national and social myths and symbols, of race, nation, state, class, and the like. With all this the making of idols is always going on. Values are turned into idols with extraordinary ease: indeed even civilization itself may be turned into an idol, as the state, the nation, the race, as the proletariat or as one social order or another. Is the difference between civilization and culture only a matter of terminology?

The distinction between culture and civilization became popular from the time of Spengler onwards, but it is not his invention. The terminology in this connection is a matter of convention. The French, for example, prefer the word civilization and understand by it culture. The Germans prefer the word culture. The Russians in earlier days used the word civilization but from the beginning of the twentieth century gave their preference to the word culture. But the slavophils, Leontiev and Dostoyevsky and the rest understood admirably the difference between culture and civilization. The mistake of Spengler consisted in the fact that he assigned a purely chronological sense to the words civilization and culture, and saw in them a difference of epoch. Whilst culture and civilization will always exist, in a certain sense civilization is older and more primitive than culture, culture takes shape later. The invention of technical equipment, even of the most elementary tools by primitive man is civilization, just as civilization is the whole socializing process. The Latin word 'civilization' points to the social character of the process indicated by that word. By civilization must be meant a process which is more social and collective, by culture, a process which is more individual and one which goes deeper. We say, for instance, that such and such a person is a man of the highest culture, but we cannot say that such and such a person is a man of very high civilization. We speak of spiritual culture, but we do not speak of spiritual civilization. Civilization indicates a higher degree of objectivization and socialization, whereas culture is more closely linked with personality and spirit. Culture indicates the fashioning of material by the action of spirit, the victory of form over matter. It is more closely connected with the creative act of man, although the difference here is relative, as are all differences which arise from classification.

We may call an epoch of civilization *par excellence* one in which the predominating importance belongs to the masses and to technique. This is commonly said about our own epoch. But as in an epoch of civilization, culture exists, so also in an epoch of culture, civilization exists. Technics which embrace the whole of life act destructively upon culture, they depersonalize it. But in such an epoch there are always elements which rebel against the victorious march of technical civilization. That was the part played by the Romantics. There are creative geniuses of culture; but the cultured milieu, cultured tradition and cultured atmosphere are based also upon imitation, just as civilization is too. The highly cultured man of a certain style usually expresses imitative opinions upon every subject: they are average opinions, they belong to a group, though it may well be that this imitativeness belongs to a cultured *élite* and to a highly select group. A cultured style always includes imitativeness, and assimilation to tradition. It may be that socially it is original in appearance, but individually it is not original. Genius has never been completely able to find a place for itself in culture, and culture has always striven to turn genius from a wild animal into a domestic animal. It is not only the barbarian who is subject to socialization; the creative genius is also. The creative act, into which there enters an element of savagery and barbarism, is objectivized and changed into culture.

Culture occupies a middle zone between nature and technics, and it is often crushed between these two forces. But wholeness and harmony never exist in the objectivized world. There is an eternal conflict between the values of culture and the values of the state and society. On the whole, the state and society have always aimed at achieving totalitarianism, they have issued their orders to the creators of culture and required service from them. Creators of culture have always had difficulty in defending their freedom, but it has been easier for them to do it in a less unified and more differentiated form of society. Values of a lower order, the state, for instance, have always striven to subject and enslave to themselves values of a higher order, for instance, the values of the spiritual life, of knowledge and of art. Scheler has tried to arrange a scale of values: the value of what is noble in character is higher than the value of what is pleasant; spiritual values are higher than vital values; the values of holiness are higher than spiritual values. But it is absolutely beyond doubt that the values of holiness and spiritual values have much less power than the values of what is pleasant or vital values, which are often despotic. The structure of the objectivized world is like that.

It is of great importance that we should define the inter-relations which exist between the aristocratic and the democratic principles in culture. Culture is founded upon the aristocratic principle, upon the principle of qualitative selection. The creativeness of culture in all spheres struggles towards perfection, towards the attainment of the highest quality. It is so in knowledge, it is so in art, it is so in the working out of nobility of soul, and in the culture of human feelings. Truth, beauty, right, and love, do not depend upon quantity; they are qualities. The aristocratic principle of selection forms a cultured *elite*, a spiritual aristocracy. But the cultured *élite* cannot remain confined within itself, isolated, self-affirming, in its fear that it may become remote from the sources of life; the power to create may become exhausted in its fear of degeneration and death. All forms of aristocracy which are embodied in a group inevitably degenerate and wither away. It is true that the creativeness of cultural values cannot be spread all at once among the unqualitative mass of mankind, but nevertheless the process of the democratization of culture cannot fail to take place.

Truth is aristocratic in the sense that it is the attainment of quality and perfection in knowledge, independently of quantity, opinion and the demands of human majorities. But this in no way means that truth exists for the select few, for the aristocratic group. Truth exists for the whole of mankind and all men are called to enter into communion with it. There is nothing more repellent than the pride and contempt of a closed *élite*. Great geniuses have never been like that. It may even be said that the formation of a caste of culturally refined and complex people who have lost touch with the breadth and depth of the life process is a false development. The isolation of people who venerate themselves as those who belong to a cultured *élite*, is a wrong isolation. It is the isolation of a herd of animals, even though the herd may be a small group. It is not the solitariness of the prophets

[124]

and the geniuses. The genius lives near to primary reality and to real existence, whereas the cultured *élite* is subject to the laws of objectivization and socialization. The worship of culture is elaborated within it and that is one of the forms which idolatry and human slavery assume. True spiritual aristocracy is connected with a sense of service, not with the consciousness of one's own privileged position. Real aristocracy is nothing less than the attainment of spiritual freedom, of independence of the surrounding world and of human quantity, in whatever form that may take. It is nothing less than hearkening to the inward voice, the voice of God, and the voice of conscience. Aristocracy is personality in an aspect which refuses to acquiesce in mingling, in compliance, in slavery to an unqualitative world. But the human world is full, not of this sort of aristocracy, but of the aristocracy of isolation, of self-confinement, pride, contempt, of a haughty attitude to those who stand on a lower level, that is to say, a false aristocracy, an aristocracy of caste, an outcome of the social process.

It might be possible to establish a distinction between the democratic values and the aristocratic values within culture. Thus religious values and social values should be regarded as democratic, while values which are connected with philosophy, art, mysticism, and cultural emotions should be regarded as aristocratic. Tarde has some interesting ideas about conversation as a form of communion. Conversation is a product of high culture. A distinction can be made between conversation which is formal, conventional, utilitarian, and conversation which is intellectual, of no practical use, and sincere. It is just that second type of conversation which is an indication of high culture.

But the tragedy of culture lies in the fact that no high qualitative culture has a prospect of endless development before it. The flowering of culture is followed by decline. The fashioning of a cultural tradition implies a high culture, and in it not only creators of culture but a cultured *milieu* makes its appearance. Cultural traditions which on the other hand have become too hardened and too stereotyped indicate a weakening of cultural creativeness. Culture always ends in decadence, that is its role. The objectivization of creativeness means that the creative fire is dying down. The egocentricity and isolation of the cultured *élite* which has become a consumer rather than a producer, lead to the substitution of literature for life. An artificial literary atmosphere is created in which people lead an unreal and visionary existence. Cultured people become the slaves of literature, slaves of the last word in art. That is why aesthetic judgments are not personal, but belong to a group, an *elité*.

Culture and cultural values are brought into being by the creative act of man and the natural genius of man is revealed in them. Man has endowed culture with the immensity of his gifts. But here again the tragedy of human creativeness is brought to light. There is a lack of correspondence between the creative act, the creative intention and the creative product. Creativeness is a fire, while culture is already the quenching of that fire. The creative act is an upward flight, it is victory over the burdensome weight of the objectivized world, over determinism. The product of creativeness in culture, is a downward pull. It is a process of precipitation. The creative act, the creative fire, are in the realm of subjectivity, whereas the product of culture is in the realm of objectivity. In culture there takes place, as it were, all the time the same estrangement, the same exteriorization of human nature. That is the reason that man becomes a slave of cultural products and values. Culture is not in itself the transfiguration of life and the appearance of the new man; it denotes the return of man's creativeness back to that same objectivized world from which he desired to break away. But this objectivized world appears enriched. For the rest, the creativeness of great geniuses has always been a break-through beyond the limits of the objectivized determined world, and this has been reflected in the products of their creativeness. This was the theme of the great Russian literature of the nineteenth century, which always moved out beyond the limits of literature and art. It is the case with all philosophers of the existential type, beginning with St. Augustine. It is the subject matter too of the eternal difference between classicism and romanticism which goes on age after age. Classicism is simply this, the assertion of the possibility of attaining to the perfection of the creative product in the objectivized world, with the absolute exteriorization of that product from the very creator of it. Classicism is not interested in the existentiality of the creator and has no wish to see the expression of that existentiality in the creative product. Classicism, therefore, requires finiteness in the giving of a finish to the product of creativeness. It sees in the finite the mark of perfection and it fears the infinity which is revealed in the existential sphere and cannot be expressed in the objectivized sphere as perfection of form. Pure classicism has never existed and the greatest creators have never been pure classicists. Could it be said that the Greek tragedies, the dialogues of Plato, Dante, Cervantes, Shakespeare, Goethe, Leo Tolstoy, Dostoyevsky, Michael Angelo, Rembrandt, Beethoven, belong to the pure classical type? Of course not.

Romanticism does not believe in the possibility of attaining to the perfection of the creative product in the objectivized world. It is bent upon infinity and desires to express it. It is immersed in the world of subjectivity and values the existential and creative impulse itself, the creative inspiration, more than the objective product. Pure romanticism also has never existed, but the spirit of romanticism is wider than the romantic school in the proper sense of the word. In romanticism there is much that is bad and weak, but the eternal truth of romanticism lies in the blow it deals to the falsity and wrong of objectivization, in its awareness of the lack of correspondence between the creative inspiration and the creative product.

It is necessary to understand more clearly what the objectivization of creativeness in the values of culture means, and in what sense it is necessary to rebel against it. Here a great misapprehension is possible. The creative act is not only a movement upwards but also a movement towards an other, towards the world and towards men. The philosopher cannot but express himself in his books, the scholar in his published investigations, the poet in his verse, the musician in symphonies, the artist in pictures, the social reformer in social reforms. The creative act cannot be stifled within the creator and find no outlet for itself. But it is absolutely untrue to identify the realization of the creative act with objectivization. The objectivized world is only a condition of the world in which the creator is obliged to live, and every expression of creative action in the external falls into the power of that world. It is important to recognize the tragic situation of the creator and the tragedy of creativeness which is brought about by him. The struggle against slavery to the objectivized world, against the quenching of the creative fire in the products of creativeness, by no means consists in the fact that the creator ceases to express himself and to realize himself in his creations. That would be an absurd requirement. The conflict consists in the maximum break-through by the creative act, out of the closed circle of objectivization, in the maximum existentiality of the creator's creations, in the irruption of the maximum of subjectivity into the objectivized world. The meaning of creativeness is to be found in the anticipation of the transfiguration of the world, not in the fixation of this world in objective perfection.

Creativeness is a fight against the object world, a fight against matter and necessity. The conflict has its reflections in the most outstanding phenomena of culture. But culture wishes to leave man in this world. It casts a spell over him by its values and its achievements of immanent perfection. Whereas the creative fire, flaming up behind the façade of culture was a transcension, a broken-off transcension. The whole problem lies in this, how is the transition from the path of objectivization to the path of transcension to be made? Civilization and culture are created by man and they enslave man; they bring about his enslavement through their highest qualities, not their lowest.

It would be absurd simply to reject culture and especially so to appeal to a pre-cultural state, just as it would be absurd simply to repudiate society and history. But it is important to understand the inconsistencies of culture and the inevitability of a supreme judgment upon it, as upon society and history also. This is not an ascetic attitude to culture and creativeness but an eschatological attitude. I would call it a revolutionary eschatological attitude. But creative irruptions and transfigurations are still possible within the confines of culture itself. The triumph of music, the greatest of the arts, is possible, of music both in idea and in apprehension. In society itself again, irruptions into freedom and love are still possible; transcension is still possible in the world of objectivization; the irruption of metahistory is still possible in history; the attainment of a moment of eternity is still possible in time. But in the massive processes of history, in the congealed and crystallized conditions of culture, and in the fixed and ordered organizations of society objectivization triumphs, and man is laid under the spell of an enchantment by slavery which he does not recognize and which he experiences as pleasure. Man is enslaved by the standards of science and art. The academic spirit has been the instrument of this enslavement. It is a systematic and organized quenching of the creative fire, a demand that creative personality should be completely subjected to the social group. The demand of 'objectivity' is in no way the demand of truth, but socialization, it is subjection to the average man, and to the commonplace. Man is enslaved to the mind and reason of civilization, but this reason is not the divine Logos. It is the reason of the average standard of socialized consciousness which adapts itself to the average spiritual level and to a lower degree of spiritual community among men. Thus, the whole personality is crushed and there is no scope for the exercise of its supra-rational powers.

The good also in civilization enslaves man, the good which has been turned into law and socialized and made to serve the social commonplace routine. Man falls into slavery to ideal cultural values. He turns all the qualities of culture into idols of science and art and this makes him a slave. The spirit of the sciolist, and of the aesthete, snobism in the cultural sphere, are so many forms of human slavery. Behind the ideal values there stood prophets and geniuses in their day, with creative inspiration and fire. But when monuments have been erected to the prophets and the geniuses and streets have been called by their names, a chilled and mediocre culture comes into shape which no longer endures a new prophetic spirit and a new spirit of genius. A legalism and pharisaism of culture always emerges and the prophetic spirit always and inevitably rebels against it. Culture is a great blessing, it is a path that man must take, and the barbarian must not be allowed to reject it. But there is a supreme judgment upon culture which is not to be avoided, there is an apoca-lypse of culture. Culture must be transfigured into a new life, as the whole earth must be. It cannot linger on indefinitely in its medio-crity, in its cold legalism. We shall speak of this in the last chapter.

There is a falsity to which civilization and culture compel us. Poulain truly says that this falsity is a discord which is systematized and hidder from view. Superficially indeed unity reigns. Lies are necessarily opposed to the truth, even if the truth has shown itself to be dangerous and destructive. Truth is always dangerous. The lie accumulates because the end is replaced by the means. And the means have for so long been turned into the end that it is now impossible to reach the end. Civilization arose as a means but it was turned into an end and has become a power which controls man despotically. Culture with all its values is a means to the spiritual life, to the spiritual ascent of man, but it has been turned into an end in itself which crushes the creative freedom of man. This is the inevitable result of objectivization, which always tears the means and the end apart. The realism of civilization demands of man an ever-growing activity, but by this demand it enslaves man and turns him into a mechanism. Man becomes a means to an inhuman realistic process, technical and industrial. The result of this realism by no means exists for the sake of man; man is made to exist for the sake of the result. The spiritual reaction against this realism is a demand for the right of contemplation. Contemplation is a respite, the finding of a moment in which man emerges from his enslavement by the stream of time. In the old culture disinterested contemplation played an enormous part. But the exclusive culture of contemplation may be passivity on the part of man, it may be the repudiation of an active rôle in the world. Therefore, the union of contemplation and activity is necessary. The chief thing of all, however, is that man both in relation to culture and in relation to technics should be a master and not a slave. When on the other hand the principle of force is proclaimed and force is placed on a higher level than truth and exalted above value, that means the end and death of civilization. And then it is necessary to wait for new and mighty beliefs which will grip man and a new spiritual impulse which will conquer crude force.

6. THE SLAVERY OF MAN TO HIMSELF AND THE LURE OF INDIVIDUALISM

The last truth about human slavery is the fact that man is a slave to himself. He falls into slavery to the objective world, but this is slavery to his own exteriorizations. Man is the slave of various sorts of idols, but they are idols which he has himself created. Man is always a slave of that which lies, as it were, outside himself, which is estranged from him, but which is an inward source of slavery. The struggle between freedom and slavery is carried on in the outer, objectivized, exteriorized world. But from the existential point of view it is an inward and spiritual struggle. This follows at once from the fact that man is a microcosm. The conflict between freedom and slavery is carried on in the universal which is contained in personality and this conflict is projected in the objective world. The slavery of man consists not only in the fact that external force enslaves him; but still more profoundly in this, that he consents to be a slave, that he in a servile way accepts the action of the force which enslaves him. Slavery is characterized as the social position of people in the objective world. Thus, for example, in a totalitarian state all the people are slaves. But this is not the final truth of the phenomenology of slavery. It has already been said that slavery is in the first place a structure of consciousness and that a certain kind of objective structure of consciousness. 'Consciousness' determines 'being', and only in a secondary process does 'consciousness' fall into slavery to 'being.' A servile society is the outcome of the inward slavery of man. Man lives under the sway of an illusion which is so powerful that it appears to be normal consciousness. This illusion finds expression in the usual awareness of the fact that man is in slavery to an external force, at the same time as he is in slavery to himself. This illusion of consciousness is different from that which Marx and Freud detected.

Man defines his relation to the 'non-I' in a servile way, in the first place because he defines his relation to himself in a servile way. That servile social philosophy according to which man ought to put up with external social slavery and emancipate himself inwardly only, by no means follows from this. Such a philosophy is an absolutely false interpretation of the relation between 'inward' and 'outward'. Inward liberation inevitably demands outward liberation also, and the destruction of servile dependence upon social tyranny. The free man cannot put up with social slavery. But he remains free in spirit, and in that case if it is not within his power to overcome the external social slavery it is a struggle which may be very hard and long drawn out. Freedom presupposes superable resistance.

Egocentricity is the original sin of man, a violation of the true relation between the ego and its other, God, the world, and men, between personality and the universe. Egocentricity is an illusory, distorted universalism. It sets the world and every reality in the world in a false perspective, it is the loss of capacity for the true reception of reality. Egocentricity is under the power of objectivization, which it seeks to turn into an instrument of self-affirmation: it is the most dependent of existences and is in eternal slavery. Here there is hidden the greatest mystery of human existence. Man is the slave of the surrounding external world, because he is the slave of himself, of his egocentricity. Man slavishly submits himself to external slavery, which issues from an object, precisely because he in his egocentricity affirms himself. Egocentrics are usually conformists. He who is a slave of himself, torments himself. Personality is the antithesis of slavery, but egocentricity is the dissolution of personality. The slavery of man to himself is not only slavery to his lower, animal nature. That is a crude form of egocentricity. Man becomes a slave also to his higher nature and that is much more important and disturbing. Man becomes the slave of a refined ego which is very far removed from the animal 'I', he becomes a slave to his most lofty ideas, to his highest feelings, to his talents. He may entirely fail to notice, or recognize, that he is turning even the highest values into instruments of egocentric self-affirmation. Fanaticism is precisely that sort of egocentric self-affirmation. It is explained in books on the spiritual life that humility may be converted into extreme pride. There is nothing more hopeless than the pride of the humble. The typical Pharisee is the type of man in whom devotion to the law of goodness and purity, to an exalted idea, has been turned into egocentric self-affirmation and self-satisfaction. Even holiness can be converted into a form of egocentricity and self-affirmation and become false holiness. An exalted ideal egocentricity always means the setting up of idols and a false relation to ideas as a substitute for relations to the living God. All forms of egocentricity, from the basest to the most exalted, always denote the slavery of man, the slavery of man to himself, and through that, slavery to the surrounding world also. The egocentric is a being both enslaved and enslaving.

[132]

There is an enslaving dialectic of ideas in human existence, it is an existential dialectic, not a logical. There is nothing more terrible than a man possessed by false ideas, and affirming himself on the ground of those ideas, he is a tyrant both over himself and over other people. This tyranny of ideas may become the foundation of a régime in state and society. Religious, national and social ideas may play that sort of rôle of slave makers, equally so whether they are reactionary or revolutionary ideas. In a strange way ideas enter into the service of egocentric instincts and the egocentric instincts give themselves up to the service of ideas which treat man with contempt. And slavery, interior and exterior, always triumphs. The egocentric always falls into the power of objectivization. Looking upon the world as an instrument for his service, the egocentric always ejects himself into the external world, and becomes dependent upon it. But most frequently of all the slavery of man to himself assumes the form of the lure of individualism.

Individualism is a complex phenomenon which cannot be appraised in a simple manner. It may have both a positive and a negative significance. Personalism is frequently called individualism as the result of inaccuracy in the use of words. A man is called an individualist on the ground of his character, or because he is independent, original, free in his judgments, because he is not mingled with his environment but rises above it, or because he is isolated in himself, not apt for communion, a despiser of other people, an egocentric. But in the strict sense of the word, individualism comes from the word 'individual', and not from the word 'personality'. The affirmation of the supreme value of personality, its defence of freedom and the right to realize the possibilities of life, its reaching out towards completeness, is not individualism. Enough has already been said about the distinction between individual and personality.

In Ibsen's *Peer Gynt* an existential dialectic of individualism is displayed with genius. Ibsen posed this problem: What does it mean to be oneself, to be true to oneself? Peer Gynt wanted to be himself, to be an original individual, and he entirely lost and ruined his personality. He was simply the slave of himself. The individualistic aestheticism of a cultured *élite* which is revealed in the present day

[133]

novel, is the dissolution of personality, the fall of the whole personality into a disintegrated state and the slavery of the man to this disintegrated state. Personality is inward completeness and unity, mastery over self, victory over slavery. Dissolution of personality is its falling apart into separate self-affirming intellectual, emotional, sensory elements. The central core of the man is broken up. The spiritual principle alone maintains the unity of the spiritual life, and builds up personality. Man falls into the most varied forms of slavery when he can oppose to the enslaving force only the disintegrated elements and not a complete personality. An inward source of slavery for man arises from the autonomy of the sundered parts of man, which goes with the loss of the inward centre. A man who is broken up into parts readily succumbs to the temporary insanity of fear, and fear is that which more than anything holds a man in slavery. Fear is overcome by an integrated centralized personality, by an intensive experience of the dignity of personality. The intellectual, emotional sensuous elements in man cannot conquer it. Personality is a whole, whereas the objectivized world which is in opposition to it, is partial. But only an integrated personality, the image of the highest existence, can be conscious of itself as a complete whole which offers resistance on all sides to the objectivized world. The slavery of man to himself which makes him a slave to the non-ego, always denotes disintegration and dismemberment.

All possession, whether it is possession by base passion or by lofty ideas denotes the loss of the spiritual centre in man. The old atomistic theory of the life of the soul is false, that theory which derives the unity of the soul process from a special sort of psychical chemistry. The unity of the soul process is relative and is easily overthrown. An active spiritual principle synthetizes the soul process and brings it to unity. It is an operation at which personality works until it is complete. It is not the idea of the soul which holds the central place of importance but the idea of the integral man embracing the principles of spirit, soul and body.

An intense vital process may destroy personality. The will to power is dangerous not only to those upon whom it is directed but also to the possessor of this will himself. It acts destructively and enslaves the man who has allowed the will to power to gain the upper hand of him. According to Nietzsche truth is established by the vital process, by the will to power. But this is a most antipersonalistic point of view. The will to power provides no possibility of recognizing truth. Truth renders no service of any sort to one who is bent upon becoming powerful, that is to say, bent upon enslavement. In the will to power the centrifugal forces in man are in operation, an incapacity to control the self and to resist the power of the object world are disclosed. Slavery to self and slavery to the objective world are one and the same slavery. The pursuit of mastery, power, success, glory, the enjoyment of life, is always slavery; it is a servile attitude to self and a servile attitude to the world as an object of desire and lust. The lust for power is a slavish instinct.

One of the illusions of men is the conviction that individualism is the resistance of the individual man and his freedom to the surrounding world which is always bent upon doing violence to him. In actual fact individualism is objectivization and is connected with the exteriorization of human existence. This fact is to a large extent screened from view and is not immediately evident. The individual is a part of society, a part of the race, a part of the world. Individualism is the isolation of the part from the whole, or the revolt of the part against the whole. But to be a part of any kind of whole, even if it be in revolt against that whole means to be exteriorized already. Only in a world of objectivization, that is to say a world of alienation, impersonality and determinism, does that relation of part to whole exist which is disclosed in individualism. The individualist isolates himself and asserts himself in his attitude to the universe; he accepts the universe solely as violence offered to himself. In a certain sense individualism is the reverse side of collectivism. The refined individualism of modern times which, as a matter of fact, has grown very old, the individualism which comes from Petrarch and the Renaissance, was an escape from the world and society to the self, to its own soul, to the lyric, to poetry and music. The life of man's soul was much enriched, but the processes of dissociation of personality were put in train. Personalism means something entirely different. Personality contains the universe within it, but this inclusion of the universe takes place not in the sphere of the object world but in the sphere of the subject world, that is to say of existentiality. Personality is aware of itself as rooted in the realm of freedom, that is, in the realm of the spirit, and from that source it draws the strength for its conflict and activity. This is the very meaning of being a person, of being free.

The individualist, on the other hand, is essentially rooted in the objectivized social and natural world and thanks to this rootedness wishes to isolate himself and to oppose the world to which he belongs. The individualist is in fact the socialized man, but one who experiences this socialization as violence, who suffers from it and isolates himself and impotently rebels. This is the paradox of individualism. For instance, a false individualism is to be seen in the liberal ordering of society. In that system, which has in actual fact been a capitalist system, the individual was crushed by the play of economic forces and interests, he was himself crushed and he crushed others. Personalism has a communal tendency, it desires to establish brotherly relations among men. Individualism in social life, on the other hand, establishes wolfish relations among men. It is remarkable that great creative men have in fact never been individualists. They have been solitary and unrecognized, they have been in sharp conflict with their environment, with established collective opinions and judgments. But they have always thought of themselves as called to service, they have had a universal mission. There is nothing more false than to regard one's gifts and one's genius as a privilege and as a justification of individualistic isolation.

There are two different types of solitariness—the solitariness of creative personality which experiences the conflict of inward universalism with objectivized universalism, and the solitariness of the individualist who sets his desolation and impotence in opposition to that objectivized universalism to which he in fact belongs. There is a solitariness of inward plenitude and a solitariness of inward emptiness. There is a solitariness of heroism and a solitariness of defeatism, a solitariness which is strength and a solitariness which is weakness. The solitariness which finds nothing but passive aesthetic consolation for itself belongs as a rule to the second type. Leo Tolstoy felt himself very much alone, alone even among his followers, but he belonged to the first type. All prophetic solitariness belongs to the first type. The astonishing thing is that solitariness and estrangement which are properties of the individualist commonly lead on to subjection to a false sense of community. The individualist very readily becomes a conformist and makes his submission to an alien world to which nothing can offer any resistance. Examples of this are provided in revolutions and counter-revolutions, and in totalitarian states. The individualist is the slave of himself, he is under the spell of slavery to his own ego and, therefore, he cannot resist the slavery which comes from the non-ego. On the other hand, personality is emancipation both from slavery to the ego and from slavery to the non-ego. Man is always a slave of the non-ego through the ego, through a condition in which the ego is found. The enslaving power of the object world can make a person a martyr but it cannot make him a conformist. Compliancy, the spirit of the conformist, which is a form of slavery always makes use of this, that or the other of man's temptations and instincts, one form or another of enslavement to one's own ego.

Jung establishes two psychological types—the introverted which faces inwards, and the extroverted which faces outwards. This distinction is relative and conventional as all classifications are. As a matter of fact, there may be both introversion and extroversion in one and the same man, but at the moment it is another question which interests me. To what extent may introversion mean egocentricity and extroversion mean estrangement and exteriorization? Distorted introversion, that is to say introversion which has lost personality, is egocentricity, while distorted extroversion is estrangement and exteriorization. But introversion in itself may denote going down into the depths of oneself, into the spiritual world which is revealed in the depths, as extroversion can denote creative activity directed towards the world and man. Extroversion may denote also the ejection of human existence into the external and mean objectivization. This objectivization is created by a certain directing tendency of the subject.

It is worthy of note that the slavery of a man may be the result alike of his being exclusively engulfed by his own ego and concentrated upon his own condition without taking note of the world and other people; and of his being ejected exclusively into the external, into the objectivity of the world and losing the consciousness of his own ego. Both the one and the other are the result of a breach between the subjective and the objective. The 'objective' either entirely engulfs and enslaves human subjectivity or it arouses repulsion and disgust and so isolates human subjectivity and shuts it up in itself. But such estrangement and exteriorization of the object in relation to the subject is again what I call objectivization. Engulfed entirely by his own ego the subject is a slave, just as a subject which is wholly ejected into an object is a slave. Both in the one case and in the other personality is disintegrated or else it has not yet taken shape. In the primitive stages of civilization the ejection of the subject into the object, into a social group, into a horde, into a clan, predominates. At the summit of civilization the engulfing of the subject by his own ego prevails. But at the summit of civilization there takes place also a return to the primitive horde. Free personality is a flower that blooms but rarely in the life of the world. The immense majority of people is not made up of persons. In this majority personality is either still potential or else already disintegrated. Individualism certainly does not mean that personality is rising into prominence. Or it implies that only as the effect of an inaccurate use of language. Individualism is a naturalistic philosophy, whereas personalism is a philosophy of the spirit. The emancipation of man from slavery to the world, from his enslavement by external forces, is his emancipation from slavery to himself, to the enslaving powers of his own ego, that is to say, it is emancipation from egocentricity. Man ought at the same time to be both spiritually introverted, interiorized, and extroverted by going out in creative activity to the world and to men.

PART III

1. *A.* THE LURE OF SOVEREIGNTY. THE TWOFOLD IMAGE OF THE STATE

The greatest temptation of human history is the temptation to exercise sovereignty and in it there is concealed a most powerful enslaving force. The temptation of sovereignty takes very varied forms in history. It changes its shape and it leads men into error. This temptation to achieve great power never leaves man alone throughout the extent of his history—the Empires of the ancient East, the Roman Empire, Papal Theocracy, the Holy Byzantine Empire, the Tsardom of Moscow, the Third Rome, the Empire of Peter, the Communist State, the Third German Reich. The whole disquieting and tangled problem of sovereignty is bound up with the fact that man has a natural disposition to dominate others. Man is in search of his kingdom, in the grip of a dream of sovereignty. He is in search of his kingdom and he devotes his strength to the establishment of it, but his kingdom makes him a slave. Man does not always notice this and a slavery which is pleasant does not seem to him to be slavery. In his search for sovereignty man expresses his passion for the universal. He identifies his longed-for kingdom with world unity, with the final unification of humanity.

The temptation of sovereignty is one of the temptations which Christ rejected in the wilderness. The devil showed Christ from a high mountain, 'all the kingdoms of the world and the glory of them', and proposed that He should fall down and worship them. Probably among these kingdoms presented to the spiritual vision of Christ were all those kingdoms of the world which were to call themselves Christian, all the changing forms of sovereignty till the end of time. Christ rejected that temptation and He rejected it for ever and in reference to all the kingdoms of the world. Christians have not followed the example of Christ, and they have bowed down before sovereignty, in mocking travesty confusing, combining and uniting the Kingdom of Christ with the kingdoms of the world.

[139]

Christ called upon them to seek first the Kingdom of God and His righteousness'. Christians, however, have all the while sought all the things that 'shall be added unto' them, they have been afraid, they have been in terror that the search for the Kingdom of God would prove destructive to the kingdom of the world. In this way they have corrected the action of Christ, as the Grand Inquisitor as Dostoyevsky says. In the *Legend of the Grand Inquisitor* there is revealed with the skill of a genius, the existential dialectic of the age-long temptation of sovereignty. It provides the firmest foundation for Christian anarchism, although Dostoyevsky himself was not free from the temptation of sovereignty (in the form of Orthodox theocracy).

'Render unto Caesar the things that are Caesar's and unto God the things that are God's.' This is commonly interpreted in a sense which reconciles the kingdom of Caesar and the Kingdom of God; it is given a meaning which abolishes the conflict. But the life of Christ was precisely this conflict carried through to the utmost limit of intensity. The 'kingdom of Caesar' has in fact never agreed to recognize the Kingdom of God as an autonomous region and has always demanded service from the 'Kingdom of God', has always been bent upon making a mere tool of it. The kingdom of Caesar has tolerated Christianity when Christianity had been adapted and adjusted to it and has rendered it service. When there has been such subservience the sovereignty of Caesar has conferred every kind of privilege upon it.

That weird and horrible phenomenon of human life which today is called the totalitarian state, is certainly not a temporary and accidental phenomenon of a certain epoch. It is a revelation of the true nature of the state, of sovereignty. The totalitarian state itself wishes to be a church, to organize the souls of men, to exercise dominion over souls, over conscience and thought, and to leave no room for freedom of spirit, for the sphere of the Kingdom of God. But the state by its very nature lays claim to a universal all-embracing significance. It is willing to share its sovereignty with no-one, with nothing. A distinction must be made between sovereignty, empire and the state. The state still has a particularist character. It is still conscious of its boundaries, and elements and functions of the state are to be found in every expression of human life lived in common. But the will to power is built into the very foundation of the state, the poison of imperialism is already in it. The expansion of a state leads on to empire, which no longer has a particularized, but a universal character. This is the fatal dialectic of the state. England is a small state but the British Empire is a world dominion. The Holy Byzantine Empire and the Russian Empire laid claim to universal significance. The First, Second and Third Rome were universal sovereignties. In fact, the emperor, if he regards his mission and his title as holy, is an oecumenical emperor. If the state aspires to be the empire, then the empire aspires to be an oecumenical empire. The imperial sovereignty recognized its own oecumenicity, not because it was extended over the surface of the whole earth, but because it was founded upon the true and oecumenical faith. The communist state which is one of the manifestations of imperialism has the same properties as the Holy Empire of Byzantium or of Moscow. The state has always striven to be totalitarian. All the theocratic states have been totalitarian; all the empires have been totalitarian. Plato's Republic was a totalitarian state. That state was absolute and denied all independence and freedom to human personality. It was a proto-type which prefigured at the same time mediaeval theocracies and the present-day totalitarian state including the communist state. Here we have to deal with a world principle, with a phenomenon of world significance. It follows from the Gospel that the 'Prince of this world' always rules, that he places himself at the head of states and empires. But the 'Prince of this world' is not a neutral figure placed in a neutral zone between the Kingdom of God and the kingdom of the devil. He is a figure in the highest degree aggressive and ready to take the offensive; he is always encroaching upon the freedom of the spirit and upon the sphere of the Kingdom of God. The prince of this world is at the extreme limit of the objectivization, the exteriori-zation and the alienation of human nature. The conflict between the Kingdom of God and the kingdom of Caesar is in philosophical terms, the conflict between subject and object, between freedom and necessity, between spirit and objectivized nature. It is all the while the same problem of the slavery of man.

A radical break has taken place between personal morality, especially the morality of the Christian Gospel, and state morality, the morality of sovereignty, the moral practice of the 'Prince of this world'. That which has been considered immoral for a person has been considered entirely moral for the state. The state has always used evil means—espionage, falsehood, violence, murder; there have been distinctions in this respect in degree only; these methods, indisputably very evil, have always been justified by a good and exalted end in view. But not to speak for the moment of the quality of that end, it must be said that this so-called good and exalted end has never been realized. The life of mankind has been filled to capacity with those very means, those thoroughly evil means, whereas the end has in the meantime been forgotten. Yes, and to speak truly, a nend can justify nothing; it is entirely abstract and is a product of violent disruption. No-one can ever clearly explain and justify the fact that undoubted vices and sins in an individual person—pride, self-conceit, egoism, cupidity, hatred, blood-thirstiness, brutality, lying and theft should assume the appearance of virtues and gallantry in the state and nation, nor can anyone justify their doing so. This is the very greatest falsity in world history. No-one has ever in any way justified on metaphysical and religious grounds the ethics of the state, the morality of communities, of which morality the principle that 'everything is permitted' is a characteristic. When Christian thinkers have endeavoured to do it, the falsity that such an attempt represents is evidence of their lack of scruple, and their slavery. It is only the voice of slavish morality that has been heard. It has been left unintelligible in what way a nearer approach to the Kingdom of God comes about, and in what way the Kingdom of God benefits, from organized lying, from organized espionage, from executions, from predatory wars, the seizure of foreign lands and brutality to their peoples, from the growth of national egoism and national hatred, from monstrous social inequalities and from the power of money. If it is good for individual people to repent and be humbled, it would be still better for communities, states, nations, and churches, to enter upon the path of repentance and humility. This would be both a wider and a deeper repentance and humility on the part of the people who constitute these communities. The arrogance of an individual person is not so terrible as the arrogance of a nation, a state, a class, or of an ecclesiastical confession. The self-assertion of a group is the form of self-assertion from which there is least hope of escape.

Those who have no thought for the Kingdom of God or the righteousness of God in any shape or form and show respect for nothing but earthly power have obvious advantages. The Christian conscience does not allow a man to devote himself to the attainment of power and glory, to try to dominate other men, to seek for pride of place. But all this is allowed and approved and even recommended when it is transferred to the state and the nation. If the state and nation be regarded as a person and to this personality a different and non-human code of ethics is applied, then man is not personality, man is a slave. There is nothing more repellent than to apply a pantheistic line of thought to the state, society and nation, and then on the basis of that to regard them as taking supremacy over man. It needs to be said that politics are always based on lies, and, therefore, the expression of moral principle, not Christian only but simply human, ought to mean a demand for the reduction of politics and their fictitious power over human life to the very minimum. Politics are always an expression of the slavery of man. The astonishing thing is that politics have never been an expression even of intelligence, to say nothing of nobility, or of goodness. The so-called great among statesmen and political figures have said nothing wise and intelligent; they have usually been men of ordinary current ideas, of banalities adapted to the average man. Even Napoleon said nothing particularly clever. He took the idea of a world democracy—of a United States of Europe—from the French revolution—and his own contribution was to add to this a demonic will to power and the devouring imperialism which brought him to ruin. It is only a hypnosis which makes people think that Napoleon said things that showed profound thought. Tolstoy was very well aware of the worth of great historical figures. He understood the insignificance of historical greatness. The majority of these great figures, these politically-minded men, are distinguished by the same criminality, hypocrisy, craftiness and insolence. It was only upon those grounds that they were regarded as statesmanlike minds. They will be the last and lowest of mankind at the Judgment Day. An exception must be made in favour of the social reformers who emancipated man from slavery.

The moral and religious question which faces the personal conscience can be put in a very simple and elementary way: is it permissible to execute a single innocent person for the sake of the safety and wellbeing of the state? In the Gospel this question was put in the words of Caiaphas. 'It is better for us that one man should die for the people than that the whole nation should perish.' It is well known what sentence was decided by these words. The state always repeats the words of Caiaphas; it is the state's confession of faith. Statesmen have always given the answer that in the interests of the safety of the state and the increase of its strength, an innocent man may and should be put to death. And every time that happens a voice is raised in favour of the crucifixion of Christ. The demoniacal stamp which is imprinted upon the state is due to the fact that the state always gives its vote for the execution of Christ: it is its destiny. The same question was put in the Dreyfus case. The point at issue was: may an innocent man be condemned if this appears advantageous to the French State and to the army? It does great honour to the French that they made this question a question of honour, a question of the moral conscience of the nation.

It is a question of fixing the scale of values. Not only is the existence of the state not the highest value, but even the existence of the world, of this objectivized world, is certainly not the highest value. The death of one man, of even the most insignificant of men, is of greater importance and is more tragic than the death of states and empires. It is to be doubted whether God notices the death of the great kingdoms of the world; but He takes very great notice of the death of an individual man. All the while it is the same problem which was raised in Sophocles in the clash between Antigone and Creon. It is the clash of personal human morality which makes a stand in defence of the right to bury one's brother, and the impersonal inhuman morality of the state which denies that right. Personal morality has always been right in comparison with state morality, it has been a human and existential morality as opposed to an inhuman and objectivized morality. Nietzsche whom it is now desired to make the founder of fascist and national-socialist morality, that is to say the morality of Caiaphas, Creon and the rest, said the state is the most cold-blooded of monsters and that man begins where the state ends.

We are on the eve of a radical, revolutionary, personalist transvaluation of values in the world and then only will profound social changes be possible.

It is beyond dispute that the state exercises very great power over human life and it always shows a tendency to go beyond the limits laid down for it. This is sufficient indication that the state represents a reality of some sort. The state is not personality, it is not a being, it is not an organism, it is not an entity (*essentia*). It has no existence of its own, its existence is always to be found in people; existential centres are in people. But for all that how unconquerable the hypnosis of power is. The state is, of course, a projection, an exteriorization, an objectivization of a condition of the people themselves. The power of the state proves to be inevitable given a certain condition of the people, given a certain character of their existence. And that is a fallen condition. At the same time men bring their creative instincts to the making of the state. Men not only need the state and cannot do without the services it renders, but they are seduced by it, they are taken captive by the state, they connect their dreams of sovereignty with it. And there lies the chief evil and a source of human slavery.

The state has a functional significance in the public life of men. The rôle of the state has varied at different periods. The state is twofold; it has a twofold expression. It may both liberate man and enslave him, and the enslaving rôle of the state has always been due to a wrong attitude towards it, to an inward slavery of man who has acquiesced in hypnosis and suggestion, to a deceitful dream of sovereignty. The origin of the hypnosis of the state is not rational, it is irrational. Power always has an irrational character, and relies upon irrational beliefs and irrational emotional life.

In its work of giving actual expression to the will to power, the state always needs myths; it cannot exist without irrational symbols. Even the most rational democratic state relies upon myths, such, for example, as Rousseau's myth of the indefectibility of the *volonté générale*. The great danger consists not in the actual idea of the state, which exercises necessary functions, but in the idea of the *sovereignty* of the state, the sovereignty of theocracy, monarchy, aristocracy, democracy, or communism. The idea of sovereignty in all its forms

B.S.F.

is slavery for man. The very seeking after sovereignty is in itself a great delusion, it is a slavish search; it is a dream of slaves. The idea of sovereignty is an illusion arising out of the objective world which is the world of slavery. There does not exist any sovereignty at all. Sovereignty belongs to no-one and it is essential to break free from this slavish idea. Sovereignty is an hypnosis. It always regards itself as sacred; whereas there is nothing whatever sacred in the object-ivized world; there are only false sanctities and idols. Spirit is never incarnate in states and in historical bodies politic; spirit is incarnate in the human body, in human communion, in human creativeness, in a person and in personality, not in a state and not in the great bodies politic of history. In the objectivized world there are only necessary functions, nothing more than that. And this is an emancipating thought. Sovereignty does not belong to the people either, any more than it belongs to monarchy.

At the foundation of power and dominion there lies a totemistic idea of monarchy. The monarch was a totem. This is abundantly clear in ancient Egypt. From that time men have always tried to find religious sanction as a support for power, and even in the twentieth century they are by no means free from this idea. A sovereign people, a sovereign class, a sovereign race—all these are new and changing forms of the totem. The führer, as dictator, also is a totem. At the dawn of history, as Fraser has shown, the magician and healer was turned into the king. But the leader dictator of the present day is again turning himself into a magician and soon probably will lay hands upon the sick in order to heal them. The king regarded him-self as of divine extraction in the ancient world, for example, in Sparta; but in the twentieth century the dictator Caesar likewise regards himself as of divine extraction, as an emanation of the nation, considered as a deity, or of the state or social community accepted as a divinity. Everywhere alike we meet with this mystical idea of sovereignty, this mystical idea of the nation, of the community, of the party. It is an age-long manifestation of human slavery. The appearance of dictatorships and tyrannies means that the old basic idea of power in its exercise of authority has disintegrated and col-lapsed, A new symbolism of sacred power is taking shape. Dictator-ship and tyranny are usually the reverse side of inward anarchy and lack of unity of faith, and thus the new power, everywhere consolidating its symbols, usually displays a greater will to power and to domination than the old power which relied upon age-long tradition. This is characteristic of the *parvenu*. Individual thinkers have tried to reject the idea of sovereignty but with no great force. Benjamin Constant, Royer-Collard, Guizot, rejected sovereignty. They affirmed that sovereignty belongs not to the will (of a monarch or a people) but to reason. But they kept within the circle of liberal ideas, which have no dynamic force, and they were associated with bourgeois privileges. The anarchists also have rejected sovereignty, although they have not followed it out with sufficient consistency, since the majority of them have been collectivists.

Anarchism is one of the poles of thought in the subject of the relation between personality and the state, and between society and the state. An estimate of anarchism must be twofold because there are two different sides to it. There is absolute truth in anarchism and it is to be seen in its attitude to the sovereignty of the state and to every form of state absolutism. It is an exposure of the wrongness of despotic centralization. There is religious truth in anarchism; but anarchism is materialistic and as such it has in fact frequently become absurd. What the basis is of that freedom which man ought to oppose to the despotic power of society and of the state is left entirely incomprehensible. And indeed a great number of anarchist doctrines do not set the freedom of human personality in contrast with the power of society and the state, but the freedom of the elemental masses, whose will is left as undisputed master. Such, for instance, was the communist anarchism of Bakunin. Thus the domination of the stateless communist society can be still more totalitarian than the domination of the state which meets with limits to its power. Anarchism may be alike ferocious and armed with bombs, or benign, idyllic, and given to believe in the goodness of human nature. It must be admitted that the anarchism of Max Stirner goes deeper, and so, from another side, does the anarchism of Tolstoy.

Anarchism touches upon a problem of the metaphysical and religious order. The religious truth of anarchism consists in this, that power over man is bound up with sin and evil, that a state of per-

[147]

fection is a state where there is no power of man over man, that is to say, anarchy. The Kingdom of God is freedom and the absence of such power; no categories of the exercise of such power are to be transferred to it. The Kingdom of God is anarchy. This is a truth of apophatic theology; the religious truth of anarchism is a truth of apophatics. The state and power are bound up with evil and sin: they are not transferable to any state of perfection. The emancipation of man from slavery is the attainment of absence of power of man over man. There is a sublime truth in the fact that man is a self-governing creature. He should govern himself and others should not govern him. A reflected glimmer of this truth is to be seen in democracy, in that positive eternal side of democracy which in actual experience is always distorted. The self-government of man always means that concord has been attained between inward and outward freedom. Power over man is an evil and even the source of all evil. Tolstoy alone carried the idea of anarchism into the heart of religion. That heart is to be found in his doctrine of non-resistance to evil by force, a doctrine which is not well understood. Tolstoy in actual fact accuses Christians of this, that they arrange their affairs in every case in such a way that they will go well even if there is no God and, therefore, they take refuge in power and violence. He proposes to stake everything on his belief in God and in nature as divine. Tolstoy believed that if people stopped using force and having recourse to power, a historical miracle would take place and God Himself would intervene in human life and divine nature would come into its right. Human resistance and violence hinder the working of the true human nature.

This is at any rate a profound statement of the problem, more profound than that of the materialistic anarchists who always appeal to force and bring in power and compulsion from the other end. Tolstoy's mistake consisted in this that he had so little interest in the victim of violence and compulsion. It seemed as though he did not consider it necessary to protect him. With this is connected the impossibility of finally eliminating the state in the conditions of our existence in view of the flood of evil which arises from the aggressive will of man. Here we come up against the negative side of anarchism with its misleading and fanciful dreaming, The state ought to defend freedom and right. That is the justification of its existence. But every process by which the state is made absolute is a great evil. The power of the state possesses no sovereignty of any kind. The state should be limited, it should be brought within bounds which it ought not to go beyond. It is impossible to admit that final objectivization of human existence which the state demands, possessed as it is by the will to power. A totalitarian state is the kingdom of Satan. The state should not presume to concern itself with the spirit and spiritual life; but it does always show a tendency to demand from thought and creativeness and from spiritual life some degree of adaptation to itself (theocracy, absolute monarchy, the secret dictatorship of money in sham democracy, Jacobinism, communism, fascism).

The idea of the totalitarian state is by no means new, it is only a more consistent and extreme manifestation of a perpetual tendency in the state, of the everlasting will to power and the endless enslavement of man. Anarchism is right when it rebels against the idealization and exaltation of the state, against doctrines which see in power the ideal dignity of that which should be. (Frank.) Power has too often created evil, and rendered service to evil, and the men in power have too often been an assortment of the worst rather than of the best. A St. Louis is a rare phenomenon in history, and men in authority who have devoted their efforts to social reforms for the sake of man and not to the increase of authority itself and the growth of the might of the state and nation, have also been rare. Too often they have used the majesty of the state to palliate the self-seeking interests of men and classes. There is no baseness which has not been held to be justified by the interests of the state. For the sake of the majesty of the state and the prestige of authority they have tortured individual men and women and whole nations. The state has respected the rights of man less than anybody, although its one and only task consists in the protection and preservation of those rights. The privileged and ruling classes have commonly been regarded as the representatives of the interests and unity of the state. The rightness of anarchism as against the wrong of the state consists in the fact that the state ought not to set 'great' ends before itself and sacrifice men and women and the people as a whole for the sake of these supposedly great ends. Great kingdoms and mighty empires are nothing in comparison with a man. The state exists for man and not man for the state. This is a particular case of the truth that the 'sabbath was made for man'. Power, government, is only the servant, simply the defender and guarantor of the rights of man and nothing more. And only those states are to be tolerated which might take as their symbol the value of man and not the majesty of the state. But the power of the state keeps its relative and functional importance intact. The anarchist Utopia of an idyllic stateless life is a lie and a seductive delusion.

The Utopia of anarchism rests upon a naïve monistic philosophy and by no means wishes to have any acquaintance with the tragic conflict of personality with the world and society. It certainly does not mean the emancipation of man, because it is based not upon the supremacy of human personality but on the supremacy of the stateless society, of the social community as a whole. It is amazing that anarchist doctrines have never been personalist. The anarchist Utopia is in the last resort one of the forms assumed by the dreams of sovereignty. The dream of sovereignty may be a dream of stateless sovereignty. But in this stateless sovereignty human personality can be violated and enslaved. The refusal of the dream of sovereignty which enslaves personality is the refusal also of the anarchist Utopia, as indeed of every earthly Utopia, in which the enslavement of man is always to be found. Liberation from slavery is in the first place liberation from all will to power, from all power as a right. The right to power belongs to no-one. Nobody has the right to exercise power, neither an individual man nor a selected group of people, nor the whole nation. What exists is not a right to power but a burdensome obligation to power as an organic function for the protection of man.

There are a number of respects in which the function of the state ought even to be broadened, for example in economic life. It is not to be permitted that there should be hungry people, people oppressed by want, and unemployed; the exploitation of man cannot be permitted. To prevent these things should be the principal purpose of the state. The state is before all things an institution which guarantees, mediates and checks, and the concern of the state with political economy rests not on the rights of the state in economic life, but on the supremacy of individual economic right, on the guarantee of those individual rights. This is the emancipation of the individual man, of human personality, by means of the abolition of economic privileges. The state has a duty to guarantee the free development of autonomous life. The state is evidently a necessary thing, it is a necessity for human beings, but this simply points to the fact that in the hierarchical scale of values it belongs to those of the lowest order. The whole question lies in this scale of graduated values. Everything necessary, everything which is urgently indispensable in human existence belongs to the lowest values. Such is the value of economics. We must stop continually telling people from their childhood onwards that the state is a higher value than human personality and that the vigour, majesty and glory of the state is the highest and most worthy end. The souls of men have been poisoned by having these slavish ideas instilled into them. In actual fact the state should in the exercise of its true functions remind one of a co-operative association.

Man ought not to be bound to any particular form of the state. The love of freedom with which all human dignity is connected is not liberalism, nor democracy, nor anarchism, but something immeasurably more profound and connected with the metaphysics of human existence. The state is sometimes defined as the organization of chaos and the creation of a social cosmos in a hierarchical order. It is true that the state does not allow a final chaotic collapse of the social life of men, but all the same, beneath the constraining organization of the state, the chaos which it conceals is stirring, and under a despotic state chaos is stirring most of all. Fear is always chaos, the disclosure of inward chaos, of the dark abyss.

The idea of democracy, according to Montesquieu, consists in founding the state upon virtue. But chaos is stirring beneath the democracies also, and therefore fear makes its appearance too, although in a less degree than in the other political systems. Political life is distorted most of all by fear of an enemy, by the fear of hurt. The state has always been occupied with conflict against the enemy both internal and external. The power of the state is disfigured by fear; it not only inspires fear but it also suffers from fear. There is nothing more terrible and dangerous than a man possessed by fear and especially there is nothing more terrible than political power which is possessed by fear. It is precisely the man possessed by fear who perpetrates the greatest violence and cruelty. The tyrant has always been possessed by fear. The demonic principle in the state is due not only to the will to power but also to fear. Freedom is the victory over fear. Free men do not feel fear themselves nor do they inspire it in others. The greatness of Tolstoy's thought is to be seen also in his desire to free the social life of men from fear. Revolutions are possessed by fear and, therefore, perpetrate violence. Political Terror is fear, not only to those upon whom it is exercised, but also to the very men who practise it. Terror is built into the fabric of the state and of revolution. Terror is the outcome of the objectivization of human existence, of ejection into the external; it is socially organized chaos, that is to say, it is collapse, alienation, absence of freedom.

The authorities and the people are in a state of mutual dependence and slavery. The idea of 'leadership , which is so profoundly opposed to the principle of personality, is also a form of reciprocal slavery. The 'leader' is a slave in the same degree as the people who drag the 'leader' along. But perhaps the most repellent feature in the state, a disease which arises from the very principle of state authority, is bureaucracy. Bureaucracy which no state of any kind is able to dispense with, has a fatal tendency to develop, to expand, to extend its power and to look upon itself not as the servant of the people but as a master who demands obedience. Bureaucracy is the outcome of a process of political centralization. Only decentralization can ward off the danger of the development of bureaucracy. Bureaucracy corrodes even socialist parties. We shall see that the most dangerous and negative side of the socialist state is the tendency which is inherent in it to increase the power and scope of bureaucracy, and the one and only communist state which has been actually realized in the world has shown itself to be the most bureaucratic state in the world. Bureaucracy is the most extreme form of depersonalization. It is a realm which has no knowledge of personality, it takes cognizance of number only, of the impersonal unit. It is a fictitious paper realm to the same extent as the sovereignty of money is in the capitalist world. Only in the world of objectivization, that is to say, of alienation, determinism, impersonality do bureaucracy and money, espionage and falsehood hold sway. This is an inevitable characteristic of a world which has lost freedom and unity in love and kindliness. But these properties are to a greater or less degree inherent in the state, and every state which insists upon regarding itself as a sacred ideal and decks itself with sacred symbols, is fated to acquire those same properties of bureaucracy, lying, espionage, and bloodthirsty violence.

Ideologists of the state who are captivated by the ideal of sovereignty are fond of using such expressions as 'this is the mind of the state', 'he is a man of statesmanlike mind'. In the majority of cases the expression means nothing whatever. What it really means is that a man who is regarded as having a statesmanlike mind is devoid of feelings of humanity and looks upon man as merely a tool to serve the power of the state and will place no hindrance in the way of any kind of violence and bloodshed. That is what all 'statesmanlike minds' have been like; they are slaves and idolators. The idols to which they have been faithful have demanded bloody human sacrifices.

There is nothing more repugnant to the moral sense and at the same time more fashionable and more banal, than to give the name of sentimentalists to those who are opposed to the cruelties and violence perpetrated by authority, and who resist the triumph of crude force. This is playing upon the very basest of human emotions. The Gospel must be viewed as a sentimental book, and we must recognize as sentimental all ethics which are founded upon the dignity of the human person, and upon compassion for human suffering. As a matter of fact, sentimentality is sham sensitiveness and sentimental people can be extremely cruel. Robespierre, Dzherzinsky, Hitler are all sentimental. Cruelty can be the reverse side of sentimentality. What needs to be preached is a sterner, I would even say, a colder ethic of humanity and compassion. We need a heroic love of freedom which lays stress upon the value of every human creature and of every creature in general, which is filled to the full with compassion and sympathy but a stranger to false sentiment. Those people from whom the charge of sentimentality comes are commonly idolators, possessed, and slaves. We need a merciless exposure of these savage and ferocious anti-sentimentalists, and a pitiless fight against them. They are sadists, perverts, and they ought to be made to wear straight jackets. And above all the philosophical

falsity of those who set cruelty and violence in antithesis to sentimentality must be exposed. Every cruel and violent man is a weak
man, he is feeble and sick. The strong man is the man who gives, who
helps, liberates, and loves. Every enslaver is a man enslaved, a man of
ressentiment in one form or another.

To found the majesty and power of the state upon sadistic instincts
is simply an extreme case of the loss of freedom, of personality and of
the human image in the objectivized world. It is an extreme expression of the Fall of man The state has made attempts to christianize
and humanize. This has never been completely successful, as it has
been impossible to apply Christian and humanist virtues to the state.
But it has been partially successful. In the nineteenth century a
number of processes in the humanizing of the state took place. At
least a number of human principles were proclaimed in the sphere
of thought. But they ended in the acute dechristianization and
dehumanizing of the state. The worship of crude force and violence
is being proclaimed as the basis of the greatness of the state. A
demoniacal principle in the state is being disclosed. The rights of man
are more and more trampled under foot, and the more the state is
bent upon being a great sovereignty, the more the imperialist will
triumphs, so much the more the state becomes inhuman, the rights
of man are denied and demoniacal possession triumphs. Every kingdom is opposed to the Kingdom of God and those who seek for
sovereignty cease to seek for the Kingdom of God. Sovereignty,
great and powerful sovereignty, cannot but enslave man, and for
that reason it is necessary to desire the end of all sovereignty. The
metaphysical basis of anti-étatism is determined by the supremacy of the
freedom over being, of personality over society.

1. *B*. THE LURE OF WAR. THE SLAVERY OF MAN
TO WAR

The state, in its will to power and its expansion creates war. War
is the fated destiny of the state. And the history of societies as
states is full of wars. The history of the human race is to a notable

[154]

degree a history of wars and it is now arriving at total war. The outward aspect or 'style' assumed by the state is essentially military rather then civic. The authority of the state is always surrounded by the symbols of war, by armies, flags, orders, and military music. Monarchs have always been soldiers, they have gone about in military uniform, and appeared surrounded by their guards. Presidents of democratic republics go about in mere civilian clothes, that is an enormous advantage, but behind them also there stands an army, and behind them too are assistants in military uniform. The symbolism of power is always military, authority is always ready to resort to force in order to uphold its prestige. If authority is not waging war against external foes, it is always getting ready for it, and it is always in readiness for war against the enemy within. The state disburses monstrous sums on armaments and this exhausts its finances and imposes a heavy burden on its people. The law of life for national states is:—Man is a wolf to man. In organized civilized states, men spend their strength in the first place upon preparation for mass murder, and the sacrifices that they make are primarily to this inhuman end. It would be a mistake to say that war exists for the sake of men and not men for the sake of war.

Human societies find themselves in the vicious circle of war, and are looking for a way out of it. War is a mass hypnosis, and it is only thanks to mass hypnosis that it is a possibility. Even those who hate war and are of a pacific frame of mind are also under the influence of this hypnosis. They also are unable to break out of the vicious circle. The sovereignty of the state, nationalism, and capitalism which makes the production of munitions of war into an industry, inevitably lead to war. The question of war is in the first place a question of the scale of values. When the might of the state and the nation is looked upon as a greater value than man, war has in principle already made its appearance, everything has been made ready for it spiritually and materially, and it may break out at any moment. It is a mistake to state the problem of war in an abstract way, which separates it from the social structure and the spiritual condition of society. Given a certain spiritual condition of society, that is to say one which accepts the dominance of a particular scale of values, and given a certain social structure, war cannot be escaped and abstract pacifism can have no influence whatever. A capitalist structure of society will always give rise to war, at the back of pacifically disposed governments there will always be the men who trade in guns and poison gas, and they will always be getting ready for war.

War is possible only in a certain psychological atmosphere and this psychological atmosphere is created in a variety of ways, sometimes in unnoticed ways. Even an atmosphere of fear of war can be favourable to war. Fear never leads to any good. The atmosphere of war, alike of war itself and of preparation for it, is a collective atmosphere, an atmosphere of the mass subconscious in which personality, personal consciousness and the personal conscience are paralysed. War and everything connected with it, is not only the most extreme form and the utmost limit of violence, it is also the most extreme form and the utmost limit of anti-personalism, it is a denial of personality. In consenting to war, man ceases to be personality and he ceases to regard other people as personalities. An army is a sort of hierarchical organism of which everyone in it feels himself to be a part, where each takes a share in the common life of the whole and occupies a definite place in it. This precipitates human personality into an entirely special atmosphere, in which slavery and violence are experienced organically and may even be felt to be pleasurable. This is the particular temptation, and the special lure of slavery to war, which arouses the elemental forces of human nature.

War and the army cannot fail to regard human personality as a means to an end, as a subordinate part of a superhuman whole. States desire the increase of population and encourage the birth of children solely from the point of view of the provision of cannon fodder and to add to the strength of the army. This is a piece of cynicism on the part of the state which represents itself as a lofty and patriotic ideal. A false scale of values, which enslaves man, inevitably leads to a perversion of moral feeling. The human masses can only be made to go to war by paralysing their consciousness through a system of hypnosis, of psychological and physical poisoning, and by Terror which is always introduced in time of war. A military 'style' of society always means violence and the enslavement 'of man psychologically and physically. A military 'style' has predominated in societies in the past, and our contemporary society is returning to it, for it already recognizes nothing but force. Spencer thought that the military type of society would be replaced by the industrial, a type which would not be favourable to war. But he did not realize that the industrial, that is to say, the capitalist type of society, was to bring into being a new type of imperialistic wars, more horrifying still than those which had occurred before. The world has not emerged from that vicious circle, the circle is still more tightly closed. The world has never been so much depersonalized. At the present time, war, and the preparation for it, have left no room whatever for the principle of personality.

The romance of war, to which even the young people of today surrender, is the most repugnant form of romanticism, for it is connected with murder and what is more, it has no basis at all. Present day war is frightful prose, it is not poetry, and in it a completely unmitigated boredom predominates. If the wars of previous centuries were associated with personal bravery and heroism, and if honour and gallantry found a place in them, this certainly does not apply to the total warfare of today. Furthermore, just as in the present-day state the cult of crude force and of a demoniacal will to power is laid bare, so also in present-day war there is disclosed a demoniacal world slaughter house which destroys mankind and civilization on a grandiose scale. Previous wars were localized and kept within bounds. Present-day war is total and absolute in the same way as present-day states desire to be total and absolute. It is ludicrous to talk about deeds of martial gallantry in the chemical warfare of today which is destroying the population of the world. It will soon be the case that even the army will have no significance whatever. War is absolutely mechanized and industrialized. It corresponds with the character of contemporary civilization. In such conditions the technique of war is such that it is scarcely possible for there to be any victors, everyone is defeated and destroyed. Into the hands of men possessed by the will to power, and led on by the lure of false values, there fall the most terrible weapons, in comparison with which previous weapons were the toys of children. And the fate of mankind comes to depend entirely upon a spiritual revolution, upon the moral condition of men.

A gang of bandits always draws a sharp distinction between the members of its own circle and those who are outside it, a different code of morality is applied to each of these circles. In this respect a state which is waging war is very like a gang of bandits. But with this difference, that among the bandits there do exist their own conception of honour, their own ideas of justice, and their own code of morals and manners, things which do not exist in a state possessed by the will to power. Present-day believers in the romance of war are fond of talking about the tragic acceptance of war. War has become too base a thing, too absolutely evil to give rise to tragic conflict. I do not think it would be true to speak of just and unjust wars. That would be the application of a moral appraisement to a phenomenon which lies outside any sort of morality. In the past there have been wars which were evil in but the smallest degree, sometimes they were waged in defence of righteousness. Nowadays a war cannot be an evil in just a small degree, nowadays its satanic nature is laid bare.

The idea of a 'holy' war was a blasphemous mockery even in the past. If there has never been anything 'holy' in objectivized history at all but merely a false bestowal of the name, to apply the quality of 'holiness' to that which is the expression of the extreme of world evil is a temptation of the devil. States have never been really 'holy' and all the less could wars be 'holy'. And the force of all this is augmented when it is a question of present-day life, and the wars of today, which remind one more of a cosmic catastrophe. Military conceptions of honour have always been unchristian and opposed to the Gospel, but present-day wars stand on an immeasurably lower level than those conceptions of honour. They are reminiscent not of a duel but of a back street murder. Totalitarian states cannot have any conception of honour and neither can totalitarian wars. The idea of honour is bound up with personality; it does not exist in the depersonalization of the present time, When all men are looked upon as slaves or as mere material, there can be no talk about honour. We are witnesses in our day of a transition to a new military society, but how naked and bare it all is in comparison with the old military societies! Nowadays they kill off their enemies and accord them no military honours. From the time of the Renaissance men began to hold the opinion that thought, knowledge, science, literature, and the printing of books had an immense and commanding importance. With our time the reverse movement begins. Again men consider that the commanding effectiveness is that of the sword, and what is more of how repulsive a sword, that soldiers form the front rank of mankind, that war and murder are the principal means to achieve an end.

But those who act by the sword are not kept within bounds by any of the higher principles, which was, at least, the case in the Middle Ages. The very distinction between a state of war and a state of peace is being obliterated. A state of peace is also a state of war and wars are carried on without any declaration of war. At the present time war is too debased a state for war to be declared, men are on too low a moral level. The lure of military heroism and might still continues to tempt, but it is mere propaganda, and always lying propaganda. No authentic, absolute heroism is any longer possible, for heroism presupposes the existence of personality. The present-day state, and the warfare of today recognize no personality at all. In Nietzsche there is to be found the idea of pure heroism which leads to no end, and which has no continuation either in this life or in the life to come. Pure heroism is the ecstasy of the moment of heroic action, an emergence from time. It is the temptation of such people as, for instance, Malraux. This type of heroism is opposed to the exaltation of thought which has existed in recent centuries. In the last resort heroic experience of that kind is connected with war (it matters nothing whether it is war between nations or war between classes) and is applied to war. But war itself is of a character which leaves no room for heroism and has no need of it. Heroism of that sort finds its place more readily in present-day technical inventions which are connected with victory over the elemental processes of nature.

The warlike instincts of man cannot be uprooted and dislodged. They can only be switched over into some other region and sublimated. When the satanic technique of war, the technique of world-wide destruction, makes war finally impossible (probably this will be after a considerable part of the human race has been destroyed), the combative instincts of man in the noble sense of the word, will be obliged to seek some other outlet for themselves. Courage was the first virtue in human society. It will remain a virtue, but the direction of its application will be different. Further, courage is a complex phenomenon. The man who distinguishes himself by bravery in war may display the most shameful moral cowardice as a citizen. And it is just the totalitarian states which struggle for power and demand bravery in war, which do not permit moral and civic courage and train cowards and slaves.

The division of the world into two camps, which is the principal method employed for the concentration of the forces of communism and fascism, is a military division and one which is adapted to the purposes of war. But this division is the greatest of errors. It is Manichaeism adapted to the utilitarian ends of strife and war. This intensified division fills men with hatred and prepares the psychological atmosphere of war. The human race is not divided into the Kingdom of Ormuzd and the Kingdom of Ahriman. In every man there are two kingdoms, of light and of darkness and of truth and of falsehood, of freedom and of slavery. The real division of the world and mankind is much more complicated. The national enemy, the social enemy, or the religious enemy is not a concentration of world evil, he is not a villain, and he is not and cannot be nothing but an enemy, an object of 'holy' hate. He is a man with all the human properties of a national, social or religious group of people. One must stop considering 'ours' as invariably good while the 'foreign' is invariably bad. The Gospel alone has proclaimed that one must love one's enemies and escape from the vicious circle of hatred and desire for vengeance. And this means a revolution in the world and a turning to the other world, it means a radical denial of the laws of the natural world and of the natural order which reigns in it. There is a fundamental antagonism between the divine order and the order of the world and here mutual adaptation is impossible, only change is possible here.

The distinction between the absolute and the relative is an outcome of abstract thought. The truth which is revealed in the Gospel is concrete and belongs to the realm of subjectivity, not to the realm of objectivity, it reveals the freedom of the Kingdom of God. Obedience to the command 'Thou shalt not kill' as the voice of God, is within the power not only of individual men and women but also of human societies. But in order that human societies may obey this commandment they must turn aside from the way of the slavery of man, and enter upon the path of the subjectivization of human existence, that is the path of emancipation. With this is combined a radical change in the scale of values, the personalist transvaluation of values. The creation of the idea and form of 'the enemy' which plays such a rôle in world history is dehumanizing, depersonalizing objectivization. The application of the morality of the Gospels to human societies is personalism; it is the act of placing human personality at the centre, the recognition of it as the supreme value. 'The enemy' is an objectivization of existence in which the form of man disappears and, therefore, there is nothing more monstrous than the blessing of war by the Christian Church, or the very phrase 'Christ-loving soldiers'. Man ought to be a warrior, he is called to warfare; but this has nothing in common with a body of soldiers, which is an extreme form of the servitude and enslavement of man.

This point of view must be sharply distinguished from bourgeois pacifism which is not only powerless to overcome war, but may even indicate a baser condition than war. Bourgeois pacifism may denote simply a love of quiet and a care-free life, the fear of catastrophe, and even cowardice. There is a sort of peace which is more abject than war, it cannot be admitted that peace should be purchased at any price. The real struggle against war is itself also war, it is the true martial spirit, courage and willingness to accept sacrifice. The martial spirit does not invariably mean war against men as the enemy, against those who hold a different belief, against people of another social class. Warfare must be waged, for example, against the class society, against the existence of classes founded upon the unjust distribution of property and money, but not against the people who constitute the classes, not against men and women who have become simply and solely 'enemies'. Christ brought peace, but He also brought the sword. Separation is necessary, but not hatred. And here is an astounding thing. Many Christians reject revolution with horror because it presupposes murder and the shedding of blood. But they accept and even bestow their blessing upon war which sheds more blood and commits more murder than revolution. And

[161]

this is due to the fact that values are determined according to a different standard. They consider the state and nationality to be such high values, even putting them as the highest values of all, that for the sake of them, they think it is worth while to kill and shed blood. Whereas social righteousness and liberation are not recognized as values for the sake of which killing and the shedding of blood are worth while. But such an attitude to values is simply not to be tolerated by the Christian conscience. Freedom and justice are higher values than the might of the state and nationality. But the chief point is that murder and bloodshed are evil and sinful whatever the end in view may be. Revolution can be much less of an evil than war. But only a Christianity which has been purified, and emancipated from historical slavery is in a position to raise the question of war and revolution.

Tolstoy describes how Nikolai Rostov recognized a Frenchman as an enemy and what his experiences were as a result of this shock. But Nikolai Rostov was a man made for war, he had the servile war psychology. Warfare is possible only against an object. You cannot make war on a subject. If in your enemy you recognize a subject, a concrete living being, human personality, war becomes impossible. War means that men have been turned into objects. In warring armies there are no subjects, no personalities. It is sometimes said in defence of war that there is no personal hatred in it. But can there be hatred which finds its outlet in a thirst for killing, yet is not directed against another man, against a person? Is the one whom it is desired to kill out of hatred, viewed as a subject? I think not. The hatred which kills a man, converts that man into an object, that against which hatred is expressed ceases to be a subject, and a person. If the one who hates and is thirsting to kill, could recognize in his enemy an existential subject, if he could enter into communion with the secret personality of the other, his hate would be a thing of the past, and the act of killing would become impossible. Hatred and murder exist only in a world where men have become objects, where human existence has become objectivized. There is an eternal conflict between 'war' and 'peace', between 'historical' life and 'private' life, between life which is 'objectivized' and life which remains in 'subjectivity'.

The problem of war in the life of the world is not only the problem of war which has been declared and has broken out, it is to an even greater extent the problem of preparation for war. Human societies can perish as a result of a militarist psychology, of the endless piling up of armaments, of the will to war, and of the fear of war. It is in reality an atmosphere of increasing madness. In the strict sense of the word, a war may not actually break out, but human life becomes intolerable; men cannot breathe freely. Not only war itself, but the preparation for war means that the freedom of man has reached its minimum. Mobilization means the limitation of self-controlled movement. War in actual fact is determined by the structure of consciousness. Triumph over the possibility of war presupposes a change in the structure of consciousness. The direction of consciousness is changed. This is a spiritual victory over the slavery of man, over a servile consciousness. But the servile consciousness still has the mastery in the world and war is one of its expressions, the most terrible. The satanic nature of war is open to no doubt. The blood which is shed in war does not flow for nothing; it disseminates a poison, conscience is troubled by it.

By its very nature war is irrational, it relies upon irrational instincts, but it presupposes rationalization. Preparation for war is in the highest degree rational, and it presupposes the deliberately reasoned arming of states. This is a self contradiction of war. The human masses are inoculated to produce a most irrational condition of the soul. War presupposes the arousing of erotic conditions, its nature is erotic, not ethical. In this particular case, I include in *eros*, *anti-eros* also, which has the same nature. Hate is an erotic phenomenon. And the mass of mankind is brought to a most irrational state of mind, to the madness of rational arming, it is upheld by rational discipline, it works on a technical basis. It is a demoniacal combination of extreme irrationalism, with extreme rationalism. People live in the enslaving power of the myth of war, a myth which arouses evil erotic conditions. In a rationalized and technical civilization myths continue to play an enormous part. They are born of the collective subconscious. But these myths are made use of in a very rational manner. The myth of the beauty and heroism of war, of the martial *eros*, which rises above the prosaic routine of everyday life, is an aspect of human slavery. This myth is connected with other myths, the myth of the chosen race, the myth of the majesty of sovereignty and so on. All these myths stand out in opposition to the truth of personalism, they are always hostile to the humanization of life, they are all in revolt against the spirit of the Gospel, they all legalize the slavery of man.

1. C. THE LURE AND SLAVERY OF NATIONALISM.
NATION AND PEOPLE

The spell of nationalism and slavery to it, constitute a deeper form of slavery than slavery to the idea of the state. Of all the 'suprapersonal' values it is to the value of the national that man is most easily induced to subject himself, he most readily feels himself to be a part of the national whole. This is very deeply rooted in the emotional life of man, more deeply than his relation to the state. But nationalism, which is advocated by all parties of the right, is itself a complex phenomenon. We shall see that the very idea of the nation and nationality is a product of rationalization. Vladimir Solovyev who in the eighties of the last century carried on a fight against Russian zoological nationalism, draws a distinction between the national and nationality, analogous to the distinction between egoism and personality. He insists that national egoism (the same thing as nationalism) is as reprehensible from the Christian point of view as personal egoism. It is commonly supposed that national egoism is a moral duty of personality and that it does not denote the egoism of personality but its readiness for sacrifice and its heroism. This is a very remarkable result of objectivization. When the very thing which is evil for man is transferred to the collective realities which are recognized as ideal and suprapersonal, it becomes a good and is even turned into a duty. Egoism, self-seeking, self-conceit, pride, the will to power, hatred of others, violence, all become virtues when transferred from personality to the nation as a whole. To the nation everything is permissible. It is permissible even to commit crimes in its name, it is so to speak made justifiable even from the point of view of the ordinary man. The morality of the nation shows no inclination to give any recognition to human rights. The life of the individual man is short, whereas the life of the nation is long; it may last for thousands of years. The life of the nation makes actual the link between periods of time, which the individual man cannot do. The individual man is conscious of the link with preceding generations through the life of the nation. 'The national' overawes by its deep-rootedness in a prolonged life. Here we are faced by what is all the while the same problem. Where is the existential centre, where is the organ of conscience—in personality or in the nation? Personalism denies that the existential centre, the centre of consciousness, is to be found in the nation or in any kind of collective body, or non-human reality. It is always in personality.

Personality is not a part of the nation. A sense of nationality is a part of personality, and it is to be found in personality as one of the elements in its qualitative content. The nation enters into the concrete man. This is but a particular application of the truth that the universe is in personality and not personality in the universe. A sense of nationality is a means of fostering personality, whereas nationalism on the other hand is a form of idolatry and slavery which arises from exteriorization and objectivization. *Eros* is connected with the ideas of deficiency and want. Nationalism, which is one of the forms of slavery which arise from the falling away of the universe from man, is of an erotic character. It is set in motion by *eros* and *anti-eros* and is in its nature anti-ethical. The application of ethical values to the life of a nation makes nationalism impossible. This is one of the conflicts between *eros* and *ethos*. Nationalism which is fundamentally an erotic spell is always nourished upon lies, and it cannot do without lies.

National self-conceit and pride is a lie, just as much as it is by the way ludicrous and stupid. National egocentricity, national self-containment, and xenophobia, are in no degree better than personal egocentricity, self-containment and hostility to other people, and they also precipitate men into a fictitious and illusory life. Nationalism is an idealized form of the self-exaltation of man. Love for one's people (we shall see that the people is not the same thing as the nation) is a very natural and good feeling. But nationalism insists upon hatred, it requires hostility towards and contempt for other nations. Nationalism is already potential war. But the principal lie which is the outcome of nationalism, arises from the fact that when men speak of the 'national' ideal, of the good of the 'national' whole, of 'national' unity, of the 'national' vocation, and so forth, they always associate the word 'national' with a privileged, dominating minority, commonly with the class which possesses property. By 'nation', and 'national', men and women are never understood, concrete beings, but an abstract principle which is pleasing to certain social groups. In this fact is to be found the root of the distinction between nation and people. 'The people' is always connected with men and women. National ideology is usually manifested as a class ideology. While appealing to the national whole they desire to suppress the parts which consist of men and women, beings who are capable of suffering and joy. 'Nationality' is turned into an idol, and it demands human sacrifice as all idols do.

The ideologists of nationalism pride themselves upon representing a whole, while various other currents of thought represent parts, this or that class. But as a matter of fact it is possible to put forward the interest of a class falsely as the interest of the whole. This is to deceive both oneself and other people. In this connection the comparison of national ideology with class ideology is of immense interest. The ideology of a class has a very unprepossessing exterior and rhetorical triumphs over it are very easy. The nation as a whole, existing as it does for thousands of years, has a higher value than a separate class, which did not exist in the past and perhaps will not exist in the future. The Russian, French or German nation taken as a historical whole is a more profound reality than the Russian, French or German proletariat. But the problem is by no means solved, nor even stated, when men make such general observations. At a certain historical moment the problem of a class may be more acute, and demand a solution which admits of no delay, more than the national problem and precisely for the sake of the very existence of the nation. The national in personality is a deeper thing than 'class'. The fact that I am a Russian goes deeper than the fact that I belong to the gentry. Yet none the less in objective fact the 'class' interest can be more human than the 'national' interest, that is, within the sphere of class interest it is possible to talk about the despised and violated dignity of man about the value of human personality. Whereas within the 'national' interest one can talk about the 'common' which has no relation at all to human existence.

With this is connected the appraisement of nationalism and socialism. It is not to be disputed that nationalism is of pagan origin whereas socialism is of Christian origin. Socialism (not the communist, that is to say not the fascist type) is interested in people, in the value of man, unless there is some distortion arising from a false outlook upon the world. Nationalism on the other hand has no interest in people. To it the highest value is not man but objectivized collective realities which are not an existence but a principle. 'Socialism' can be more spiritual than 'nationalism', for 'the social' may constitute a demand that man shall be a brother to man and not a wolf, whereas the common national life can be wolfish. Nationalists certainly do not want human life to be more communal; more just and humane. With the triumph of nationalism the strong state dominates over personality and the rich classes dominate over the poor. Fascism and national socialism want more community life within a given nationality, but they realize this but poorly. They lead to a monstrous étatism and behave like a wild beast to other nationalities. National socialism is possible; but in it the social element is the more human while the racial and national element means dehumanization.

We shall speak about socialism again later on. It must be emphasized once more that nationalism is by no means the same thing as patriotism. Patriotism is the love of one's native land, of one's soil, of one's people. Nationalism, on the other hand, is not so much love as a collective egocentricity, self-conceit, the will to power and violence over others. Nationalism is a fiction of the mind, an ideology, which does not exist in patriotism. National self-conceit and egoism are just as sinful and stupid as personal self-conceit and egoism, but their effects are much more fateful. In the same way family egoism and self-conceit have more ominous a character than personal egoism and self-conceit. German national messianic self-conceit, even as found in men of genius, such as Fichte, for example, is of a ludicrous character. It is simply intolerable. Every projection and objectivization of personal evil and sin is a transference to the collective and gives rise to the maximum of evil and expresses the maximum of sin. Thus the slavery of man is reinforced.

To draw a distinction between nation and people, between what is of the nation and what is of the people, is not a mere matter of words. It is still more evident in other languages (*nation* and *peuple*; *Nation* and *Volk*). The people is a much more primary and natural reality than the nation. In the people there is something which lies beyond the rational. The nation is a complex product of history and civilization, and so it is a product of rationalization. The most important thing of all, however, is that the people is a reality which is more human than the nation. The people means men and women, an enormous quantity of men and women who have attained to unity, taken a definite shape, and acquired their own specific qualities. The nation on the other hand is not men and women. The nation is a principle which dominates over men and women, it is a ruling idea. It might be said that the people is concretely real while the nation is abstractly ideal. The word 'ideal' is not in this particular case a commendation. On the contrary it indicates a greater degree of objectivization and estrangement of human nature, a greater degree of dehumanization. The nation is more intimately connected with the state than the people are. *Narodnitchestvo** has frequently had an anti-state and anarchic character, whereas nationalism has always been the affair of the state and always desires a strong state, always in fact values the state more than culture. The people is eager to give expression to its own nature and being, it establishes customs and a style, while the nation is bent upon expressing itself in the might of the state, it constructs the vehicles and agencies of power. The people has a facial expression while the nation wears a mask. Nationalism of the fascist type means the loss of the national self-portrait (if this word 'national' is used, as it frequently is, in a sense identical with 'belonging to the people'), there is nothing whatever national in it. It means the acute rationalization of the life of the people and its organization on a technical basis. In no degree does it set any store by culture. All present day forms of nationalism are as like one another as two drops of water. All dictatorships; all organizations of

* See note on p. 4.

political police; all plants for production of armaments; all organizations for sport, how absolutely alike they are!

Before its decisive victory German national socialism was one of the forms of *narodnitchestvo* which set the organic and communal character of the common life of the people in opposition to the formal organization of the state. It stood for *Gemeinschaft* as against *Gesellschaft,* but after its final triumph national socialism became possessed by the will to state power, and the *narodnik* elements in it were weakened. The tradition of German culture was broken up. Nationalism attaches not the least value to spiritual culture and it always persecutes the creators of it. Nationalism always leads on to tyranny. The nation is one of the idols, one of the sources of human slavery. The sovereignty of the nation is the same error as the sovereignty of the state and as all sovereignties upon earth. This sovereignty of the nation has its left wing expression just as it has its right wing expression and it always tyrannizes over man. The people does at least stand nearer to labour as the foundation of social life and nearer to nature. But even the people can become an idol and a source of human slavery. *Narodnitchestvo* is one of the lures and it easily assumes mystical forms—such as the soul of the people, the soul of the soil, the mystical surge of the people. Man can be completely lost in this elemental surge. It is an inheritance from, and a survival of, primitive collectivism before the awakening of spirit and personality. *Narodnitchestvo* always belongs to the soul and not to the spirit. Personality as the existential centre, as the centre of consciousness and conscience may take its stand in opposition even to the people. In personality there is a maternal bosom, and that which is of the people (the national) is in fact that bosom. But the revolt of personality is the victory of spirit and freedom over the natural and elemental surge in the people. Slavery to the people is one of the forms of slavery. It must be remembered that the people cried out 'Crucify Him, crucify Him', when there stood before them the Son of Man and the Son of God. It has demanded the crucifixion of all its prophets, teachers and great men. This is sufficient evidence of the fact that the centre of conscience is not in the people. In *narodnitchestvo* there is its own truth and right but there is also a great falsity, which is expressed in the reverence paid by personality to the collec-

[169]

tive, by quality to quantity, by the minority to the majority. Truth is always to be found in personality, in quality, in minority. But this truth must in its living manifestation be connected with the life of the people; it does not mean isolation and self-containment. National messianism is a temptation; it is incompatible with Christian universalism. But belief in the vocation of one's people is necessary for its historical existence.

In actual experience 'national' and 'belonging to the people' are confused and are often used in one and the same sense, just as *Gesellschaft* and *Gemeinschaft* are. The 'national' contains a higher degree of rationalization than 'belonging to the people', but both the one and the other rely upon the collective subconscious, upon very powerful emotions whch lead to the exteriorization of human existence. Man needs a way out of his loneliness in the prevailing freezing strangeness of the world. This takes place in the family; it takes place in nationality, in the national community. The individual man is incapable of feeling directly that he belongs to mankind. It is necessary for him to belong to a narrower and more concrete circle. Through national life man feels the link of the generations, the link of the past with the future. Mankind has no existence outside man; it exists in man and in man is the greatest reality. With this reality humanness is connected. The nation appears to be more existent outside man. But in the last resort this is an illusion. The nation also exists only in man. The objective reality of the nation is exteriorization. It is one of the results of objectivization and no more. But various degrees of objectivization give various degrees of nearness, completeness, fullness. Mankind appears as though it were remote and abstract while all the time it is humanness, the humanity of man. Nationalism crushes man, human personality and humanity alike. It crushes not the actual quality of 'nationality' in man but the objectivization of this quality and turns it into a reality which stands above man. Both 'nation' and 'people' are readily turned to idols. Objectivization of powerful emotions takes place. The most mediocre and the most insignificant man feels himself exalted and raised through his share in what is 'national' and of the people.

One of the causes of enslaving enchantments lies in this that they give man a greater feeling of power. While making himself the slave

[170]

of an idol he feels himself exalted on high. Man becomes a slave but without slavery he would feel himself upon a still lower level. When man is impersonal and there is revolt in him, any sort of universal content, enslavement of various kinds, gives him by objectivizations the feeling of completeness. The only thing to set against this slavery is personality with spiritual content. The 'national' fills the vacuum more easily than anything else. It is a possibility for enormous masses of people and presupposes no qualitative attainment at all. At the same time, negative feelings, hatred for the Jews or other nationalities, play a greater part than positive feelings. The so-called national question cannot in actual fact be justly solved. Conflict is always connected with it. All history is unrighteous annexation. Nationalities were created by unjust and violent assortment, as were the historical aristocracies. The suppression of the sovereignty of national states might facilitate the solution of the national question, but 'national' lies beyond national states and indicates another degree of objectivization. Nationalism denotes the making absolute of a certain degree of objectivization. At the same time the irrational is rationalized, the organic is mechanized, human quality is turned to non-human reality. While what is national and of the people enters into the concrete universal, while all degrees of individualization are taking place, nationalism not only is hostile to the universal but even destroys it. In the same way universalism is hostile to personalism. Nationalism must be rejected both in the name of the personal and in the name of the universal. This does not mean that there is no degree between the personal and the universal, but it means that the degree of the national which is to be found between them ought not to swallow up either the personal or the universal but ought to be subordinated to them. In any case precedence ought to be given to what is 'of the people' over the 'national'. Christianity is a personalist and universal religion but not a national, not a racial religion. Every time that nationalism proclaims Germany for the Germans, France for the French, Russia for the Russians, it reveals its pagan and non-human nature. Nationalism does not acknowledge the value and rights of every man because he is a man and bears the image of man and the image of God and carries a spiritual principle within him.

Nationalism is the most widespread emotion in the world, the most human since it is the most characteristic of man; and the most anti-human, the most enslaving of man to exteriorized power. It is mistaken and superficial to suppose that the defence of a German, of a Frenchman or of a Russian is the defence of a concrete being; whereas the defence of a man, of every man, because he is a man, is the defence of an abstraction. It is just the opposite. The defence of national man is the defence of the abstract properties of a man and not the very deepest at that, while the defence of man in his humanity and in the name of his humanity is the defence of the image of God in man. That is to say it is the defence of the integrated form in man, of that which is deepest in man and not liable to alienation, like the national and class properties of a man. It is precisely the defence of man as a concrete being, as personality, of a unique and unrepeatable being. The so-called national and social qualities of man are repeatable; they are liable to generalization, to abstraction, to conversion into quasi realities which stand above man. But behind this is hidden the inmost core of man. The defence of this human depth is humanness; it is a work of humanity. Nationalism is treason and perfidy in relation to the depth of man; it is a terrible sin in relation to the image of God in man. He who does not see a brother in man, but another nationality, who, for example, refuses to see a brother in a Jew, such a one is not only not Christian, but he is losing his own proper humanity, his own human depth. The emotions of nationalism eject man on to the surface and, therefore, make man a slave of the object world. The emotions of nationalism are much less human than the social emotions, and are in a much smaller degree evidence of the fact that personality is growing in man.

1. D. THE LURE AND SLAVERY OF ARISTOCRACY. THE TWOFOLD IMAGE OF ARISTOCRACY

There is a special lure of aristocracy, a satisfaction in belonging to the aristocratic stratum of society. Aristocracy is a very complex phenomenon and requires a complex appraisement. The very word 'aristocracy' invites a favourable estimate. Aristocrats are the best, the well-born. Aristocracy is a selection of the best, the well-born. But in actual fact historical aristocracy has not by any means meant the best and the most well-born. It is necessary to make a distinction between aristocracy in a social sense and aristocracy in a spiritual sense. Aristocracy in the social sense takes shape in everyday social life and is subject to the laws of that social routine. In this sense aristocracy belongs to the realm of determinism and not to the realm of freedom. Aristocrats in the sense of a race which has crystallized out in the course of history, are men who are in a special degree determined; they are determined by inheritance and family tradition. The aristocratic principle in social life is a principle of inheritance, and inheritance is determinism weighing down upon personality; it is even more than determinism, it is the fate of race, the fate of blood. Social aristocracy is a racial and not a personal aristocracy, a matter of racial qualities, not personal qualities, and so racial pride is connected with it, pride of origin, which is the principal vice of aristocracy. A brotherly attitude to people is extremely difficult for the aristocracy.

An aristocracy is a group which has been sorted out in the course of the racial process, a group the properties of which are handed on through inheritance. In this sense aristocracy is profoundly opposed to personalism, that is to the principle of personal, not racial qualities, of qualities which do not depend upon the determinism of the hereditary principle. A spiritual aristocracy as distinguished from a social aristocracy is a personal aristocracy, an aristocracy of personal nobility, personal qualities and gifts. Personalism presupposes an aristocracy of personal qualities which are opposed to any form of mixture with the unqualitative masses, an aristocracy of freedom as opposed to the determinism under which the race and the caste live. Social aristocracy affirms an inequality which is certainly not personal, not due to personal qualities, but a racial inequality, the social class inequality, an inequality of caste. It would be ridiculous to assert that the gentleman who defines his worth in terms of inheritance, of blood, or the bourgeois who defines his worth in terms of the inheritance of money, by that very fact are higher in personal qualities than the man who has received neither the inheritance of blood nor the inheritance of money and can lay claim to no

[173]

inequality which bestows privileges upon him. A man's gifts are received from God, not from his family and not from property. The personal inequality of men and their social inequality are distinct and even antithetic principles. The social levelling process which is intended to abolish the class privileges of society may all the same contribute to the appearance of effective and real personal inequalities in men, that is to say to the disclosure of a personal aristocracy. How does a social aristocracy take shape? The higher qualities and attainments cannot be achieved all at once by vast human masses. The emergence of qualities takes place to begin with in small groups of people. In them a higher cultural level is worked out, more refined feelings and more refined morals. Even the bodily form of man becomes nobler and less coarse. A culture always takes shape and reaches higher levels by way of aristocracy.

It would be unjust and untrue to regard social aristocracy as always evil. There has been much positive value in it also. In aristocracy there have been admirable characteristics of nobility, of magnanimity, good breeding, capacity for a self-sacrificing understanding of other people, things of which the *parvenu* has no conception as he struggles to climb upwards. The aristocrat makes no effort to raise himself higher; he feels himself to be at the top from the beginning. In this sense the principle of aristocratic selection actually contradicts the aristocratic principle of origin. The struggle for success and advance is not aristocratic. Selection is a naturalistic principle; it is of biological origin. Christianity does not acknowledge selection. In contrast to the laws of this world it proclaims that 'the last shall be first; the first shall be last'. All the old values are reversed in a revolutionary manner. But side by side with the attractive characteristics of aristocracy there have been also the repellent. A peculiar insolence, a haughty behaviour to their social inferiors, contempt for labour, racial pride which does not correspond with personal qualities, exclusiveness of caste, aloofness from the living movement of the world, an exclusive preoccupation with the past ('whence' and not 'whither'), self-isolation.

The exclusive aristocratic group cannot maintain itself indefinitely however much it struggles for its own preservation. The basis becomes broadened. New strata enter into the privileged aristocratic stratum. Democratization takes place and the qualitative level is lowered. Then new qualities emerge. The exclusiveness of the aristocratic group inevitably leads to degeneration. The renewal of exhausted blood is necessary. After mingling and democratization, after the process of levelling there takes place a reverse process of aristocratic selection. But it can take place according to various criteria, not necessarily on the basis of family, inheritance and birth. The aristocracy of the chosen race is doomed to disappearance but an aristocracy may be formed out of the bourgeoisie, as it may be formed out of the working peasant masses. In this case aristocracy will assume different psychological properties.

In the social process various groups are formed by way of selection and differentiation, and every group which crystallizes out has its own forms of enslavement for man. Bureaucracy takes shape in every society which is organized into a state. It has a tendency to spread and to increase its importance. Bureaucracy is formed on an entirely different principle from aristocracy, that is to say it is formed on the basis of the professions and functions to be found in a society which has been made into a state. But it is inclined to regard itself as being also an aristocracy. Bureaucracy is meant to render services to the people, but it shows a disposition to consider itself as a self-sufficient authority, to regard itself as master in the house of life, and in this lies the inward contradiction of its existence. It is easily turned into a parasite with the possibility of unlimited expansion. Bureaucracy may take shape in any kind of social structure of society. A revolution overthrows the old bureaucracy and immediately creates a new one still more expanded, and in fact for this purpose makes use of the cadres of the old bureaucracy which are prepared to take service in any kind of régime. The fate of Talleyrand and Fouché is symbolic. The Russian communist revolution created a bureaucracy to an extent which had never existed before. It is the formation of a new bureaucracy or a new proletarian aristocracy. An authentic historical aristocracy is closed and limited; it had no wish to expand and adapt itself to new conditions. A bureaucracy expands indefinitely; it sets no store by exclusiveness and the preservation of quality; it readily adapts itself to all conditions and to every régime. That is why it can never be called an aristocracy. The upper layer of the bourgeoisie which imitates an aristocracy and climbs into the aristocracy also can never be called an aristocracy. The bourgeoisie has an entirely different psychological structure. But of that later.

The real aristocracy was formed not by way of amassing wealth and power and not by way of functions rendered to the state but by the sword. The origin of aristocracy is war. Laurence Stein even says that caste is the absolute triumph of society over the state. Aristocracy is a caste and it adapts itself with difficulty to the organization of the state. In a certain sense it is anti-state. State absolutism has grown up in conflict with feudalism, with aristocracy and its privileged freedoms. It might even be said that freedom is aristocratic and not democratic. Freedom in the past was a privilege of aristocracy. The feudal knight defended his freedom and independence in his castle with his weapons in his hand. The drawbridge was the defence of the freedom of the feudal knight. It was not freedom within society and the state, but freedom from society and the state. Ortego writes very truly on this subject. It is frequently forgotten that freedom is not only freedom within society but also freedom from society, that it is a frontier which society does not wish to recognize in relation to human personality. The masses of the people set little store by freedom and have little sense of the lack of it. Freedom is a property of spiritual aristocracy. Chivalry was an enormous creative achievement in the sphere of moral consciousness. The aristocrat was the first person in human society to have the feeling of personal dignity and honour. But his limitation lay in the fact that he felt this for his own caste only. The aristocracy of freedom, the aristocracy of personal dignity ought to be transferred to the whole people, to every man because he is a man. But few people who have issued from the aristocracy have recognized this. But here the question is precisely of the transference of positive aristocratic qualities to the broad human masses. It is a question of the inward, it is a question of the formation of an interior aristocracy.

At one time in Egypt the dignity of immortality was attributed only to the king; all the rest of the people were mortal. In Greece to begin with only gods or demi-gods or heroes and supermen were regarded as immortal; the people were mortal. Christianity alone has recognized all men as worthy of immortality, that is to say it makes

the idea of immortality absolutely democratic. But a process of
putting the life of the people on a democratic basis which does not
mechanically place men on a level, which does not deny quality, is
to make an aristocracy. It is the communication of aristocratic
qualities and aristocratic rights to others. Every man ought to be
recognized as an aristocrat. It is precisely the proletarian as such that
a social revolution ought to destroy, it should destroy proletarian
deprivation and humiliation. Christianity has overthrown the principles of Greco-Roman culture, and in so doing has affirmed the
dignity of every man, of his sonship to God. It has affirmed the image
of God in every man, and Christianity alone is able to unite democracy, the equality of man in the sight of God, with the aristocratic
principle of personality, the spiritual equality of persons, which is
not dependent upon society and the masses. Christian aristocracy
has nothing in common with caste aristocracy. Pure Christianity is
profoundly antithetic to the spirit of caste which is the spirit of a
double slavery, the slavery of the aristocratic caste itself and the
slavery of those over whom the caste desires to dominate. The aristocracy of Cato is exclusive and finite. Christian spiritual aristocracy is
thrown open and infinite.

The working out of personality is the working out of an aristocratic type, that is to say of the man who does not allow himself to be
blended with his impersonal world environment, who is inwardly
independent and free, who rises to every higher qualitative content
of life, and descends to the lower world which is suffering and
abandoned. The principal mark of true aristocracy is not exaltation
but self-sacrifice and magnanimity, which are derived from inward
riches, a readiness to descend, inability to feel *ressentiment*. Racial and
family aristocracy as it is seen in history, lives in slavery to the past,
to ancestry, to tradition and custom. It is ceremonious. It is hidebound. It lacks all power to select values and freedom of movement.
Personal aristocracy, on the other hand, is just that freedom of appraisement and freedom of movement. It is not hidebound. It is
independent of social environment. With this the twofold form of
aristocracy is connected. Personal aristocracy, that is to say the
qualitative attainment of personality, is socialized and transferred to

the social group. The aristocracy of the social group may take shape in accordance with various characteristics. It may be a clerical caste, a hierarchy of princes of the Church. It may be a caste in the proper sense of nobility of family. It may be an aristocratic selection within a class which is not aristocratic, for example, the bourgeoisie and the peasantry. It may be the formation of an aristocratic social group in accordance with intellectual and spiritual qualities, which cannot extend to larger bodies of people; for example, an *élite* of academicians, scholars and writers may be formed. Every intellectualist *élite* is inclined to self-exaltation and isolation. It also is an aristocratic caste, and displays all the marks of a caste. All sorts of occult orders may represent themselves to be aristocratic castes and the initiated ones, so may freemasons who have a similar shade of mysticism about them.

The forms of social aristocracy which transfer the aristocracy of personality to the aristocracy of a social group are of very various kinds but they always give rise to the slavery of man. In religious life, for example, personal aristocracy, that is to say, special personal gifts and qualities, find expression in prophets, apostles, saints, spiritual guides, and religious reformers, while a social religious aristocracy finds its expression in a settled and crystallized ecclesiastical hierarchy which does not depend upon personal qualities, personal spirituality, that is to say personal aristocracy. Personal religious aristocracy comes under the category of freedom, while social religious aristocracy comes under the category of determination and ʌasily passes into enslavement. Here we are met with the same phenomenon as everywhere else. The fountain-head of slavery in man is objectivization. This objectivization is brought about in history by way of various forms of socialization, that is to say the alienation of personal qualities and their transference to social groups, where these qualities lose their real character and acquire a symbolic character. Social aristocracy is a symbolic aristocracy and not a real one. Its qualities which evoke feelings of pride are not personal human qualities but mere signs and symbols of origin. It is for this reason that the form of aristocracy is twofold.

The aristocratic formation of personality is above all antithetic to the *parvenu* type—a bourgeois is a *parvenu* in origin, although among people who come from the bourgeois classes there may be those who are by no means *parvenu* in type, but very fine and noble people. The typical aristocrat always comes down from his level, the typical *parvenu* is always pushing and insinuating himself upwards. The feeling of guilt, and the feeling of pity, are aristocratic feelings. The feeling of being injured and offended and the feeling of envy are plebeian. I use the word 'plebeian' here in the psychological sense. The whole meaning of the existence of the aristocratic spiritual type lies in the existence of a type of people who are not disposed to experience a sense of injury and envy, *ressentiment,* and of whom it is more characteristic to feel guilt and pity and sympathy. But the socialization of the aristocratic spiritual type, that is to say the creation of an aristocratic caste always leads to this, that instead of truly aristocratic spiritual properties, quite different properties make their appearance, pride, self-exaltation, contempt of the lower classes, defence of their own privileges. The average man of all social classes and groups never has very high personal qualities; he is determined by his social environment and is under the sway of the common social spirit. Caste is always an enslavement of man, depersonalization, the aristocratic caste, the bourgeois and proletarian castes alike. The proletariat also may become a caste, a false aristocracy, and then the same bad properties make their appearance in it—self-exaltation, denial of human dignity in people of other classes. There are no good classes, there are only good people. They are good to the extent that they overcome the spirit of class in themselves, and the spirit of caste, to the extent that they reveal personality. Caste is an enslavement of man. True aristocracy is a vision of the image of personality, not of the image of a social group or class or caste.

There is one more important problem connected with aristocracy, and that is the distinction between the rare people who are great and the usual mediocre people. There are people who have a thirst for an uncommon life, one that does nor resemble the everyday life which overwhelms man on all sides. This does not altogether coincide with the question of gifts, talents, and genius. A man with uncommon gifts can be mediocre and ordinary. The realm of routine knows its geniuses. Such are the majority of the so-called great actors on the stage of history, statesmen, geniuses of objectivization. And that man is to be called unusual, and remarkable, who is unable to reconcile himself to the commonplace routine and limitations of existence, the man within whom there is a break-through into infinity, who does not consent to the final objectivization of human existence. Objectivization knows its great men, but they are ordinary mediocre people. This fact makes its appearance also in science and the arts. There are aristocratic theories which see the meaning of human history in the appearance of notable and great men, men of genius, while they look upon all the rest of mankind, the mass of mankind, as a fertilized soil, manured as the means of producing this blossoming of humanity. The superman of Nietzsche is the final expression of this sort of doctrine. It is the spell of false aristocracy which is intolerable alike to Christian consciousness and to simple human consciousness. Not one single human being, though he be the most insignificant of men, can be the means, the fertilized soil for the production of unusual and remarkable men. This too is that objectivization of personal aristocracy which creates slavery. True aristocracy remains in the realm of infinite subjectivity; it establishes no sort of objective sway. True aristocracy is not a right or a privilege; it asks nothing for itself; it gives; it imposes responsibility and the obligation of service.

The rare and notable man who is endowed with special gifts is not a man to whom everything is permitted. On the contrary, he is a man to whom nothing is permitted. It is fools and insignificant people to whom everything is permitted. But aristocratic nature like the nature of genius (genius is the entire nature and not only a sort of immense gift) does not occupy any particular position in society; it denotes the impossibility of occupying any particular position in society; the impossibility of objectivization. Real aristocratic breeding is by no means a breed of masters, a vocation to domination, as Nietzsche, with his hatred of the state thought, in opposition to his own self. The real aristocratic breed is a breed of men who cannot occupy a position in those relations of master and slave which the ordinary objective world holds by. The aristocratic breed is extraordinarily sensitive and suffers much. Masters are coarse and insensitive and inconsiderate. The master, in fact, is a plebeian, domination is a plebeian affair. In the process of objectivization spirit takes on a plebeian aspect. The formation of an objectivized society is a plebeian

[180]

affair. But does this mean that a personal aristocracy remains, as it were, shut up in itself and in no way finds expression in the external? Of course not. But it expresses itself in a different perspective, not in the light of society, but in the light of communion, not in the light of socialization but in the light of communication, in the personalist community of people, the communion of 'I' with 'thou', but not with 'he', not with an object. This is an eschatological perspective in relation to this world, but it denotes the changing of this world, a break-through, an interruption of that inertia which is due to object-ivization. It means also that man will no longer play the master over man.

1. *E*. THE LURE OF THE BOURGEOIS SPIRIT. SLAVERY TO PROPERTY AND MONEY

There is a spell and a slavery of aristocracy. But still more is there a spell and slavery of the bourgeois spirit. The bourgeois spirit is not only a social category, it is connected with the class structure of society, but it is also a spiritual category. I shall be concerned at the moment principally with the bourgeois spirit as a spiritual category. Perhaps Léon Bloy, himself a bourgeois, has done more than anyone else for the service of wisdom in his astonishing book *Exégèse des liens communs*. The antithesis between the bourgeois spirit and socialism is very relative and does not touch the depth of the problem. Hertzen very well understood that socialism can be bourgeois. The general outlook of the greater number of socialists is such that they do not even grasp the fact that there is a spiritual problem in the bourgeois spirit. The bourgeois in the metaphysical sense of the word is a man who firmly believes only in the world of visible things, which enforce recognition of themselves, and who desires to occupy a strong position in that world. He is a slave of the visible world and of the hierarchy of position established in that world. He forms his estimate of people not by what they are, but by what they have. The bourgeois is a citizen of this world, he is a king of the earth. To have conceived the idea of becoming king of the earth is to be bourgeois.

In that has been his mission. The aristocratic has taken possession of the world, by the power of the sword he has promoted the organization of kingdoms. But even so he was not able to become king of the earth, a citizen of this world, for him there were limits, which he has never been able to overstep.

The bourgeois is deeply rooted in this world, he is content with the world in which he has established himself. The bourgeois has little sense of the vanity and futility of the world, and of the insignificance of the good things of this world. The bourgeois takes economic power very seriously and not infrequently worships it disinterestedly. The bourgeois lives in the finite, he is afraid of the expanse of the infinite. It is true that he acknowledges the infinity of the development of economic power, but this is the only infinity of which he desires to take cognizance. He screens himself from spiritual infinity by the finiteness of the order he has established in life. He recognizes the infinity of growth in prosperity, of the development of organized life, but this merely shackles him to finiteness. The bourgeois is a being who has no desire to transcend himself. The transcendent hampers him in settling down on earth. The bourgeois may be 'believing' and 'religious', and he even calls upon 'faith' and 'religion' to safeguard his position in the world. But the 'religion' of the bourgeois is always a religion of the finite, shackled to the finite, it always conceals spiritual infinity. The bourgeois is an individualist, particularly when property and money are the matter in question, but he is antipersonalist. The idea of personality is foreign to him. In reality the bourgeois is a collectivist, his consciousness, his conscience, his judgments are socialized; he is one who belongs to a group. His interests are individual, while his consciousness is collective.

If the bourgeois is a citizen of this world, the proletarian is a being who is deprived of the citizenship of this world and has no consciousness of that citizenship. There is no room for him on this earth, he must look for his place in a transformed earth. With this is connected the hope which is attached to the proletarian that he will transfigure this earth and create a new life in it. This hope in the proletarian is commonly not fulfilled, because when the proletarian is victorious he becomes a bourgeois, a citizen of this transformed world and the king of the earth. And then the same endless story begins all over again. The bourgeois is a perpetual figure in this world, he is not necessarily connected with any particular structure of society, though it is in the capitalist regime that he reaches his clearest expression and achieves his greatest triumphs. The proletarian and the bourgeois are correlatives and pass over one to the other. Already in his youthful works Marx defined the proletarian as a man in whom his human nature was estranged to the utmost. His human nature ought to be restored to him. But the easiest thing of all is to restore it to him as bourgeois nature. The proletarian wants to become a bourgeois, but to become not an individual bourgeois but a collective, that is to say, in a new social structure. Socially the proletarian is absolutely right in his quarrel with the bourgeois. But there ought not to be social opposition to the fact that he has become a bourgeois, there ought to be only spiritual opposition. Revolution against the kingdom of the bourgeois spirit is spiritual revolution. It is by no means opposed to the truth and right of the social revolution, to a change in the social position of the proletariat, but spiritually it changes and transfigures the character of that revolution. The bourgeois is a being who has been objectivized to the utmost, completely ejected into the external, in the highest degree estranged from the infinite subjectivity of human existence. Bourgeois nature is loss of freedom of spirit, the subjection of human existence to determinism. The bourgeois wants everything for himself, but from out of his own self he produces nothing in thought or speech; he possesses material property, but he has no spiritual property.

The bourgeois is an individual and at times a very inflated individual, but he is not a personality. He becomes a personality to the extent to which he gets the better of his bourgeois spirit. The essential element in the bourgeois spirit is impersonal. Every social class displays a tendency to enter the impersonal bourgeois atmosphere. The aristocrat, the proletarian, the member of the intelligentsia, many of them become bourgeois. The bourgeois cannot overcome his bourgeois nature. The bourgeois is always a slave. He is the slave of his property and of his money, he is a slave of the will to enrichment, a slave of bourgeois public opinion, a slave of social position, he is the slave of those slaves whom he exploits and of whom he lives in fear. To be bourgeois is to be unemancipated in spirit and in soul, it means the subjection of the whole of life to external determination. The bourgeois creates a realm of things, and things take control of him. He has done a frightful amount for the dizzy development of technique, and technical knowledge has control of him, he makes man a slave with the help of it.

The bourgeois has rendered services in the past, he has displayed immense initiative, he has made many discoveries, he has developed the productive powers of man, he has overcome the power of the past and turned towards the future, which presented itself to him as an endless growth of power. To the bourgeois the principal matter is not 'whence' but 'whither'. Robinson Crusoe was a bourgeois in his day. But in the period of his creative youth the bourgeois was not yet a bourgeois. He settles down to the bourgeois type later on.

The fate of the bourgeois must be understood dynamically, he has not always been one and the same. That turning of the bourgeois to the future, that will to rise, that will to enrichment, to secure the first place, creates the type of the arrivist. Arrivism is the bourgeois general outlook upon life *par excellence*, and it is profoundly antithetic to any form of aristocracy. There is no sense of origin in the bourgeois, he has but a poor memory of his origin and his past, as compared with the aristocrat who remembers them all too well. Chiefly he creates a vulgar luxury and makes life the slave of it. In bourgeois luxury beauty perishes. Luxury desires to make beauty the tool of riches and beauty perishes under such treatment. In bourgeois society, which is based on the power of money, luxury develops, chiefly thanks to the bourgeois love of women. Woman, the object of bourgeois desire, creates a cult of luxuriousness which knows no limit. And this is also the extreme of depersonalization, and of the loss of personal dignity. The human being in his inward existence disappears, and is replaced by an environment of luxury. Even the bodily form of man becomes artificial and it is impossible to distinguish the human face in him. The bourgeois woman for whose sake the bourgeois creates a world of fantastic luxury and commits crimes, reminds one of a doll, a creature which is a work of art. Carlyle's philosophy of clothes must be remembered here.

Marx saw a positive mission for the bourgeois, that is the development of material productive forces, and also a negative, even a criminal rôle, the exploitation of the proletariat. But to him the bourgeois was an exclusively social category and he looked no deeper. The bourgeois has an insurmountable tendency to create a world of fancy which enslaves man, and causes the disintegration of the world of true realities. The bourgeois' most fantastic creation, the most unreal, the most uncanny and horrible in its unreality—is the kingdom of money. And this kingdom of money in which all real substance disappears, possesses a terrible power, holds a terrible sway over human life, sets up governments and overthrows them, makes wars, enslaves the labouring masses, gives rise to unemployment and destitution, renders the life of people who are successful in this kingdom more and more fantastic. Léon Bloy was right. Money is a mystery, there is something mystic in the power of money. The kingdom of money, the extreme of impersonality makes even property itself fictitious, Marx was right in saying that capitalism destroys personal property.

The bourgeois has a particular attitude to property. The problem of the bourgeois is a problem of the relation between 'being' and 'having'. The bourgeois is defined not by what he is but by what he has. By this criterion he also forms his judgment of other people. The bourgeois has property, money, wealth, the means of production, a position in society. But that property with which he has to such an extent grown together, does not constitute his personality, that is, it does not make him what he is. Personality is what a man is, and that is left remaining when he possesses nothing at all. Personality cannot depend upon property, upon capital. But property must depend upon personality, it ought to be personal property. The repudiation of the bourgeois capitalist structure of sociey is not the repudiation of all property, it is rather the assertion of the personal property which is lost in that structure. But personal property is property which belongs to labour and is authentic property. Property is inadmissible if it becomes an instrument of enslavement and oppression of man by man. Property considered in its reality from the point of view of personality cannot be the creation of the state or of society. The state and society cannot be a subject in relation to property, for it cannot be a subject at all. The transference of property to them is objectivization. The state and society are merely a middle-man, a regulator, a guarantor, which ought to prevent property from becoming an instrument of exploitation. The individual man cannot be an absolute owner of property, neither can society, nor the state. Property is in this respect like sovereignty. The absolute sovereignty of a monarch cannot be transferred to the people, all sovereignty must be limited and overcome. Absolute property cannot be transferred from a private person to the state and society. This would mean the creation of a new tyranny and slavery. Property is by its very nature limited and relative, it has only a functional significance in relation to personality. The only permissible and real form of property is possession. One can approve property only as possession, no more than that. Property is always relative to man, it is functional, human, it exists for man. There is nothing whatever sacred about property, it is man that is sacred.

The bourgeois world has given another twist to the meaning of property, it enslaves man to property, it defines its relation to man in terms of property. And here we meet with an astounding phenomenon. The opponents of socialism, the defenders of the capitalist structure of society are fond of saying that the freedom and independence of man are linked with property. Take his property away from a man, hand his property over to society or to the state and man becomes a slave, he loses all independence. But if that is true, it is a terrible condemnation of the bourgeois capitalist structure of society which deprives the greater part of the people of property. It recognizes that the proletariat is in a servile condition and is devoid of all independence. If property is the guarantee of a man's freedom and independence then every man, everyone without exception, ought to possess property, it is not admissible that a proletariat should exist. It is a judgment which does not square with bourgeois property, which is a source of slavery and oppression. But the bourgeois wants property only for himself, as the source of his own freedom and independence. He knows no other freedom than that which is conferred by property.

Property has a double rôle to play. Personal property can be a guarantee of freedom and independence, but on the other hand property may make a man a slave, a slave of the material world, a slave of objects. Ownership always loses more and more of its individual character. Such is the character of money, the great enslaver of a man and of mankind. Money is a symbol of impersonality. Money is an impersonal bartering of anything for anything. Even the bourgeois in spite of having his own proper name as the owner of property, ceases to exist and is replaced by the label of the firm. In the kingdom of money, which is entirely unreal and a paper kingdom of figures and bank account books, it is unknown who is the owner and of what he is the owner. Man is more and more transferred from a real kingdom to a fictitious kingdom. The horror of the kingdom of money is twofold, the power of money is not only an outrage upon the poor and destitute, it is also the plunging of human existence into the fantastic and the visionary. The kingdom of the bourgeois ends in the triumph of fiction over reality. Fiction is the extreme expression of the objectivization of human existence. Reality is connected not with the objective, as is often supposed, but precisely with the subjective. Subject not object is the firstborn.

That all is not going very well with property is to be seen from the fact that people shift their gaze in an odd manner if the subject of their property or money is referred to, they feel awkward and uncomfortable. It would be unfair to say that the bourgeois is always covetous and thinks about nothing but profits. The bourgeois can be an entirely disinterested person and by no means egoistic, he may have a disinterested love for the bourgeois spirit, even a disinterested love of money and profit is possible. Max Weber has sufficiently shown that in the early stages of capitalism there existed what he calls 'innerweltliche Askese'. The bourgeois may be an ascetic and by no means think about personal pleasure and satisfaction and the amenities of life, he may be a man of ideas. It is true also to say that the life of the bourgeois is happy. The sages of the whole world have at all times said that riches and wealth do not bestow happiness, this has become common ground. To me it is a fact of the first importance that the bourgeois is himself a slave and that he makes slaves of others. Impersonal power enslaves, and both the bourgeois and the proletarian are under the sway of it, it is a power which ejects human existence into the world of objects. The bourgeois may be a great philanthropist and benefactor, he may be, and commonly is, a

[187]

defender of normal standards. But the power to dominate demoralizes the bourgeois. Every dominating class becomes demoralized. And domination which results from the possession of money demoralizes more than anything else.

It is naïve to suppose that the bourgeois can be overcome and eliminated simply by a change in the structure of society, for example, by replacing the capitalist order by socialism or communism. The bourgeois is eternal, he will remain to the end of time, he is transformed and adapted to new conditions. The bourgeois may become a communist, or the communist become a bourgeois. It is a question not of social structure, but of structure of soul. It does not follow from this, of course, that there is no need to alter the social structure. But it is not to be believed that the social structure will automatically create a new man. Socialism and communism may be bourgeois in spirit. Socialism and communism may give effect to a just and equitable distribution of the bourgeois spirit! The bourgeois does not seriously believe in the existence of the other world, he does not believe in it even when he makes a formal profession of some religious faith. For him the quality of religion is measured by the services which it renders to the organization of this world and to the conservation of his position in this world. The bourgeois will risk no sacrifice of anything in this world for the sake of the other world.

The bourgeois is fond of saying that the world is perishing and coming to an end when an end comes to his economic power, when his property is shaken, when working men demand a change in their position. But this is only *ad hoc* rhetoric. The bourgeois has no feeling for the end and the last judgment. He is a stranger to the eschatological perspective, and has no feeling for eschatological problems. There is something revolutionary in eschatology, a notification of the end of the bourgeois sway of mediocrity. The bourgeois believes in the endlessness of his power and shows hatred of everything which reminds him of the end. And at the same time the bourgeois himself is an eschatological figure, in his own person he figures as one of the ends of world history. The world will come to an end partly from the fact that the bourgeois exists; if there were no such person as he, the world might pass over into eternity. The bourgeois does not want an end, he wants to remain in an unending middle position and precisely for that reason there will be an end. The bourgeois wishes for a quantitative infinity, but he does not wish for qualitative infinity, which is eternity. The realization of the bourgeois spirit, which takes place along various lines, is opposed to the realization of personality. But the bourgeois remains a man, the image of God remains in him, he is simply a sinful man who takes his sin as a norm, and he must be treated as a man, as a potential personality. It is impious to regard the bourgeois exclusively as an enemy who is meant to be exterminated. This is what is done by those who wish to take his place and themselves become new bourgeois in the course of social upheavals. Bourgeois domination and the bourgeois spirit must be combated, wherever they may appear. But one must not become like a bourgeois and regard him as a means to an end. The bourgeois is a traitor to his humanity, but one must not betray humanity in one's relation to him.

2. *A*. THE LURE AND SLAVERY OF REVOLUTION. THE TWOFOLD IMAGE OF REVOLUTION

Revolution is a perpetual phenomenon in the destinies of human societies. There have been revolutions in all epochs, they happened in the ancient world. There were many revolutions in ancient Egypt, and it is only from an immense distance that it appears as a whole, and striking in its hierarchical order. There were no fewer revolutions in Greece and Rome. At all times the lower, oppressed, labouring classes of society have revolted, refused to suffer abasement and slavery any longer, and overthrown the hierarchical order which seemed to be everlasting. There is nothing everlasting, nothing ordained by God, in the objectivized world. The only thing possible is the attainment of a temporary equilibrium and a precarious apparent felicity. After a comparatively short period of time men grow accustomed to the absence of crises, wars, and revolutions. But the soil always remains volcanic. The years of relative equilibrium and calm soon pass. The lava is thrown out from the womb of the earth, insurmountable contradictions become acute. Revolutions, which are inevitable in the existence of societies, inspire one person with horror and repulsion, while to another they suggest the hope of a new and better life. The prince of this world controls human society and controls it in falsehood and wrong. For this reason it is natural that rebellions against this control should take place from time to time. But the prince of this world very quickly secures control over these rebellions against wrong, and creates fresh wrong. In this lies the twofold nature of revolution.

In a revolution the judgment of God is accomplished. In a revolution there is an eschatological moment, the approach, as it were, of the end of time. But revolution is a malady, it bears witness to the fact that there has been no creative power for the reformation of society, and that the forces of inertia have triumphed. There is a demoniacal element in revolution; an outburst of desire for vengeance, of hatred and murder occur in it. In revolution an accumulated *ressentiment* always comes into operation, and vanquishes creative feelings. The sort of revolution may be desired in which there shall be no demoniacal element, but at a certain moment it always triumphs. A revolution takes its stand beneath the flag of freedom to but a very small degree; to an incomparably greater extent it stands beneath the banner of fate. Revolution is the fate of human societies. In revolution man desires to set himself free from slavery to the state, to an aristocracy, to the bourgeoisie, to lying sanctities and idols, but he immediately creates new idols, new false sanctities and falls into slavery to a new tyranny.

Hertzen was a revolutionary and a socialist. But he was free from optimistic illusions and he had a keen sight into the future. He summoned men to 'the struggle of free man against the liberators of mankind'. He said that 'the masses understand by equality, equal oppression' and that 'truth belongs to the minority'. He exclaimed 'there will be no freedom in the world until what is religious and political are turned into what is human and simple', and 'it is but a little thing to hate a crown. What is necessary is to give up reverencing the Phrygian cap. It is a little thing not to recognize an insult to majesty as a crime. What is necessary is to recognize *salus populi* as a crime.' That means that Hertzen was a personalist. His theory of revolution was personalistic. Although personalist, the philosophical basis of his personalism was very naïve and feeble. It means also that Hertzen was absolutely free from the revolutionary myth. He wanted to make revolution without myth; he wanted to be a revolutionary without taking the freedom of man into consideration, and preserving for himself complete freedom of judgment. This is extremely difficult. The most difficult revolution, which has never yet been achieved and which would be more radical than all revolutions is the personalist revolution, revolution for the sake of man and not for the sake of one society or another. In reality and looked at profoundly revolution is a change in the principles upon which society rests, and not the bloodshed of this or that year and day. And in reality and regarded profoundly personality is revolutionary while the masses made up of average folk are conservative. The elemental surge of revolution has always been antipersonalistic, that is to say reactionary. It has always been unfavourable tó freedom of the spirit, freedom of personality, freedom of personal judgment. Revolution has always been directed against despotism and tyranny, but at a certain moment in its convulsion it has always created dictatorship and tyranny and the abrogation of forms of freedom. Revolution is war. It divides society into two camps and is realized by means of military dictatorship. Revolution can use only democratic slogans, but democracy is suitable only for a peaceful life and is certainly not suitable for revolution.

Revolution indicates a rupture in the development of society. Uninterruptedness or, as they are sometimes fond of saying, 'organicness', of development is a utopia. The organic is much more utopian and more unrealizable than a revolutionary outburst. Catastrophe is much more realizable than the peaceful development which is the guardian of faith in traditions. Extreme tendencies are much more realizable than moderate tendencies. In its development human society passes through death. In order to come to life again it is necessary to die. A sinful past is lifted up on the cross. And revolution is partial death. In it too much and too many die. A new life comes through death. But this new life is not the same as the revolutionaries imagined it. Both the individual man and the nation pass through an experience of dichotomy and unhappiness (Hegel's unhappy consciousness); harmony and completion are unattainable

[191]

without this. In this world a peaceful growth of happiness is impossible. Those classes which enjoy relative well-being and happiness must inevitably go through unhappiness and ruin. The illusion of endless happiness and well-being is one of the most absurd of illusions, especially if it is based upon injustice. There is in this world no human justice, but there is harsh merciless inhuman justice, the justice of fate.

It is ludicrous and naïve to judge revolution from the point of view of religious and moral standards. It always appears unreasonable and non-moral. Revolution is irrational by nature. Elemental and even mad forces operate in it, forces which always exist in the human masses but are restrained to a certain degree and up to a certain moment. In revolution, just as in counter-revolution, the sadistic instincts which potentially are always to be found in man, are unbridled and let loose. Here we meet with the chief paradox of revolution. Revolution is irrational. It gives rein to° irrational instincts and at the same time it is always subject to rationalistic ideologies and processes; rationalizations are going on in it. Irrational forces are made use of in order to realize rational slogans. Irrational and often absurd and unjust traditions of the past, which have accumulated through many centuries and hindered the development of life, are in revolution overthrown and replaced by rational organization. The future which revolution claims to establish is always a rational future. In the future reason must triumph. But reason triumphs thanks to the revolt of irrational forces. We see such a relation between the irrational and the rational in the two greatest revolutions—the French and the Russian.

A feeling of vengeance grips the actors in revolution and this is to be explained. But it assumes forms which are elemental and irrational and even mad. Revolution is always linked on to a cherished hatred of the past and it cannot exist, cannot develop and grow without an enemy who arises out of the hated past. When such an enemy does not really exist then he is invented. Men are nourished and nourish others on the myth of the enemy. Good depends upon evil; revolution depends upon reaction; hatred becomes an inspiration. In revolution, as is the case in history in general by the way, myth undoubtedly plays a greater part than reality. But there is another state of temporary insanity which plays a determining rôle in revolution, and that is the temporary insanity of fear. The men who lead a revolution and find themselves on the crest of its wave always live in deadly fear; they never feel themselves secure.

Power in general is always linked up with fear. It is by this fear above all that the cruelty of revolution is determined, and the inevitability of the Terror which assumes control of it. A man who is possessed by fear always begins to persecute. The man who is possessed by a persecution mania is a dangerous man, persecution is always to be expected of him. There is nothing more terrible than men possessed by fear, men who see on all sides of them dangers and conspiracies and attempts upon them. It is just these men who are in the grip of an insane fear, which may be animal and mystic, who set up courts of inquisition, inflict torture, and use the guillotine; they burn at the stake and they guillotine and they shoot an uncountable number of people. The persecution, torture and execution of heretics also are the result of fear. Fear, when confronted by an evil or by many evils (that is to say, by what is regarded as evil by a certain belief and view of life) is one of the greatest evils in human life and human history. This fear distorts human nature, darkens the human conscience and frequently turns a man into a wild beast. This happens in revolutions and counter-revolutions which psychologically are very much alike, and it happens in war. It is a very dangerous situation when a man is under the control of a purely negative reaction, when he is concentrated upon a single evil which holds universal sway within his consciousness.

A revolution may begin as the result of a decline of personal dignity which has been set at naught and outraged by the old life, as the result of a growing and improving personal judgment upon life. But in the actual surge of revolution personal judgment and personal conscience are always weakened and are replaced by collective consciousness and the collective conscience. In revolution a process of objectivization takes place, a process of the alienation of human nature into the object world, whereas a real and radical revolution ought to be a triumph over all objectivization and a transition to free subjectivity. Fear as a result of the ejection of existence into the external, leads to a division of the world into two warring camps.

[193]

The hostile world appears united and universalized; in it it is impossible to meet 'thou'; only 'not-I' can be met. Into this hostile 'not-I' there enter very various worlds. Fear always harbours a Manichaean consciousness and divides the world into the kingdom of Ormuzd and the kingdom of Ahriman. In this way there is built up a greater concentration of consciousness, a greater tenseness of conflict. Really in all camps more or less the same people are active, with their instincts, their capacity to suggest and infect, with their outbursts of cruelty, and with their instinct of humanity and their capacity for sympathy and kindliness. And evil usually prevails over good.

There are, of course, those who reveal themselves as a concentration of evil instincts. Nothing so distorts human nature as maniacal ideas. If a man is possessed by the idea that all evil in the world is to be found in the Jews or in the masons or the bolshevists, in the heretics or in the bourgeoisie (and these not the real people but an idea of them invented by the imagination) then the best of men will be turned into a wild beast. This is a remarkable instance of human slavery. Marat probably would always have been a wild beast, but it was said of Robespierre that if he had lived in quiet and peaceful times he would probably have been a virtuous philanthropic and humane provincial scrivener; and had he lived at some other time Dzherzhinsky would very likely have been an admirable man, not only not a man of blood, but a man full of tenderness and love. It is known of Torquemada that he was by nature rather a kindly and lovable person.

Revolutions pursue the great end of liberating man from oppression and slavery. The men who have prepared the way for revolution have been heroic people, who were capable of sacrifice and of giving their lives for an idea. But at the period of their triumph revolutions entirely obliterate every trace of freedom. They tolerate it to a much smaller extent than the period which preceded the revolution, and the makers of the revolution when they have power in their hands become ferocious and cruel, and stain themselves with human blood. One and the same revolutionary is an entirely different man before the revolution and in the flaming outburst of it. He is two quite distinct persons. Even his face is altered. You cannot recognize his face. The horror which is associated with revolution certainly does not belong to the ends which it usually pursues; these ends are commonly freedom, justice, equality, brotherhood, and the like exalted values. The horror is associated with the means it employs. Revolution seeks triumph at all costs and whatever may happen. Triumph is achieved by force. This force inevitably turns into violence. There is a fateful mistake of the makers of revolution which is connected with their relation to time. The present is regarded exclusively as a means, the future as an end, and on this account violence and enslavement, cruelty and murder are affirmed for the present, but for the future, freedom and humanity. For the present, life is a nightmare, in the future, life is a paradise.

But there is a great mystery concealed in the fact that the means are more important than the end. It is precisely the means they employ, the way they take, which bear witness to the spirit by which people are imbued. By the purity of the means they employ, by the cleanness of the road they follow, you will know what manner of spirit they are of. The future in which the exalted end was to be realized never comes. In it there will again be those same repulsive means. Violence never leads to freedom. Hatred never leads to brotherhood. A general repudiation of human dignity because of a single hostile part of humanity will never lead to the universal affirmation of human dignity. In the world of objectivization a breach between means and ends is brought about, and that cannot take place in true existence, in the world of subjectivity.

The destined fate of revolution is that it inevitably leads to Terror and Terror is the loss of freedom, the loss of everybody's freedom, the loss of freedom for all. At the outset revolution is pure and single-minded; it proclaims freedom, but as the development of its immanent forces goes on, in the power of the fateful dialectic which takes place in it, freedom disappears and the reign of Terror begins. The fear of counter-revolution takes possession of the revolution and in consequence of this fear it goes out of its mind. The fear grows in proportion to the victory of the revolution and it reaches its maximum when the revolution is finally victorious. This is a paradox of revolution. Perhaps it is a paradox of victory in general. The victor does not become magnanimous and humane; he becomes merciless and cruel; he is possessed by a thirst for extermination.

Victory is a terrible thing in this world. Woe to the victorious, not to the vanquished! It is usually observed that the vanquished become slaves. A more profound phenomenon is not usually observed, that is that the victors become slaves. Least of all is the victor a free man. He is an enslaved man, his conscience and consciousness are disturbed and confused. Terror is one of the very basest things in human life, it is a fall of man, and it obscures and distorts the expressed idea of a human being. One who practises Terror ceases to be a person; he is in the power of demoniacal forces. I have in mind chiefly the organized collective Terror which is put into practice by people who have attained to power. Terror is the offspring of fear; in a Terror it is always the slavish instincts that are triumphant, and a Terror cannot be actually realized without monstrous falsehood. It always has recourse to the symbols of deceit. Revolutionary and counter-revolutionary Terror are phenomena of the same order. Counter-revolutionary Terror is still more base and still less justifiable. It is the fate of revolution that it always bears within itself the seed from which Caesarism grows; the tyranny of the masses is always Caesarism. All revolutions have ended in that way. Fear never leads to good. Caesar, the dictator, the tyrant, are born of fear and Terror. All revolutions which are not spiritual revolutions, are like that, all which depend upon the objectivized world, that is to say a world which has lost freedom. Revolution ought always to introduce a new life. But the nature of the objectivized world is such that in it the worst evils of the old always enter into the new. It is an illusion that revolution breaks with the old; it is only that the old makes its appearance with a new mask on. The old slavery changes its dress, the old inequality is transformed into a new inequality.

A myth is always created about revolution, and the revolution is moved by the dynamic of the myth. The astounding thing is that it is not only the imagination of the masses of the people that creates a myth; scholars create it also. Man feels an unconquerable need to personalize various forces and qualities. Revolution also is personified and represented as a being. Revolution is also regarded as sacred, it becomes just as sacrosanct as monarchy was, and the pre-revolutionary régime. This personification of revolution and looking upon it as sacrosanct is also a relic of the past in it. In actual fact revolution is not sacrosanct any more than monarchy is sacrosanct or any more than anything else in the objectivized world is sacrosanct. The sacrosanct is to be found only in the subjective world. True emancipation from slavery does not allow of all these personifications and hallowings. A revolution may be necessary, it may be just, but it cannot be sacrosanct. It is always sinful, just as that order of society against which it was directed was sinful.

The sovereignty of revolution is the same falsity as every sovereignty in the world. Psychologically revolution is a reaction; it bursts out when things can no longer be endured. At the very height of a revolution, when the temperature is raised to the highest degree, destruction is stronger than creativeness. Positive construction begins later.

The most interesting thing about the metaphysics of revolution is its relation to time. If time in general is a paradox, in the relation of revolution to time this paradox reaches its most acute form. The revolution takes place in the present, and the men who take part in it are under the sway of an elemental surge in the present; and yet at the same time it must be said that revolution knows no present and has no present. It is wholly concerned with the past and the future. Revolution is rancorous, but it has no memory. Revolution supposes at first that it is possible to annihilate the past so that nothing remains of it, *du passé faisons la table rase*—a stupid illusion. It is possible to annihilate various sorts of injustice and enslavement which belong to the past, it is possible to obliterate what belongs to historical time, but it is not possible to obliterate what belongs to existential time. One can annihilate history but one cannot annihilate metahistory. Bit by bit memory begins to return to revolution; it begins to call the past to mind. History is built up by memory; the loss of memory is the disappearance of history. It is an astounding thing that memory begins to be lost within the very revolution itself. Revolution strikes with the weapon of ingratitude; it feels no gratitude to those who created it, to those who were the men that inspired it; it kills them out of hand one after the other. This is perhaps the very basest characteristic of revolution. During the period of revolution, especially at the time of its ending, the history of the revolution cannot be written; its principal actors disappear from the scene. This is a typical phenomenon. It is explained by the fact that a revolution is an acute malady of time; it is aware of nothing but a process of transition and it appraises everything according to the service it renders to that process of transition. It is characteristic of the relation of revolutionaries to time that they are usually extreme pessimists in their attitude to the past and extreme optimists in their attitude to the future. This indeed is 'a leap from the kingdom of necessity into the kingdom of freedom'. Such an attitude to the past and the future is particularly characteristic of Marxism. In actual fact since the past and the future are only fragments of time which is diseased and torn asunder, there is no basis either for an optimistic attitude to the past, as in conservatism, or for an optimistic attitude to the future, as in the case of the revolutionaries. An optimistic attitude is possible only in relation to the eternal, that is to say only in relation to the subjugation of broken-up time.

But the truth and right of revolution lie in the fact that it always destroys the excessively false and corrupt past which was poisoning life. Revolution always brings realities to light, it reveals the unreality of that which gave itself out as reality. It puts an end to many fictions, but it creates new fictions. It destroys by force the right which had ceased to be a right and had turned into brute force. Revolution is a paradox of right and might. The old right is turned into violence upon consciousness because it has lost its might. Revolution becomes might and seeks to create new right. Objections to revolution from the point of view of conventional right which regards itself as everlasting whereas in actual fact it belongs to the disintegrated past, are ridiculous. Revolution is the formation of a new association which, as Poulain truly says, is accompanied by the embarrassment, the destruction, the suppression of the other, that is to say of the old association. The enemies of revolution, the counter-revolutionaries, are fond of talking about the horrors and evil of revolution, but they have no right to speak. It is the old pre-revolutionary life and its defenders who are more than anyone else responsible for the horrors and evils of revolution. The responsibility always lies upon those who are above, not on those who are below. The horrors of a revolution are but the transformation of the horrors of the old régimes, only the working of the old poisons. It is precisely those old poisons which appear as the evil in revolutions. That is why counter-revolutionary forces can only strengthen the evil in revolutions. They can never bring about freedom from that evil.

Every great revolution makes the claim that it creates the new man. The creation of the new man is incomparably greater and more radical than the creation of a new society. A new society after the revolution is as a matter of fact created, whereas the new man does not make his appearance. In this lies the tragedy of revolution and its destined failure. All revolutions in a certain sense have been ruined by the old Adam, who appears in a new dress at the end of the revolution. This old Adam, a man of sin, makes both revolution and counter-revolution. But the slavery of man shews itself unconquerable; only the forms of slavery are changed. This does not mean that revolution is devoid of meaning and that to bring about a revolution is a senseless act. Revolutions have meaning and are important moments in the destiny of peoples. Revolutions represent a great attempt at experiment which both impoverishes man and enriches him. The very impoverishment is an enrichment. Some forms of slavery after all are destroyed in revolution. The possibility of historical activity is always conferred upon new strata of society. The chains which fettered energy are struck off.

But the slavery of man is not destroyed at the root. The new man is not an article of manufacture; nor can he be a product of social organization. The appearance of the new man is a new spiritual birth. Christianity, viewed as a whole, has been nothing else than a call to a new spiritual birth, a call for the appearance of the new Adam. But instead of the new man the world has been given signs and symbols of the new man, worn by the old Adam, by the old man. In this lies the tragedy of every historical actualization which is not a realization but an objectivization. Objectivization never is realization, objectivization is symbolization. And this is the essential nature of the historical tragedy which demands an end of history. A real deep-rooted revolution is a change in the structure of consciousness, a change of attitude to the objectivized world. Historical revolutions never do bring about such a change in the structure of consciousness. They remain within the scheme of determination and they are determined not so much by freedom as by fate. But the importance of great revolutions lies in this, that there is an eschatological moment in them which always becomes so wrapped up in historical determination, so much precipitated into historical time, that almost nothing of it is to be distinguished. Existential time in revolutions is but a momentary flash; it is carried away on the stream of historical time. Revolutions always end badly. Determinism triumphs over freedom, historical time overcomes existential time. The spirit of revolution shews itself to be hostile to the revolution of the spirit. The tragedy of a revolution is banal and commonplace to a horrible degree. The bloody horrors of revolution are banal and commonplace.

Revolutions are made by the average man and for the average man who by no means desires a change in the structure of consciousness, does not want a new spirit, does not wish to become a new man, has no desire for a real triumph over slavery. Terrible sacrifices are needed for the attainment of very small results. Such is the economy of the life of this world; and it is useless to talk about the teleological nature of the world process and the historical process. Those who defend a teleological view of things in general like to affirm an objective teleology in the world. But an objective teleology, even if it exists, has nothing in common with subjective human existential teleology. Objective teleology crushes man, and man is compelled to set his subjective teleology, his freedom, in opposition to it. God acts only in freedom, only in subjectivity; He does not act in the objective determined world. Objective teleology is the slavery of man. The way out to freedom is a break with objective teleology.

2. B. THE LURE AND SLAVERY OF COLLECTIVISM. THE ENTICEMENT OF UTOPIA. THE TWOFOLD IMAGE OF SOCIALISM

In his helplessness and dereliction man naturally seeks safety in communities. Man consents to renounce his personality in order that his life may be more secure, he seeks a crowd in a community of people so that things may be less terrible for him. The life of human societies, of primitive clans, arose from crowded communities, from a primitive communism. Totemistic cults were connected with social communities. And at the height of civilization, in the twentieth century, communities that are taking shape anew demand cults in which the experience of primitive totemism may be brought to light. The sociological religion which was preached by Durkheim, is an experience of the totemism which he discovered among the societies of savage tribes. The spell and the slavery of collectivism occupy a principal place in human life. In human personality there takes place an intersection of various social circles and groups. Simmel speaks of this; he saw in society merely the reciprocal action of individuals. Man belongs to various social groups—family, class, profession, nationality, state, etc. In objectivizing this arrangement of groups, which have only a functional relation to him, he imagines them to be communities of which he feels himself a subordinate part and in which he is dissolved. But the period of time when partial and differential social groups are generalized and universalized is the time which one must call the age of collectivism. There is formed, as it were, a single centralized community as the supreme reality and value. It is then that the real lure of collectivism begins.

The community begins to play the rôle of a church, with this difference, that the church has at any rate recognized the value of personality, and the existence of the personal conscience, while collectivism on the other hand, requires the final exteriorization of conscience, and its transference to the organs of the community. In this connection the principal difference between *sobornost** and collectivism is to be seen. Ecclesiastical *sobornost* has in history often assumed forms of human slavery and of the denial of freedom; it has often been a fiction, but the actual principle of Christian *sobornost* cannot but be personalist. *Sobornost*, as spiritual communality, is to be found in the subject not in the object; it denotes a quality of the subject, the disclosure of universality in him. The objectivization of *sobornost*, the transference of it to social institutions has always meant slavery. The spell and slavery of collectivism is nothing else than the transference of spiritual communality, fellowship, universality,

* See note on p. 4.

from subject to object, and the objectivization either of separate functions of human life or of human life as a whole.

Collectivism is always authoritarian. In it the centre of consciousness and conscience is situated outside personality in massive, collective, social groups, for example in the army or in totalitarian parties. Cadres and parties may reduce the personal consciousness to a state of paralysis. There arise various kinds of collective consciousness, which may coexist with personal consciousness. A man may possess personal consciousness and exercise personal judgment and at the same time this personal consciousness may be limited and even enslaved by collective emotions and judgments. In that case emotions on a great scale may call forth cruelty and blood-thirstiness, but they may call forth magnanimity and sacrifice. Within a community a man's fear in the face of danger and his demand for some guarantee of safety are less strong. This is one of the causes of the lure of collectivism. There is a very great danger in seeing in any sort of organization a definite end and in regarding the rest of life as an instrument and means to that end. The Jesuit order, a number of secret societies, the totalitarian parties, communist and fascist alike, have been cases of that kind. All powerful and influential organizations display this tendency, but it sometimes takes the form of fashioning a universal community, a Leviathan. Then the lure of collectivism reaches its most extreme forms of the enslavement of man. Every organization requires a certain discipline, but when the discipline demands the repudiation of personal consciousness and conscience, it is converted into the tyranny of the community. The church, the state, the nation, the class, the party may be converted into a tyranny of the community. But the community always presupposes of personality that it will expend effort and energy in conflict. An isolated personality can with difficulty struggle for its life.

Collectivism in actual fact is born of the poverty and helplessness of man. A more normal and less helpless and suffering condition leads to individualization. When the workers are accused of not understanding the supreme value of personality, and of regarding the truth of personalism with suspicion and of relying exclusively upon communities, the fact that the isolated workman is absolutely helpless and crushed is lost sight of. In a trade union or the socialist party he becomes a force and can fight for the amelioration of his position. The socialization of economic life is necessary for the defence of the worker's personality, but it should lead on to social personalism. This is the paradox of a just and righteous organization of society.

There are various degrees of communality and solidarity among people; world-wide, national, class, personalist-human. The predominance of the world-wide and personalist-human communality and solidarity over national and class communality, denotes also the victory of personality, of personal dignity and personal value over the objectivized community. Man ought to reach a condition in which he will no longer be classified, that is to say, no longer be fixed in his membership of any particular community. This means also victory over pride, over national, class, confessional, family and military pride, which are much more powerful than personal pride, and give grounds for the reinforcement of that personal pride. Social groups may both expand and contract the scope of personality. But the dominance of the social group over personality, the determination of personality by the social group in the last resort deprives personality of freedom and hinders the attainment of the universal content of life.

We speak only metaphorically when we refer to the existence of consciousness in society, of national consciousness or class consciousness. Consciousness has its existential centre always in man, in personality. But there may be the kind of exteriorization of consciousness in the process of objectivization which establishes a lasting illusion of collective consciousness. There really exists a collective unconsciousness but not a collective consciousness. *Sobornost* consciousness, or what Prince S. Trubetskoy calls socialism of consciousness also exists, but it is only a qualitative degree of universal personal consciousness, or the attainment of fellowship by personality. Society presupposes the separateness of its members, the original fusion is not society and there is no personality in it (Espinas). But this separateness is by no means opposed to fellowship and *sobornost* and does not exclude it.

It would be a mistake to say that there is no sort of reality in the community and nothing existential. But in the community this reality is distorted by exteriorization, and this existential, which is connected with the communality of men is lessened by objectivization. The separation of personal and social activities is an abstraction and an abstraction which in Christian consciousness has served as a justification of injustice and of a profoundly anti-Christian structure of society. Every personal act in human life is at the same time a social act also, there is an inevitable social projection in it. Man is not a monad shut up within himself. There always exists in human personality a social radiation, even in a man's most intimate thoughts it brings either liberation or slavery to other people. But every social act too, which is directed towards society and social groups is at the same time a personal act also. The social acts of the head of a state, of the owner of an enterprise, of the head of a family, of the leader of a party are also personal acts for which he is responsible. A man cannot be a despot and an exploiter, and also be a good Christian or simply humane in his personal life. The social is always to be found within personality.

The spell and slavery of collectivism means that the social is ejected into the external and it appears to the man that he is a part of this social which has been ejected into the external. For example, national or class pride is also personal pride, but it appears to the man that such pride is a virtue. This is the greatest of lies, and human life is full of it. National and class egoism is also personal egoism. A nationalism which hates is a personal sin. The crimes which man commits in the name of the community, identifying himself with it, are personal crimes. They are the crimes of a slave idolator. But there is an undoubted conflict between the development of personality and the development of collective groups of various degrees. Collective groups may contract the scope of personality and destroy the value of personality, by turning it into a function of its own. Nationality may do this, and so may the state and class and family and party, and religious confession and the rest. Collectivism is always possession by the false idea of abstract unity and totalitarianism. Such a unity is the slavery of man. The emancipation of man presupposes not unity but the cooperation and love of the various elements. A spiritual federalism ought to be established in opposition to spiritual centralism.

Not only is the idea of unity false, but so also is the idea of abstract

[204]

justice. There is a paradox about justice. In itself justice is not individual, it is affirmed as a 'common', as of general obligation, as a universal. But abstract, not individual, justice, as the domination of the common over the individual, becomes injustice. Real justice is individual justice. The *pathos* of justice can be the *pathos* of a community but not the *pathos* of personality, it may set the sabbath higher than man. Justice is sacred, but justice may conceal the lure and slavery of the community, the sovereignty of the common and the impersonal. Justice ought not to exteriorize the conscience of personality and make it of the 'common'. Justice becomes bad when it is not linked with the entire personality and with freedom, with pity and love. The idea of equality may at a given moment have a practically useful significance, it may be a fight for the liberation and dignity of man. But in itself the idea of equality is futile, in itself it does not mean the raising of every man, but an envious glance at one's neighbour. And all the while personalism on the other hand is based upon the equality of all men in the sight of God. The truth and right of revolution, is the truth and right of conscience and of the dignity of each man, not of all men but of each man. 'All' is common, 'each' is personal and individual. There are two ends in social life—the lessening of human suffering, poverty and degradation, and the triumph of positive values. A conflict is possible between these two ends but in the last resort they are capable of being united because to lessen human suffering. poverty and degradation means the revelation to man of the possibility of creating values.

Every man cherishes in his heart the dream of a perfect and complete life, the memory of Eden and the search for the Kingdom of God. At all times man has constructed utopias of various kinds and striven for the realization of utopia. And the most astounding thing of all is this. Utopias are much more realizable than it seems. The most extreme utopias are more actual and in a certain sense more realist than the soberly reasonable plans for the organization of human societies. The middle ages realized Plato's utopia in an aspect transformed by the Christian point of view. There is nothing more utopian than theocracy, but a theocratic society and a theocratic civilization were actually brought into being both in the West and in the East. All the great revolutions prove that it is precisely the radical utopias which are realized, while the more moderate ideologies which had seemed to be more realistic and practical, are overthrown and play no part at all. In the French Revolution it was not the Girondists who triumphed, but the Jacobins, and they tried to realize Rousseau's utopia of a perfect natural and rational order. In the Russian Revolution the communists triumphed, not the social democrats nor the socialist revolutionaries, nor simply the democrats, and their aim was to realize the utopia of Marx, the utopia of an entirely communistic structure of society. When I say that utopias are realizable and that they have been realized in theocracies, in Jacobin democracy and in Marxist communism, I do not mean that they have in actual fact been realized in the most literal sense of the word. The realization was also a failure and in the last resort led to a régime which did not correspond with the conception of the utopia. History in general is like that. But there is a dynamic force in a utopia, it concentrates and intensifies the energy of the struggle and at the height of the struggle the ideologies which are not utopian are seen to be the feebler.

A utopia always includes a project for the complete, totalitarian ordering of life. In comparison with a utopia, other theories and tendencies appear to be partial and on that account less inspiring. In this lies the attractive power of a utopia and in this is the danger of slavery which it brings with it. Totalitarianism always brings slavery with it. The totalitarianism of the Kingdom of God alone is an affirmation of freedom. But totalitarianism in the world of objectivization is always slavery. The objectivized world is partial and it does not lend itself to a complete, totalitarian ordering of things. A utopia is the distortion in human consciousness of the Kingdom of God. The lure af domination, which has already been dealt with, is the origin of utopia. Utopia always means monism, and monism in the objectivized world is always human slavery, for it is always compulsive monism. A monism which will not become slavery and compulsion is possible only in the Kingdom of God. The utopia of a perfect society in the conditions of our world, the utopia of sacred kingship, and of authority which is inviolate, the utopia of a perfect and absolute common will of the people or of the proletariat, the utopia of absolute justice, and of absolute brotherhood, all these come into collision with the supreme value of personality, with personal conscience and personal dignity, with freedom of spirit and conscience. Freedom of spirit, freedom of personality, presupposes a dualistic moment, a differentiation between the things of God and the things of Caesar. Utopia on the other hand wishes to annihilate that dualistic moment and to turn Caesar's things into God's. Such were both the theocratic utopia and the utopia of a sacred monarchy. The emancipation of man means the denial of any sort of sacredness in the objectivized historical world. Sacredness is in the world of existence alone, in the world of subjectivity. And truth is always in subjectivity, it is always in the minority not in the majority.

But this aristocracy of truth cannot be objectivized in any kind of aristocratic, hierarchical structure of society, which is always a falsity. The aristocratic utopia is not any better than any of the rest of the utopias and enslaves just as much. The aristocracy of truth does not mean privileges of any kind, it means duty. There is bitter truth in Hertzen's words, 'Why is it ludicrous to believe in God, but not ludicrous to believe in humanity, why is it stupid to believe in the Kingdom of Heaven but clever to believe in earthly utopias?' These words are directed against all utopias. And yet at the same time there is truth and right in utopia. Man ought to be bent upon reaching perfection, that is upon attaining to the Kingdom of God. But there is something terribly stifling in a utopia, there is something aesthetically repellent. When an attempt is made to realize utopia, a dream of the imperfect life makes its appearance, as something more free and more human. This is due to the fact that utopia is a mingling of Caesar's things with God's, of this world and the other. Utopia desires the perfect life, compulsory good, and the rationalization of the human tragedy, without an effective transfiguration of man and the world, without a new heaven and a new earth. Utopia raises an eschatological problem, the problem of the end.

The opponents of socialism say that socialism is a utopia and that it flies in the face of human nature. There is some ambiguity in this. It is not clear whether they do not want socialism on the ground that it is unrealizable, utopian, and a mere dream, or whether it is unrealizable because they do not want it and do everything in their power to hinder its coming into being. To say that the socialist ideal is good and just but, more's the pity, it cannot be realized, is by no means the same thing as to say that the socialist ideal is bad and hateful. Bourgeois capitalist circles confuse the two arguments and make use of both the one and the other. At one time socialism may be acknowledged to be a good and noble dream but unrealizable; at another time it is represented as a repellent slavery which must be prevented with all one's might. It is not to be disputed that there have been socialistic utopias and that there is a utopian element in socialism. There is a socialist myth just as there is a democratic myth, a liberal, a monarchical, or a theocratic myth. But socialism is not a utopia, socialism is a stern reality. If socialism could be represented as a utopia in the nineteenth century, in the twentieth century it is easier to represent liberalism as a utopia.

The argument that socialism is unrealizable because it presupposes a moral height to which the actual state of men and women does not correspond is completely bankrupt. It would be more true to say that socialism will be realized precisely because the moral level of men is not high enough and an organization of society is needed which would make impossible the excessive oppression of man by man. Liberal economics which put their trust in the natural play of human interests were founded upon an optimism which was great indeed. Socialism on the other hand contains an element of pessimism. Socialism does not want to pin its faith to the free play of forces within social-economic life, it takes a pessimistic view in its estimate of the consequences of freedom in economic life. The putting of an end to the torture of the weak by the strong cannot await the moral perfection of the strong. Social changes cannot wait until men and women are made morally perfect. The weak must be supported by actions which change the structure of society. Abstract moralism in application to social life is hypocrisy, it upholds social injustice and evil. A society composed of saints would have no need of any sort of social action to defend the weak against the strong and the exploited against those who exploit them. A socialist society is not a society of saints, it is just simply a society of sinful and imperfect men, and the manifestation of human perfection is not to be expected of it.

[208]

The problem of socialism, which is a fact of world-wide importance is very complicated and there are many sides to it. The metaphysical and spiritual side of socialism and its social and economic
side, are open to very different appraisement. The metaphysics of
socialism in its prevalent forms are entirely false. They are founded
upon the supremacy of society over personality, on the belief that
personality is fashioned exclusively by society. This is a collectivist
metaphysic, it is the lure and temptation of collectivism. Socialists
on all hands profess monism and deny the distinction between
Caesar's things and God's, between what is natural and social and
what is spiritual. Socialist metaphysics regard the common as more
real than the individual, class as more real than man; they see the
social class behind the man instead of seeing the man behind the
social class. Totalitarian, integral socialism is a false outlook upon
the world; it denies the spiritual principle, it generalizes man down to
the very depths of him.

But the social and economic side of socialism is right and just, it is
elementary justice. In this sense socialism is the social projection of
Christian personalism. Socialism is not necessarily collectivism, it
may be personalistic and anti-collectivist. Only personalist socialism
is the liberation of man; collectivist socialism is enslavement. The
socialist labour movement is charged with materialism. But it is
forgotten that the working-man has been violently precipitated into
the material world, and for that reason easily surrenders to the
materialists. Not socialist culture only but democratic culture also is
of no high quality, it has been vulgarized. This means that human
societies move forward under the spur of the necessity of solving the
elementary material problems of human existence.

Two problems lie at the roots of social life and nothing is more
difficult than the finding of a harmonious solution of the two. They
are the problem of freedom, and the problem of daily bread. It is
possible to solve the problem of freedom while depriving a man of
his daily bread. One of the temptations which Christ rejected in the
wilderness was the temptation to turn stones into bread. Here bread
becomes an enslavement of man. All the three temptations which
Christ rejected enslave man. Dostoyevsky gave expression to this
truth in that work of genius of his, the *Legend of the Grand Inquisitor*.

But it would be a false interpretation of the *Legend* to represent it as saying that the problem of bread does not demand a positive solution and that freedom alone ought to exist, without bread. People are made into slaves by being deprived of bread. Bread is a great symbol, and with it the theme of socialism is connected, and it is a theme of world significance. Man ought not to become the slave of 'bread', he ought not to surrender his freedom for 'bread'. Here we have the theme of the twofold nature of socialism, of the two socialisms. Collectivist socialism which is based upon the supremacy of society and the state over personality, on the supremacy of equality over freedom, offers bread, and takes away a man's freedom, it deprives him of freedom of conscience. Personalist socialism which is founded on the absolute supremacy of personality, of each personality over society and over the state, the supremacy of freedom over equality, offers 'bread' to all men while preserving their freedom for them, and without alienating their conscience from them.

It is sometimes put in this way, that democratic socialism is on the side of freedom, and authoritarian socialism is against it. This distinction does not go to the heart of the question. Democracy is a relative form of society. Whereas the value of personality and freedom on the other hand has an absolute significance. On one side democracy denotes the sovereignty of the people, the dominance of the majority and in this sense it is on the whole unfavourable to personality and freedom. But on another side democracy means the self-government of man, a man's rights as a man and a citizen, the freedom of man, and in this sense it has an eternal significance. People of the eighteenth and nineteenth centuries sought for the emancipation of man in society, that is to say they believed that society ought to make a man free. But the problem may be stated in an entirely different way. The liberation of man may be sought not in society but in God, and it may mean the emancipation of man from the power of society itself. This is opposed to social monism which inevitably leads to slavery; it presupposes a dualistic moment, and that spirit cannot be derived from society.

One might put forward the two types of socialism, the servile and the free, under names more in accordance with present day terminology. The servile type which is always collectivist and state socialism, is fascist socialism. This is made absolutely clear by processes which are taking place in the world and in which its determining principles appear. Fascist socialism, in which the imperialist will to power is disclosed may be 'left', and this is communism, or it may be 'right', and this is national socialism. It is precisely the fascist elements in socialism which are bad and enslaving, while the elements which are just and deserving of sympathetic interest, are not fascist. Fascist socialism inevitably leads to the reign of bureaucracy. By a paradoxical dialectic a levelling unity leads to the formation of an authoritarian hierarchical régime. This is a process which is inevitable. The grip of bureaucracy upon socialism is to be found not only in fascist socialism but also in the socialism which regards itself as democratic. The social democratic and socialist parties in Europe have been exposed to the dangers of becoming controlled by a bureaucracy and by the forces of centralization. The only force that can be put in opposition to this is to be sought in real molecular processes within human society which are founded in the values of personalism and the personalist brotherhood of man. This is also a real and not a formal democracy, that is to say it is the self-government of man, that is to say freedom which comes from below. Socialism is turned into a realm of slaves as a result of what is always one and the same objectivization. Freedom stands in opposition to this objectivization, freedom which is always in the subject and not in the object.

Can socialism be a social projection of personalism? Is personalist socialism a possibility? Personalist socialism looks like a contradiction in terms. A simplified meaning attached to the words easily inclines to the thought that the social projection of personalism is liberalism. This is a very grave error. Liberalism in economic and social life has been the ideology of capitalism. Personalism, on the other hand, is an implacable denial of the capitalist structure of society. Personalism does not allow the conversion of human personality into a thing and an article of commerce. (*Verdinglichung*—in Marx's terminology.) Working men cannot be the tools of industrial development. The wage system is a system of slavery. Personalism also cannot be reconciled with the impersonal power of money over human life.

[211]

Personalism cannot be reconciled with that distortion of hierarchical values upon which the capitalist world rests, with the valuation of a man according to what he possesses and the position he occupies in society. To regard a man exclusively as a labourer who occupies a certain position in the system of production is an intolerable slavery of man. And what is a thoroughly bad side of socialism is the supremacy it gives to economics over spirit. This failure to acknowledge human personality as the supreme value is an inheritance from capitalism, it is a continuation of the capitalist destruction of values. A false collectivism which oppresses the personal conscience, is the outcome of capitalist industrial life. The dependence of man upon the soil was less cruel. Man frees himself from slavery to the soil, but there lies in wait for him the bitter slavery to the tools by which he set himself free.

In its scale of values personalism is similar to authentic undistorted Christianity. Only Christians who have lost their conscience are capable of defending the rich against the poor. Christianity is a religion of the poor and there is no possibility of turning it into a defence of capitalists and money. Capitalism is a religion of the Golden Calf and the most astonishing thing of all is that there are disinterested defenders of it, pure ideologists. Capitalism is not only an outrage upon the 'have-nots' and the oppression of the 'have-nots', it is above all an outrage upon and the persecution of, human personality, of every human personality. And the personality of the bourgeois himself is persecuted and crushed by the bourgeois capitalist structure of society. It is not the proletarian only, it is also the bourgeois himself who is depersonalized and dehumanized. He loses the freedom of the spirit, he is a slave. Socialism raises the problem of the proletarian as a problem of world significance. The very fact of the existence of the proletarian, no less than the fact of the existence of the bourgeois also, is a contradiction of the dignity of man, of the value of human personality. The existence of the proletariat is an injustice and an evil. The process which forms a proletariat is an alienation of human nature; it is the spoliation of that nature. The service which Marx has rendered is that he revealed this fact and stated the problem in an acute form.

The position of the proletarian in this world is incompatible with the supreme value of personality. The making of a proletarian is due to taking his instruments of production from the workman and obliging him to sell his labour as an article of commerce. In this respect capitalist society stands morally much lower than mediaeval society which was associated with handicrafts and guilds. It might be said that the peasant is nearer to the sources of the world while the proletarian is nearer to the end of the world: there is something eschatological in him.

The appearance of the proletariat in correlation to the bourgeoisie is an outcome of human sin which has been socialized, and objectivized in history. There is a great responsibility for the existence in the world of people who have been made into a proletariat. The man who belongs to the proletariat is an outcast; no-one worries about him. His only salvation is to be found in union with his comrades in misfortune, only in associations of labour. The workers of the proletariat are on the average the same sort of people as everyone else, good and bad. Marx says in the writings of his younger days, that the workman is not the highest type of man, that he is a most dehumanized creature, and most particularly lacking in the riches of human nature. The myth of proletarian messianism which was destined to play so important a rôle in the history of Marxism does not fit in with this. The labouring masses are better than the bourgeois masses. They are less corrupt and are more deserving of sympathetic interest. But working men may be poisoned by a sense of *ressentiment,* by envy, and by hatred, and after their triumph they may become oppressors and exploiters. The rich torment the poor; then the poor kill the rich. Human history is a terrible comedy. Only a few men are determined by their own ideals and beliefs. The majority are determined by economic interests, by class and professional interests, by states of temporary insanity which have nothing but negative results. The Marxist proletariat is not an empirical reality, it is an idea and a myth created by the intelligentsia. As an empirical reality workers are very much differentiated and diversified and they are not the men who reveal humanity in its fullness.

The idea that the future socialist society is a proletarian society and the idea of proletarian culture are absolutely absurd and self contradictory. There ought to be no proletariat in a socialist society; but there ought to be people to whom human dignity will be restored, and the fullness of their humanity. This is the victory of humanization over dehumanization. The privileged and proud position of the noble or the bourgeois ought not to be replaced by a privileged and proud position of the proletariat. A privileged and arrogant proletarian possessed by the will to dominate is only a new bourgeois. The proletarian forms not only a social and economic but also a psychological and ethical category. The social organization of society ought to destroy the social and economic category of the proletariat. The alienation of a man's working power which is what makes the proletarian will no longer take place among mankind. Everyone who works will have equipment for production. But it is a spiritual movement in the world which ought to do away with the psychological and ethical category of the proletariat. Not the proletarian who is a heritage of evil and injustice from the past, but the integral man ought to stand out in his full stature.

Proletarian ideology is a servile ideology; it is a reaction against the past, against the servile past. What it is needful to affirm in the proletarian is not his proletarianism but the dignity of his human personality. He must be summoned not to proletarian culture but to human culture. The spirit of proletarian revolution is universal slavery and abasement. The spirit of human revolution is universal emancipation and uplifting. The inequality, injustice, and humiliations of the past create illusions in the consciousness of the oppressed. Materialism, atheism, and utilitarianism are such illusions. This is the 'opium for the people'. It is to be noted that a contraction of consciousness takes place in the oppressed (workers, countries which have suffered defeat, the conquered, political refugees) and in those who are afraid of losing their privileged position. 'The bourgeois mentality', 'the proletarian mentality' are alike a contraction and impoverishment of consciousness. The bourgeois-capitalist world and the proletarian-socialist world are abstractions. These worlds enter into each other. Capitalism cannot embrace the whole of life and the whole of culture. To point out the contrast of the bourgeois world with the world of true Christianity, of the objectivized and determined world with the world of personalism and freedom would be to make a radical antithesis. It must be said further that the concept 'proletarian' is not identical with the concept 'poor man'. The evangelical conception of poverty which reveals it as spiritually an advantage, is not the same thing as the condition of the proletarian, which cannot denote an advantage. All this leads us on to the basic theme of class and classless society.

A class society is based upon falsehood and wrong, it is a denial of the dignity of personality. Personalism is the rejection of class society, it is a demand for a classless society. In this respect both socialism and communism are right and true. But socialism fails to free itself from the heritage of class society, when it desires to be exclusively proletarian and is bent upon the establishment of a proletarian society. Personalist socialism ought not to be a matter of class, but of the people, and human, that is, free from the power of class society which gives rise to a new slavery. Classes set up distinctions and inequalities among people, which are based not on their personal worth, qualities, and callings, but on privileges which are linked with birth and blood, or with property and money. Such a classification of men is not based on any human principle and is repellent to human nature. Society must inevitably be differentiated, but not differentiated in terms of social classes. The differentiation, distinctions and inequalities ought to be human and personal, not a matter of social class and not impersonal. There were great differences and inequalities among the nobility, but each member of the nobility was possessed of noble status and socially was the equal of any other member of the nobility. In the same way the whole of society ought to consist of nobles alone, in spite of personal differences. The class distinction between the bourgeoisie and the workers is false, it is not a human or a personal distinction, it ought to disappear. All men should be working men, all should be nobles but not bourgeois, and not proletarians.

A socially levelling process is necessary, not in order to equalize and depersonalize men and women, but precisely in order to differentiate and diversify them, to bring to light personal qualitative distinctions which are concealed and suppressed by a class structure of society. A classless society is by no means a utopia, it is an inescapable reality, it denotes the humanization of society.

[215]

Aristocratic societies have not concealed the existence of classes, which were called classes; they defended inequality on principle, such inequalities as those of race and birth. There was sincerity in this, it was the open frankness of aristocratic society. Bourgeois societies conceal the existence of classes, their ideologists assert that since there is equality of citizenship, there are no more classes; they accuse the socialists of inventing the existence of classes and the class struggle. This shews the insincerity and falsehood of these societies. Classes do exist, and not only the workers but the bourgeois also carry on a class struggle, and it is a desperate struggle. The existence of class among men, the supremacy of class over man is the great evil of society and of present day society in particular.

The outstanding merit of the proletariat consists in the fact that it is bent upon self-destruction, upon its own conversion into humanity. Such is the idea of Marxist socialism also. But in practice the class self-assertion of the proletariat does exist and it prevents the creation of a new society. All class psychology is sinful and the dignity of man is expressed in overcoming it. But when the bourgeoisie makes the proposal to the proletariat that it should overcome its class psychology and put an end to the class struggle, this is hypocrisy and a subterfuge of warfare. A truly human and humane society is a brotherly society; there can be no class hierarchy in it, in it distinctions between people will be determined on another principle, in it the best, the qualitatively highest will be distinguished not by rights but by duties. But the brotherly society is not an external organization. The brotherly society requires men who have risen to spiritual heights. And never can a selection based upon personal qualities be connected with economic advantages.

At the basis of personalist society at its best there lies the idea not of the citizen nor the idea of the producer, not a political idea nor an economic idea, but the spiritual idea of the whole man, of personality. This involves the supremacy of spirit over politics and economics. The idea of the citizen and the idea of the producer are abstractions, they involve the disintegration of the integral man. Integrality is always to be found in man, not in society. The privileges of a select qualitative minority, of a spiritual aristocracy as contrasted with the non-qualitative masses, have nothing in common with class privileges; they are not liable to social objectivization. There will always be an arrangement of qualitatively distinct groups in a society, which are connected with professions, vocations, gifts, or a high degree of culture, but there is no element of class in all this. Classes should in the first place be replaced by professions. Society cannot be a homogeneous mass devoid of qualitative distinctions. In every society which has arrived at a definite form, there is a tendency towards inequality and it is not permissible to demand a levelling down to the lowest grade. The domination of a rabble might be organized in that way, but that is not a people. But personalism does not allow the class debasement of man. The advancement of man is above all a spiritual advancement; materially, on the other hand, man ought not so much to be raised as to be levelled.

In capitalist society advantages of education have been linked with financial advantages and not with the advantages of natural gifts. Socialism has in fact often been associated with an actual lowering of the level of culture, with subjection of the spirit to economics, with a dislike of any high attainment by men and of human genius. And this has not been brought about by the social and economic system of socialism, it has been due to a wrong spirit by which the leaders of socialism have been permeated. The slavery which communism brings with it is the outcome of a spirit, not of economics. The denial of the spirit is always a phenomenon of the spirit, but of spirit which has taken a wrong direction. Hitherto a combination of the social problem and the spiritual problem has still not been faced and the blame for this rests on both sides. In the social thought of the nineteenth century Hertzen among us and Proudhon in the West made some approach towards a personalist socialism, but their philosophy was bad. A development of certain ideas which Marx had in his youth might have led to it but the later development of Marxism took the opposite direction.

It is not the purpose of this book of mine to set forth a programme for the solution of the social problem. I am a philosopher and not an economist and it is the spiritual side of the social problem which interests me. My subject here is the freedom and the slavery of man. In relation to the social question, however, this becomes as concrete as the subject of daily bread, of the proletariat and of labour. The solution of the social question is not the creation of Paradise, it is rather the solution of some very elementary problems. Daily bread ought to be guaranteed for all men and for every man. There ought not to be any proletariat; there ought not to be people who have been made into a proletariat, who have been dehumanized and depersonalized; labour ought not to be exploited, it ought not to be turned into an article of commerce; and the meaning and dignity of labour ought to be discovered. It is not to be borne that there are people who are outcasts and deprived of every guarantee of existence. It is nothing but a deep-rooted lie which affirms that these elementary problems of human existence are insoluble. There exist no such things as economic laws which require the destitution and unhappiness of the greater part of mankind. These laws are an invention of bourgeois political economy. Marx was profoundly right when he denied them, and when he set up an arrangement of society which depends upon the activity of man. The answer to these questions is complex and there are no ready-made doctrines which give their solution beforehand. A doctrinaire position in general is pernicious in seeking for the solution of social questions and it always does violence to personality.

Above all it is necessary to be on one's guard against social monism. Social monism always turns into tyranny and slavery. The system of economy which is most favourable to personalism is a pluralistic system, that is to say a combination of nationalized economics, socialized economics and personal economics, in so far as it does not admit capitalism and exploitation. Only economics can be socialized, the spiritual life cannot, nor can the consciousness and conscience of men. The socialization of economics ought to be accompanied by the individualization of men and women. The brotherhood of men, which is a spiritual problem, is not to be solved by social organization, it is proximity and union not in the sphere of the abstractly-common, but in the sphere of the concretely-individual. Brotherhood presupposes the individuality of men and women and of peoples.

Personalism demands also decentralization and federalism, and a fight against centralized monstrosities. The social question is not to .be decided by the forcible seizure of power, as the majority of the movements of our time, communism, fascism, and parliamentary democracy, suppose. The forcible seizure of power means the supremacy of politics and one form or another of étatism. But politics represent to a remarkable degree the power of fiction over human life; in that respect they are like the power of money. The social question will be decided by molecular processes in the life of the people which bring the tissue of society to a new birth. It will be decided from below, not from above, as an effect of freedom, not by the act of authority. The solution of the social question by political methods which assume an absolute character, by the authority of power, is to a remarkable degree a fictitious solution, it does not create a new tissue of society. To bring justice and righteousness into actual being presupposes indeed compulsive social measures, but a brotherly community among men and a spirit of fellowship are created out of freedom, as the outcome of profound molecular processes. The social question cannot be really decided by demagogic falsehood. Personalism is a demand for truth.

Freedom, which is always rooted in the spirit, gives rise to paradoxes in its social projection. Formal freedom in social life may give rise to slavery. The freedom of labour in a capitalist society is of that sort. There are degrees and gradations of freedom. Freedom should reach its maximum in spiritual life, in conscience, in thought, in creative power, in the relation of man to God. But freedom is limited and reaches its minimum in proportion to the extent to which it sinks to the level of material life. To secure the real freedom of men and women, and the real freedom of the workers, freedom of economic life must be limited, otherwise the strong will oppress the weak and enslave him, and deny him a crust of bread. The autonomy of economics is a false and visionary freedom. But false monism or totalitarianism transfers the limitation of freedom in economic life, to a limitation of freedom and even the annihilation of freedom in spiritual life. This is the great evil of all the totalitarian systems through whose power the world is passing.

Up to the present time the world has never seen real freedom of labour or has seen it but rarely and to a very limited extent. The socialist movement fights against the crude exploitation of labour, against the economic slavery of the workers, but the deep spiritual and metaphysical problem of labour it has not even stated. Greek aristocratic intellectualism despised labour and exalted the intellectual and aesthetic view of life. Christian asceticism of the middle ages recognized the dignity of labour, but this dignity was represented not so much as creative as redemptive. At the beginning of the new age Calvinism specially exalted rational labour, but this rational labour led to the formation of a privileged bourgeoisie and to the capitalist régime. The present day world is aware of the socialistic apotheosis of labour. But strange to say this apotheosis of labour does not reveal the meaning of labour, it denotes rather liberation from the power of heavy labour over the workers. There is a contradiction in socialism here, which arises from the limitations of the socialist's general outlook upon life.

The emancipation of the workers from the enslaving power of labour, an emancipation which is entirely just and right, raises the problem of the leisure which they do not know how to occupy. The rationalization and technization of economics in the capitalist structure of society create unemployment, which is a most terrible condemnation of that structure. Other forms of social organization, more just and more humane, can give release from too long and too arduous labour, and create leisure, which will be occupied by 'innocent games and amusements'. Can it be said that complete emancipation from the burden of labour and the conversion of human life into unbroken leisure is the goal of social life? That is a wrong way of looking at human life; it is a denial of the seriousness and hardship of human life upon earth. Labour ought to be freed from slavery and oppression, but complete release from labour is not a possibility. Labour is the greatest reality of human life in this world, it is a primary reality. Neither politics, nor yet money is a primary reality, they represent the power of fictions. And the primacy of the reality of labour ought to be an accepted axiom. In labour there is both a truth of redemption ('in the sweat of thy face shalt thou gain thy bread') and a truth of the creative and constructive power of men. Both elements are present in labour. Human labour humanizes nature; it bears witness to the great mission of man in nature. But sin and evil have perverted the mission of labour. A reverse process has taken place in the dehumanization of labour, an alienation of human nature has taken place in the workers. This is an evil and injustice which belongs both to the old slavery and to the new capitalist slavery. Man has been seized with the desire to be not only the master of nature, but also the master of his brother man, and he has enslaved labour. This represents an extreme form of the objectivization of human existence. We see it for example in what Marx called the 'fetishism of goods'.

But if labour ought to be emancipated, it ought not to be deified and turned into an idol. Human life is not only labour, not only working activity, it is also contemplation. Activity is exchanged from time to time for contemplation, and that cannot be driven out of human life. The exclusive power of working activity over human life may enslave man to the flow of time, while contemplation may be a way out from the sway of time into eternity. Contemplation also is creativeness but of another kind than labour. The bourgeois general view of life does not admit any other motive for labour than personal interest. The workers labour productively and under discipline, only because of the threat of losing their employment and of being doomed to hunger, with their families. But this is also the enslavement of labour. In opposition to socialism the bourgeoisie says that the productivity of business is founded upon personal interest. Social interest does not create productive business. But the workers labour in an alien business, they have no interest in it. That means that the productivity of the business is founded upon the servile fear which the workers have of being thrown out into the street. Slavery is the motive power of labour in a capitalist society. Personal initiative in economic life is by no means identical with the initiative of the capitalist who has command of the means of production and whose initiative may be almost non-existent. The person who initiates and manages a commercial undertaking may be an engineering specialist, who is interested in it as one who takes his share in public life, as a creative man but who, nevertheless, is not the proprietor. Personal creative initiative in economic life will always remain. The subject in economic life is in any case personality and that by no means denotes that personal command of the means of production which makes possible the enslaving of other people. Personalism in any case cannot admit the domination of personal interest and competition in economic life, that is to say a wolfish relation of man to man.

But in capitalist economy itself everything is not founded upon personal interest. That is too rationalized a representation of economic and social life. In actual fact an immense part is played by sub-conscious instincts, which it is necessary to distinguish from rational interests. The bourgeois classes are often guided in the social conflict much more by these sub-conscious instincts and irrational prejudices, than by reasoned and conscious interests. In his egocentricity man often acts unreasonably. For example, in his thirst for gain he makes ready for wars in which he himself perishes. In social life no small part is played by dreams and visions which arise from the subconscious, and even by real frenzy. In politics and particularly in international politics there is much that is delirious. People rush towards ruin, they subject themselves to fate. And this is specially characteristic of the people of a dying world, of a disintegrating social structure. For the creation of a new world, for the transition to a new social order it is necessary to pass through the experience of a real and serious asceticism. It is a mistake to think that asceticism is applicable only to personal life, it is applicable also to historical and social life. To achieve victory over the lure and slavery of collectivism, over the new social slavery, the tribute paid by the subject to the object world must be made smaller. This shows the spiritual strength of personality in contrast to the temptations of the world, by which personality is enslaved. At the same time personality must be more social in the good sense of the word and less social in the bad sense, that is to say, it must be social as the effect of freedom, and not social as the result of determinism and slavery.

3. *A*. THE EROTIC LURE AND SLAVERY. SEX, PERSONALITY AND FREEDOM

The erotic lure is a lure that is particularly widespread, and slavery to sex is one of the very deepest sources of human slavery. The physiological sexual need rarely appears in man in an unmixed form, it is always accompanied by psychological complications, by erotic illusions. Man is a sexual being, that is to say, he is a divided half, he is incomplete and he feels an urge towards fulfilment, not only in his physical nature, but psychologically also. Sex is not merely a special function in man, connected with his sexual organs, it flows through the whole organism of a man. Freud has shown this to the full. It is to be noted that sex has been a hidden side of human life, there has always been something shameful about it; men have not made up their minds to bring it into the open. Man has been ashamed of his slavery to sex. Here we are faced by an astonishing paradox, that which is the source of life and its most potent urge and tension, is considered shameful and is subject to concealment. Perhaps Rozanov alone has stated this problem in all its acuteness. This attitude to sex is so strange and so unlike all the rest, that it leads to the thought of some special connection between sex and the Fall of man. Sex is, as it were, the seal of the Fall of man, an imprint which marks the loss of the integrality of human nature.

Only at the end of the nineteenth and the beginning of the twentieth century did thought, science and literature move towards a fuller unveiling of the mystery of sex and the sexual life. It is enough to mention the names of Rozanov, Weininger, Freud and Lawrence. The scientific unveiling of the unconscious sexual life by Freud at first aroused a storm of indignation against him. Lawrence was regarded as a pornographic writer. But all the same the twentieth century showed a radical change in human consciousness in its attitude to sex. If we compare the novel of the twentieth century with the novel of the nineteenth and preceding centuries, an immense difference is to be seen. Literature has always depicted love, it has been its favourite topic, but sex life remained concealed. Only in the twentieth century was the decision made to depict sex in its plain reality, no longer hidden, but revealed. It is an enormously long way from Dickens to Lawrence or from Balzac to Montherlant. Man has, so to speak, entered upon the path of unveiling, he does not wish to remain, or he cannot remain, under illusions of consciousness. The unveiling of human nature had already begun in Marx and Nietzsche, but in another way, and more profoundly in Dostoyevsky and Kirkegaard, although here too it did not touch upon sex in particular.

Christianity has screened sex behind the idea of sin, but has left a sort of ambiguity about it which Rozanov has brought to light.

I shall be concerned with this problem as it is seen in the light of the supreme value of personality and freedom and the suppression of these by the slavery of sex. We shall see that there are here two distinct problems, the sexual and the erotic (in the philosophical sense), sex and love; three problems even, sex, family, and love. There is a physical link between sexual intercourse and child-bearing, but no spiritual link, just as there is no necessary connection between sexual intercourse and love. It is open to no dispute whatever that sexual attraction and the sexual act are entirely impersonal and contain nothing specifically human, it is a bond between man and the whole animal world. Sex, which indicates a lack of completion and fulfilment in man, is the power of the race over personality, the power of the common over the individual. In resigning himself to the sway of sexual life, man loses power over himself. In non-individualized sexual attraction man, as it were, ceases to be personality, he is turned into a function of the impersonal generic process. Sexuality is of an impersonal character, while on the other hand the 'erotics' of the philosophers have a personal character, and this fact constitutes an immense difference. There is no direct and necessary connection whatever between sexual attraction and being in love. It is possible for the state of being in love even to lessen sexual attraction. The state of being in love has as its object an unrepeatedly individual being, a particular personality, and in it no substitution of one person for another is possible. Sexual attraction does admit of such substitution and does not necessarily denote any relation to personality. And in cases in which sexual attraction becomes individualized, which happens not infrequently, it does not indicate a relation to the whole personality, it takes its course through an impersonal generic element.

Sex is one of the sources of human slavery and one of the most profound of such sources, which are bound up with the very possibility of the continuance of the human race. This slavery may assume very crude forms, but it may also take forms of subtle and refined seductiveness. Sex life possesses a capacity for giving rise to erotic illusions. Schopenhauer was right when he said that man becomes the plaything of the elemental forces of race which fill his mind with illusions. To Ivan who is in love, Mary appears to be a beauty when everybody else sees that she is ugly. But not every case of the 'falling-in-love' sort of love is mere illusion, it may be a break through beyond the element of impersonal race, to personality, to the unrepeatable human person. Then it will denote victory over the slavery of sex and erotic illusion. Real love finds the personality and recognizes it, attaches itself to everything unchangeably individual in it and affirms it for eternity, that is the meaning of love. But the climate of the world is not favourable to real love, too often it is deadly to it. Love is a phenomenon which is outside the world, it arises outside the world of objectivization, it is a break through into this world of determination and therefore meets with resistance from it. On this account there exists a profound connection between love and death. This connection is one of the central themes of world literature. But first of all a distinction must be made between two types of love.

It is possible to make classifications of the types of love on the basis of various characteristic marks. But it seems to me that the most important is the distinction between the love that ascends and the love that descends. There are some very subtle thoughts in this subject in Scheler, though perhaps they do not go to the very bottom of the matter. The 'falling-in-love' type of love, *eros,* which is wider than the love between man and woman, is love which ascends. The state of being in love is an attraction upwards, rapture, it leads on to creative ecstasy. Erotic love always presupposes deficiency, unfulfilledness, yearning for fulfilment, attraction towards that which can enrich. There is *eros* as a demon, and man can be possessed by him. The winged souls, about which Plato speaks in the Phaedrus grow out of the state of being in love. In Plato *eros* has two sources of origin, riches and poverty. *Eros* is the path of ascension. But in Plato himself this path of ascension is a transition from the world of the senses to the world of ideas. The platonic *eros* is not love for a concrete living being, for personality. It is love for an idea, for beauty, for the divine height. *Eros* is anti-personalist, it does not know the unrepeatable personality and does not affirm it. This is the limit beyond which platonism does not go. And in this lies the tragedy of the 'erotica' connected with platonism. The erotics of the life of

Solovyev were of that kind. He was in love not with a concrete woman, but with eternal divine womanhood. The concrete women with whom this is connected only bring disillusionment. Upon this path the erotic illusions are insurmountable. The divine beauty alone is not an illusion. But the 'falling-in-love' sort of love does not invariably bear this platonistic character, it may be connected with the relation of personality to personality.

There is another type of love—the love that descends, the love that gives and does not ask, love which is compassion and sympathy, *caritas*. Caritative love seeks nothing for itself. It gives of its abundance to another. Erotic love is union with another in God. Caritative love is union with another in the absence of God, in the darkness of the world. It is impossible to love everyone unless we use the word in the sense of *caritas*. Love is choice. You cannot compel yourself to love. But *caritas*, lovingkindness, compassion, are possible towards all men and are not linked with choice. While *eros*-love demands reciprocity, *caritas*-love does not demand it, and therein lie its riches and its power. And real *eros*-love includes *caritas*-love, compassionate love. The erotic love which knows no compassion and charity acquires a demonic character and torments man. *Eros*, in its unmixed form, is slavery, the slavery of him who loves and the slavery of him who is loved. Erotic love can be pitiless and cruel, it perpetrates extreme violence. Christian love is not *eros*, Christian love is *agape*. The Greek language was rich in words to express the shades of meaning in love. *Eros, agape, philia*. Love is a complex state in man and the various shades of meaning in love may be blended together in it. The love which ascends, rapturous love, may be side by side with the love that descends, with compassionate love.

But completely to separate Christian love from the elements of compassion, sympathy, and *caritas*, and to regard it as exclusively erotic as they were fond of doing at the beginning of the twentieth century, is a profound distortion of Christianity and a lure. To ascribe pity and sympathy exclusively to Buddhism is not admissible, they are deeply inherent in Christianity. But it is also a distortion of Christianity to affirm spiritual love exclusively, and to separate it from the love of the soul, from attachment to a creature as a concrete being. This is anti-personalism and a denial of personality. True love proceeds from personality to personality and it is defective and distorted in abstractedly spiritual love, and in ideal *eros*-love, and in exclusive compassion directed towards an impersonal being. Love always personifies the object of love. But this may be a personification directed not towards an actual concrete being, but a personification directed towards an ideal abstract being. Real *eros* is a possibility. But erotic illusion is also possible. What is the fate in this world of authentic *eros* at the stage of falling in love? I am not now concerned with all the forms of love, or with specifically Christian love, but with love as connected with sex.

Proudhon, in whom there was nothing particularly profound, said 'Love is death'. This topic of the connection of love and death has always caused pain to those who have looked deeply into life. On the heights of the ecstasy of love is contact with the ecstasy of death. Ecstasy is in its essence a process of transcendence, it is going out beyond the limits of the everyday world. Love and death are the most important phenomena of human life and everyone even if not endowed with special gifts and without capacity for creative impulse, has experience of love and will have experience of death. Yes, and there is an experience of death even within life itself, there is a touch with the mystery of death. The greatest of all tension in human life is connected with love and death, the issue from the constraining power of everyday existence. Love conquers death, it is more powerful than death and at the same time it leads to death, it sets man on the verge of death. This is a paradox of human existence.

Love is an urge towards fullness, and in it there is a deadly sting, love is a fight for immortality and *eros* is a bearer of death. The everyday life of the objectivized world takes the keen edge off the theme of the connection of love and death. Love, personalist love, facing towards personal immortality, finds no place for itself in the everyday existence of the objectivized world. It is cast out by it, and thus placed upon the confines of death, using the word death in a wider sense than physical death. The love of Tristan and Isolde, of Romeo and Juliet leads to disaster. Platonic love is tragically without issue. The routine of social life draws love downwards, and renders it ineffective. It creates the social institution of marriage and the family, and in essence denies the rights of love as living intensity and ecstasy, and regards it as having no place in the social structure. There is nothing more absurd than the disputes about the freedom of love. The routine of social life denies the freedom of love, and regards it as immoral. And to whatever extent religion denies the freedom of love, to that extent it finds itself in the power of the routine of social life and obeys its instructions. The very statement of the question is untrue and superficial. There cannot be any other sort of love than free love; love which is necessitated, determined from without, is an absurd phrase. What ought to be denied is not the freedom of love, but the slavery of love. Love can be the very greatest slavery. The slavery is born of erotic illusion. But this has no relation at all to the social limitations upon the freedom of love, even though these limitations should have a religious character. Love cannot be, and ought not to be, renounced in the name of duty whether social or religious. That would be a slavish demand. It can be renounced only in the name of freedom or of compassion, that is in fact, in the name of another love.

On the subject of love, society can make no judgment whatever, it has no capacity for even taking note of it, and always speaks about something different. The topic of love should be entirely and radically desocialized, it is in its essence fundamentally desocialized. The family is socialized, but not love. The profound connection between love and death cannot be noted by society and by those who speak in the name of society, i.e. they do not speak opportunely or to the point. Society takes note of only the crudities of reality. And the fact that Christian theologians, teachers of the Church and official representatives of Christianity have never been able to say anything about love except commonplace trivialities and even have not noticed it, is evidence of the extent to which Christianity has been socialized in the everyday objectivized world, and adjusted to its requirements. They have spoken about sex, about sexual desire, about the sexual act, about marriage, the family and child-bearing, but not about love. What they have seen is an exclusively biological or sociological phenomenon. The subject of love has been considered more indecorous than the subject of the sexual act or the commercial side of marriage and the family.

There exists a mysterious connection of sex and family with money, with the mystery of money, but love is found outside the scheme. Such a man as St. Augustine wrote a tractate on marriage which is highly reminiscent of methods of cattle-breeding. He has not even a suspicion of the existence of love and can say nothing about that, like all Christian teachers who, in my profoundly convinced opinion, have always given utterance to immoral thoughts in their moralizing, that is to say, to thoughts which are deeply opposed to the truth of personalism. They have looked upon personality as an instrument for the service of racial and family life. It was perhaps by the Provençal troubadours that the subject of love was for the first time brought to the fore in the history of Christian Europe and they occupy an enormous tract in the field of emotional culture. Marriage and the family belong to the objectivization of human existence, whereas love belongs to eternal subjectivity.

Love has been the subject of profound discussion by three Russian thinkers, Solovyev, Rozanov and Feodorov, and they have arrived at very different conclusions. Solovyev was a platonist and his own personal erotic experience was connected with platonism. Such was his teaching about Sophia, which clashes with the doctrine of personality. But in his essay on *The Meaning of Love* perhaps the most remarkable of all his writings, he goes beyond the limits of impersonal platonism, and for the first time in the history of Christian thought connects *eros* love not with the race but with personality. To him love was connected not with child-bearing and not with the immortality of the race, but with the realization of the fullness of the life of personality and with personal immortality. Solovyev set up an opposition between love and child-bearing in distinction from all traditional doctrines of the meaning of conjugal love. The significance of love is personal, not racial. In child-bearing there takes place a disintegration of personality and the perspective of another endless racial and family life comes into view. Androgynous completeness of personality comes into being through love. Man ceases to be a dismembered, deficient creature. Love has not only an earthly meaning, but also an eternal. Love is connected with death, in the sense that it is a victory over death, and the attainment of immortality. But the question remains to what extent is Solovyev's meaning of love realizable. His personal experience of this meaning was tragic.

[229]

Rozanov is the polar opposite of Solovyev. Solovyev's doctrine of love was personalist. Death is conquered by personal love. Rozanov's doctrine of love is racial, impersonal, death is conquered by child-bearing. Rozanov is of immense importance as a critic of the Christian attitude to sex. Rozanov deifies procreative sex. He sees in sex not a mark of a fall into sin, but a benediction upon life. He professes a religion of procreation and sets it up in opposition to Christianity as the religion of death. He demands the consecration and benediction of the sexual act, as the source of life. For him the source of death is not in sex, in sex is the source of victory over death. Solovyev was conscious of the sinful element in sex. Rozanov had no feeling of the kind at all. He wants to return to ancient paganism, to Judaism which gave its blessing to procreation. Christianity established a conflict between personality and procreative sex and Rozanov becomes an enemy of Christianity. For him no problem of personality exists, so to speak. A sharpened consciousness of personality arouses hostility to procreative sex. The principal problem becomes not the problem of procreation but the problem of death. But it must be remembered that the teachers of historical Christianity always have justified conjugal love exclusively by child-bearing. Sex, the sexual act, has been under their curse as concupiscence, but the result of the sexual act—child-bearing—has had their blessing. Rozanov rightly saw hypocrisy in this and he exposed and condemned it. In any case the traditional Christian teaching about love, if indeed this can be called love, has been exclusively teaching about racial, procreative love. Love not only has no personal meaning, but a personal meaning of love is explained as immoral. Here there is a point of contact with Rozanov, but Rozanov demands consistency and sincerity: if there is a blessing for child-bearing, then there ought to be a blessing for the source of child-bearing also.

Feodorov takes a position distinct from both Solovyev and Rozanov. Feodorov is above all things grieved by death; he cannot reconcile himself to death, even it be that of one single creature. He calls men to a titanic struggle against death. In this respect there is no-one to be compared with him. He wishes to conquer death, not by personal *eros*, and not by personal immortality, like Solovyev, and not by racial *eros*, not by the procreation of new generations, but by the resurrection of the dead, not by passive waiting for the resurrection, but by active resurrection. He wants to convert erotic energy into revivifying energy; he wants a switching over of erotic energy. He believes in the possibility of turning time back, he believes in the power of man not over the future only, but also over the past. Resurrection is active change of the past. Feodorov was not a philosopher of erotics as in their different ways both Solovyev and Rozanov were, he was filled with a compassionate love for the dead. His appeal is not for racial collective procreation but for racial collective resurrection. But all three pondered deeply over love and death, over the slavery of sex and the slavery of death.

Profound contradictions in human life are connected with the surge of sex. Man experiences the degrading slavery of sex. Sex torments man and gives rise to many misfortunes in human life. But at the same time the intensity of life is connected with sex. Sexual energy is life energy and may be the source of the urge of creative life. A sexless creature is a creature of lowered life energy. Sexual energy may be sublimated, it may be detached from specifically sexual functions and be directed towards creativeness. This is even one of the ways of overcoming the slavery of sex. Erotic energy can be a source of creativeness. With sex, which is a sign of deficiency in man, is connected a particular longing. And this longing is always stronger in youth. At the same time, sex lends itself to terrible profanation, the whole of human nature is profaned through sex. The greatest triviality may be connected with sex. Not only the physical aspect of sex, but also the psychical is profaned, erotics are profaned, the very words of love become intolerable, it is with difficulty that they are pronounced. Here the slavery of sex takes the form of grim triviality and superficiality. Sex is dreadful in the sphere of the routine of ordinary life. It is dreadful in the bourgeois world and is connected with the power of money over human life. The slavery of sex is connected with the slavery of money.

In woman's nature sex is deeper and more complete than in man's nature. The slavery of sex is connected with the power of the female principle over human life. Woman is usually inclined to slavery and at the same time inclined to enslave. In man's nature sex is partial, in

[231]

woman's nature sex is complete. Therefore the slavery of sex finds much stronger expression in woman's nature. The realization of personality, which is expressed more in man's nature than in woman's, does not denote the denial or weakening of the creative life energy of sex itself, but indicates victory over the slavery of sex, the sublimation and transformation of sex. The complete and final victory over this slavery means the attainment of androgynous wholeness which by no means indicates sexlessness. Erotics play an immense part in creative natures. The universalization of erotics, the final substitution of erotics for ethics is not favourable to the principle of personality, to the dignity of personality, to freedom of spirit, and may be a subtle form of slavery. The defence of personality and freedom presupposes the ethical principle, activity of spirit. Erotics may mean passivity of spirit, the domination of the soul-body principle over the spiritual. But in what are we to find the meaning of the very life of sex, in what is the meaning of conjugal union?

The whole erotic life of man consists in conflicts which in the objectivized world cannot be finally overcome. Freud was absolutely right in affirming disharmony and conflict of the sexual life. Man suffers from traumas connected with sex. He experiences torturing conflicts between the unconscious sexual life and the censorship of society, the general attitude of the social body. The conflicts are both sexual, connected with sex, and erotic, connected with love. But with Freud the problem of eros-love is left hidden, and this is due to the limitations of his general view of life. The conflicts go on in the depth, the metaphysical depth of human existence. Sex in earthly human existence already denotes ejection into the external, objectivization, exteriorization and the breaking up of the whole being of man. By mighty unconscious attraction sex shackles man to the objectivized world in which determinism holds sway, and necessity, and determination not from within but from without, from human nature which has gone out to an object. In this lies the mystery of sex. The liberation of man is at the same time emancipation from the slavery of sex as part of the constraining world of objects. Only the object world can be compulsive, and sex is compulsive. The illusion to which man is subject consists in this that he is ready to see his freedom in the satisfaction of sexual desire at the same time as he is in a state of compulsion. Sex is the impersonal in man, the power of the 'common', the racial; love alone can be personal. It is not sexuality which is personal but erotics. Solovyev and Weininger understood this. The racial and impersonal in the sexual sense has a profound connection with the racial and impersonal in the logical and metaphysical sense. Man lives through a fundamental conflict between his sex and his personality. Sex in its manifestation encroaches upon the dignity of personality, it makes it the plaything of impersonal forces, and degrades man. Hence comes the shame which is connected with sex. This shame increases with the stature of personality and personal consciousness. The racial life of sex makes personality a means to the procreation of other personalities and personal satisfaction shows itself as an illusion, necessary for the life of the race but not for personality itself.

When sex finds an outlet for itself outside the procreation of other people, future generations, it is easily perverted into lewdness and seriously impairs the wholeness of personality. Functions which are partial are directed against the whole organism of man. There are sexual conflicts, they arise before erotic conflicts which are concerned with a higher sphere of man's existence. The phenomenon of *eros*-love is to be found at a lower level in the conflict with the impersonal life of sex, but at a higher level in relation to objectivized marriage, to the life of the family as a social institution. There exists a slavery of man to sex and a slavery of man to the family and both the one slavery and the other are the outcome of objectivization, the objectivization in the world of social routine. Man, it seems, is overwhelmed and at times crushed by a complicated network of conflicts. Nature enslaves man, and society enslaves him. And emancipation cannot be sought in a transition from nature to society, and from society to nature. Disorganized sex, which is given over to the sway of natural inclinations may be the disintegration of man and the ruin of personality. While socially organized sex, which is subjected to limitations and censorship creates new forms of slavery.

In the world of objectivization, in the world of social daily life the organization of sex in the social institution of the family seems to be inevitable. The forms which the family assumes are not of course

[233]

perpetual, they may change very much, and they are highly dependent upon the economic structure of society. This is analogous to the organization of society in the state. The family frequently enslaves personality and only the approximation of the family to the type of brotherhood can reduce this enslavement to the minimum. But at the same time the family has shown itself capable of working out a human type and has defended man from the sole and undivided power of the state. Neither the life of sex in the biological sense of the word, nor the life of the family in the sociological sense of the word, has any direct connection with the question of *eros*-love and it does not even pose this question. Love, as has already been said, does not belong to the world of objectivization, of objectivized nature, nor does it belong to objectivized society, it comes, as it were, from a different world and it is a break-through into this world; it belongs to infinite subjectivity, to the world of freedom.

And, therefore, a profound conflict is possible between love and the family, a conflict which is but a manifestation of the conflict between personality and society, between freedom and determination. The meaning of love can only be personal, it cannot be social and it remains concealed so far as society is concerned. A tyranny has been connected with the forms of the family which is still more terrible than the tyranny connected with the forms of the state. The hierarchically organized authoritarian family tortures and mutilates human personality. And a movement of emancipation directed against such forms of the family has a profound personalist meaning, it is a conflict waged on behalf of the dignity of human personality. The literature of the world has an immense significance in the fight for the freedom of human feelings, but not of sexual passions, as is slanderously said of it. This has been a fight for personality, for freedom as against determination. Freedom indeed is always spiritual. In the world of social objectivization, there must be more insistence upon the free forms of the family and less upon the authoritarian forms, less upon the hierarchical. The family also cannot be Christian, just as the state cannot be Christian, just as there can be nothing sacred in the world of social objectivization. The Gospel certainly demands freedom from slavery to the family.

In the history of the world, horror surrounds love. This horror is twofold, it is horror at the relation of the world to love, at the torture to which it is exposed from the side of society, and horror which love itself brings into the world, its inward horror. It has a social and a metaphysical source. The social horror of love which is due to the despotism of the hierarchical organization of society, may be if not entirely overcome at least reduced to a minimum. But the metaphysical horror of love is not to be surmounted in this world. There is something death-dealing in love. *Eros*-love has a tendency to turn into a universal principle of life, either to subject things to itself or to crowd out everything else. And, therefore, *eros*-love is not only the search for fullness and intensity of life, but also a compression and a decrease in the richness of life. There is despotism and slavery in love.

And most despotic of all is the love of woman, which demands everything for itself. For this reason it clashes with the principle of personality. The connection between love and jealousy gives it a demoniacal character, and this is most powerful in women, who can turn into furies. The metaphysical horror of love lies not only in the fact that there is in the world so much unshared love, nor even in the fact that there is so much love which cannot be shared (and this is much more painful), it is within the very love which is mutually shared, in what is known as happy love. This is connected with the mystery of personality, with the profound difference between female and male nature, with the lack of correspondence between the first fine rapture of love and its realization in everyday life, with its mysterious link with death. But the horror and tragedy of love have their edge blunted by the rationalization of life, by the embosoming of human existence in everyday social life, that is to say by the triumph of the world of objects over the subject world. True love, which is always a rare flower, agonizes and disappears out of the world, the world has become too abject for it. The drama of love has reached intensity as a result of hindrances which have arisen.

Today everything has become easy, but less tense and less significant. It is not a deep, but a superficial emancipation that has been reached. This is a paradox of love in the world, one of the manifestations of the paradoxical nature of freedom in the world. Freedom presupposes hindrances and conflict. Without spiritual exertion it readily becomes insipid and inane. Marriage, in its social projection, has always been closely connected with economics and not infrequently had a compulsorily commercial character. Marriage has been very far from being a sacrament. Nowadays marriage has acquired not a compulsorily commercial, but a freely commercial character. This is part of that rationalization of life which is taking place in every sphere.

The relation of love to sex in the narrower sense of the word, to sexual union, is very confused and contradictory. The stamp of the Fall of man very clearly lies upon sexual union, it is seen in everything, and it embarrasses man and disquiets him. But man endeavours to give meaning to and to justify sexual union. The simple satisfaction of a physiological necessity, like the process of nourishment, does not refer especially to human life and poses no question of its meaning. It refers to the animal life of man and raises the question of the limitation and subjugation of the animal nature.

Man has thought out three ways of providing himself with a meaning for sexual union. Child-bearing, the continuance of the race, gives a meaning to sexual union. This is the most widespread and the most virtuous point of view in the realm of everyday social life. In the face of the personalist scale of values this point of view is immoral and hypocritical in spite of its virtuous appearance. Virtue is often immoral. It is immoral to regard personality exclusively as a means of serving the race, and to exploit personal inclinations and feelings for the sake of racial ends. The totalitarian states have gone to the limit of shamelessness, they wish to organize the sexual life of men in the interests of race and state, as they organize cattle-breeding. It is hypocritical to assert that man is attracted to sexual union for the sake of the birth of children when a like end may be merely the result of reflex action, and sexual union has a meaning in itself.

To this is opposed the point of view that the meaning of sexual union lies in the immediate satisfaction and pleasure which it provides. This point of view also is immoral (though it is not hypocritical too) because it makes man a slave of his lower nature and clashes with the value of personality as free spirit. There is a third point of view: the meaning of sexual union is to be found in the union with the loved one, in the attainment of completion from this union. This

[236]

meaning is personal and the only admissible and morally and spiritually justifiable one, and it presupposes that sex is characterized in terms of spirituality. Paradoxically it might be said that only such sexual union is justifiable as means a striving for the 'personal happiness' of the lovers, although it is impossible to believe in any sort of 'happiness'.

The meaning and justification of marriage are to be found only in love. Marriage without love is immoral. The question of duty to the children has nothing in common with this, it is another question altogether. Two processes are necessary in dealing with the matter of sex and *eros*-love: external liberation from oppression and slavery to society and an authoritarian interpretation of the family on the one hand, and inward asceticism without which man becomes a slave to himself and to his lower nature on the other. All the types of love may become slavery and captivity to man, both *eros*-love and compassionate love (for example Prince Myshkin in Dostoyevsky). But *eros*-love should be united with compassionate love; otherwise it becomes an enslaver. It is only when it is united with freedom that love does not enslave. The meaning of love is always to be found in personification and idealization even when it stands in relation to principles and ideas and not to living beings. For example, love of one's country is personification. And of course love towards God presupposes personification. At its highest love is always the vision of the face of the loved one in God.

3. B. THE AESTHETIC LURE AND SLAVERY. BEAUTY, ART, AND NATURE

The aesthetic lure and slavery, which reminds us of magic, does not grip the broad masses of mankind over much. It shows itself for the most part among the cultured *élite*. There are people who live under the spell of beauty and art. This may be due to people's spiritual make-up, it may be original, and it may be the result of imitation and fashion, of infection by a certain state of their environment. At certain periods of time aesthetic fashion makes its appearance. When I say that aestheticism belongs principally to a cultured élite, I do not mean to say by this that the life of the masses of the people has no aestheticism of its own. Aestheticism is even more inherent in the masses of the people than in the bourgeoisie, but it has a different character and it is not turned into the attitude of the aesthete, which is a mark of cultural decline.

The lure and slavery of aestheticism always indicate the weakening and even the destruction of the value of personality, the displacement of the existential centre of personality, and the turning of one side of man into the whole. Man makes himself a slave of his partial states, of the emotional charms which take possession of him. On this terrain is created that type of aesthete which is possible only in a period of refinement of culture, and its detachment from the laborious and sterner foundations of life. Aesthetic values become the only ones and take the place of all the others.

Moral, intellectual, religious values can be replaced by aesthetic. In such a case the aesthete himself is seldom aesthetic. Aestheticism exists in morals, in learning, in religion, even politics may be determined by aesthetic values. Aestheticism in religion commonly assumes the form of the exclusive predominance of its liturgical aspect. Psychologically this means that a man surrenders himself to a state of stupefaction. Aestheticism in morals replaces the relation of a concrete being to concrete personality by a relation to beauty and to personal attractiveness. Aestheticism in philosophy is interested not so much in truth as in a certain emotional condition which calls forth either a harmonious or an inharmonious arrangement of feelings, depending upon the aesthetic type. Aestheticism in politics is interested not so much in justice and freedom as in emotional states which are aroused either by an idealized past or by an idealized future, and by the sharpness of the antithesis. It is connected with a mounting experience of hatred or of love.

The aesthetic seduction is the lure of passivity, the loss of capacity for activity of spirit. Even conflict in aesthetic projection may be re-incarnated in passive repulsion, and be unaccompanied by spiritual activity. The aesthetic type is the type of the passive man, who finds pleasure in passivity and lives by reaction; he is a consumer, not a creator. The aesthete may be attached to an extreme form of revolution or to an extreme form of counter-revolution—it makes no difference, he will always denote passivity and the substitution of passive aesthetic emotions for the work of conscience, which is always active. The great artist creators have never been aesthetes, even when they have had an acute and extreme aesthetic attitude to life, as for example in the case of Tolstoy.

The creative artistic act is certainly not an aesthetic act, only the consequences of a creative act can be aesthetic. The aesthetic lure makes a man an observer not an actor. And here we meet with the remarkable paradox of aestheticism. It may be thought that people who have an exclusively aesthetic attitude to life, are in subjectivity and not in objectivity. This only indicates the uncertainty and the ambiguity of the terminology.

The aesthetic lure denotes just this, that everything is converted into an object of contemplation, that the activity of the subject is absent. If the aesthete lives in a world of his feelings and emotions, this by no means shows that he is living in the existential world of subjectivity, in the world of spirit, freedom and creative activity. On the contrary, in the spiritual make-up of the aesthete, feelings and emotions are objectivized, and thrown out into the external. An exclusively aesthetic orientation to life enfeebles the sense of reality, and leads to this, that whole regions of reality fail to be taken into account. But this comes to pass, not as the effect of the activity but of the passivity of the subject. The subject takes the line of least resistance, reacts passively towards the thing that was not created by him, and has become an object to him. A clear-sighted distinction among realities presupposes activity in the subject.

The aesthetic lure denotes exclusive interest in 'how' and not in 'what', that is to say, in actual fact it means indifference to reality. This is slavery to oneself, with the loss of the reality of oneself. This is confinement within oneself together with casting oneself out into the external. The aesthete is by no means sure of his own reality, he is sure only of his passive aesthetic emotions. It could not even be said that the aesthete lives by the acceptance of beauty and the emotional excitement which beauty arouses; he is frequently indifferent to true and most real beauty, and lives by sham forms of beauty and aesthetic illusions. The lure and slavery of aestheticism inevitably brings in its train indifference to the truth, and this is its most horrifying result. People of this spiritual make-up do not seek for truth, they live under spells, which do not allow the knowledge of truth. And when man began to search for truth, he was already saved. The search for truth is activity not passivity, it is a struggle not a state of swoon.

The seduction of aestheticism is akin to the seduction of eroticism. They are intertwined with one another. Man falls under the sway of aesthetic illusions as he falls under the sway of erotic illusions. The aesthetic lure makes man a slave of the cosmos, it places him outside the logos. Personality is linked with the logos and not with the cosmos, with meaning and not with captivating natural objectivity: it pre-supposes not only *eros* but ethos also. For this reason the aesthetic lure means depersonalization. Aesthetes are by their spiritual make-up sharply-defined individualists, but they are not persons. Personality is resistance to the seductions of deluding forms of beauty. The aesthetic lure always looks backward instead of forward, such is the result of passivity, of a life which is lived by passive reactions. In the reception of beauty, the object, which is the result of the past, is always an illusory element. But it must be stated that the aesthete by no means always worships at the shrine of beauty, he may, following a fashion, even deny beauty and by no meas connect his aesthetic emotions with beauty. The aesthetic lure and slavery always lead to dissolution and decline in a literary and artistic milieu. By people who are consumers rather than creators, art is surrounded by a repellent atmosphere of snobbery which witnesses to the slavery of man, and to the loss of freedom of spirit. This is a consequence of spiritual complications and refinements, of the discovered possibility of living by passive repulsions, while considering that that life is higher and more significant than the life of everyday people, of the human masses. Here a strange self-affirmation accompanies the loss of self.

But the existence of the aesthetic lure means the rejection of true beauty less than the existence of the erotic lure and slavery means a rejection of true love. It must even be said decisively that the beautiful is more characteristic of the perfection of the world and man, than the good. A finite purpose is much more characterized as the beautiful than as the good. The good relates to the way more than to the goal. Good is the correlative of evil, and always witnesses to division and conflict.

But beauty has decidedly nothing in common with the attitude of the aesthete. I am inclined even to think that the sense of beauty has been atrophied in the aesthete. Beauty is more harmonious than goodness. In goodness there is always disharmony, there is imperfection of nature. A transfigured world is beauty. Beauty is victory over the burden and ugliness of the world. Through beauty there takes place a break-through into a transfigured world, into another world than ours. And this break-through takes place in every creative act of art and in every artistic reception of that creative act. And, therefore, the meaning of art lies in the fact that it is the anticipation of the transfiguration of the world, that it is liberation from the ugliness and burden of reality.

The liberating significance of art lies precisely in its unlikeness to this repellent and ugly life of ours, this life fettered by necessity. And this unlikeness is in art, which in its own way reveals the truth about life, the most grievous and torturing truth. What is dreadful and tormenting in art is by no means what is dreadful and tormenting in life. What is ugly in art is by no means what is ugly in life. The ugly may become artistically perfect and evoke aesthetic emotion, and not repulsion. For example the ugliness in Guyau and in Gogol. This is the mystery of the creative act which distinguishes art from reality. With this is connected the katharsis of tragedy about which Aristotle taught. Tragic suffering has a liberating and purifying significance because between our sufferings and tragedy and the sufferings and tragedy in the productions of art lies a transfiguring, creative artistic act. Art is already a transfiguration of our life, in it there is already none of the burden, the fettering, the ugliness. which degrade our everyday life. We find in it a passing over to another world, to another plane of existence, we find idealism which, as it were, anticipates a new reality. Art is not a reflexion of the world of ideas in the world of sense as idealistic philosophy has supposed. Art is creative transfiguration, not yet real transfiguration, but an anticipation of that transfiguration. The beauty of a dance, a poem, a symphony, or a picture enters into eternal life. Art is not passive but active, and in this sense theurgic.

Faguet once said that we find enjoyment in sufferings represented in a tragedy because it gives us joy that the tragic misfortune did not happen to ourselves. This is witty. But in its light way it puts the truth that suffering in a tragedy sets us free from the suffering of our own lives and transfers us to another plane of existence. Art liberates from slavery to everyday life. Art is not levity, not man's throwing aside of difficulty. Difficulty and even torment are associated with it, but of an entirely different sort from those of everyday life. Art can enslave, as happens in aesthetic seduction in the case of the aesthete. And art can set free. Beauty can be a victory over the world instead of captivity to it. So it is in true art and in true beauty. Fullness of beauty corresponds with the completeness of the nature of man. While dissipated-beauty on the other hand, beauty which is not integral, but broken up, is connected with dismemberment and not wholeness in human nature. But personality means an assembling of wholeness, and it bears a relation to integral transfiguring beauty.

In books on aesthetics the question has often been deliberated—is beauty objective, is aesthetic beauty an illusion or reality? To put the question in such a way as that is in my view due to a wrong use of the terms objective and subjective. The reception of beauty is not a passive reception of any objectivized world order. The objectivized world in itself knows nothing of beauty. It contains a mechanization which is opposed to beauty. Beauty is a break-through in this world, a liberation from its determinism. The reception of beauty in nature is not a passive reaction and it presupposes a creative act on the part of man. Beauty, like truth, is in subjectivity not in objectivity. In objectivity in itself there is no beauty of any sort, no truth, no value. This is far from meaning that beauty is subjective in the sense of illusory, to use the terminology of traditional aesthetics. Subjectivity emphatically means reality, it is objectivity which is illusion. Everything which is objectivized and is objective is from the deepest point of view, illusory. Objectivity is alienation and abstraction, determinism and impersonalism. But beauty cannot belong to the world of determinism, it is liberation from determinism, it is breathing freely. Objective beauty is just an aesthetic illusion. You cannot interpret in a naïvely realistic sense the relation between beauty and the subject who receives and experiences the beauty. Beauty does not enter into man from the objective world. Beauty is a break-through in the objectivized world, a transfiguration of the world, a victory over ugliness and over the burden of world necessity.

Man is active here, not passive. The beauty of the cosmos is connected with a creative act of man. Between objectivized nature and man stands the creative act of man. The great creative artists who have made poems, dramas, novels, symphonies, pictures and statues have always been active, and conquerors of the burden and resistance of matter. The seduction and slavery of aesthetic passivity comes not from creators but from consumers. Beauty is a break-through, it lends itself to spiritual conflict. But this break-through is not into the eternal immobile world of ideas, but into the transfigured world which is attained by human creativeness, to the world of non-being, not to 'being' but to freedom. There is in the world a process of conflict between chaos and cosmos, the world is not given to us as a beautiful harmonious cosmos. The beauty of the human form, that summit of the cosmic process, is not a fixed quality, it changes, it is even active conflict. Beauty presupposes the existence of chaos and victory over chaos. There is no beauty of cosmos without the background of chaos. Without that there is no tragedy, no climax of human creativeness, no Don Quixote, no dramas of Shakespeare, no Faust, no novels of Dostoyevsky. There is a double victory of man over chaos, an aesthetic victory and a mechanical, a victory in freedom and a victory in necessity. Only the first victory is linked with beauty. But beauty is not contemplation only, beauty always speaks of creativeness, of creative victory and conflict with the slavery of the world. It speaks of the co-operation of man, of the joint action of man and God. The problem of objectivization in art is very complex, and this complexity arises partly from confusion of terminology. What is the relation of objectivization to the aesthetic lure and slavery? With this is also connected the problem of classicism and romanticism. There is a slavery of each of these.

Classicism and romanticism refer not only to art and aesthetic appreciation, but also to the whole spiritual type and general view of

[243]

life. The distinction between classicism and romanticism in art is relative and conditional. There is a romantic element in classical art and there is a classical element in romantic art. The great creations of art cannot in fact be referred either to the classical or the romantic. Shakespeare, Goethe, Tolstoy cannot be recognized as either classical or romantic. What interests me at the moment is the philosophical problem of 'classical' and 'romantic' which is connected with the relation of subject and object, with subjective and objective. Classical art judged itself to be objective art which had reached objective perfection, while romantic art has been considered subjective and as not reaching objective perfection. Here the word objectivity is used in a sense almost identical with perfection. But both 'classical' and 'romantic' may be a lure. The creative act which produces a work of art may aspire towards perfect objectivization torn right away from the creative subject. It is presupposed that it is possible to attain perfection within the finite, and that the created product can be entirely completed. Both the created product and the creating subject are subordinated to a hierarchical objective order.

The lure of classicism is one of the forms of man's slavery. The spirit is alienated from itself, the subjective goes out into the object-ivized order, the infinite is shut up in the finite. Romanticism rose in rebellion against this lure of classicism. Romanticism means the breaking apart of subjective and objective; the subject does not wish to be a part of the object, the infinity of the subjective world is revealed. Perfection is not attained in the objectivized world, in the finite. The created product always speaks of a greater than itself, in it is a break-through into infinity. Romanticism in its torments is a struggle to set the subject free; a struggle for the liberation of man from the strength of the fetters which hold him in the finite forms of the objectivized world, from the sway of intellectualism which shackles him to a false idea of objective being, to the 'common'. But romanticism itself may become a lure and a slavery. The liberation of the subject and the struggle for the value of the very creative life of the subject, the creating existential subject, constitute the truth of romanticism. But subjectivity can become the shutting up of a man in himself, the loss of communion with reality, the mounting up of artistic emotionalism, slavery of the individual to himself. Infinite

[244]

subjectivity may be a revelation of reality in the existential sense of the word, or it may be illusoriness and submergence in a lie.

The romantics were often distinguished by falsity, ideally exalted falsity, and it means that they were in a condition of slavery to self. Romanticism is easily liable to aesthetic illusions. This is the reverse side of romanticism. The cure comes not so much from classicism, which means reaction, but from realism, which turns to truthfulness, to living truth. The Bible is not classical nor is it romantic, it is realist in the religious sense of the word. And realism, as has already been made clear, is not the same thing as objectivity. The Bible is a book of revelation because there is no objectivization in it, no alienation of man from himself. Every revelation is absolutely outside the process of objectivization. Objectivization is the concealment of revelation. For this reason a false classicism is the concealment of realities. Knowledge of reality does not permit perfection in the finite. The whole of Russian nineteenth-century literature lies outside classicism and romanticism, it is realist in the deepest sense of the word, and it witnesses to the human subjects' wrestling of spirit, to the tragedy of creativeness which issues in objectivization, it is in search of the higher creative life. In this lies its humanity and its greatness.

In all its successive spheres classicism is inhuman, it desires a non-human realm in art, in philosophy, in the state and in society. Greek tragedy, the most perfect of all human creations is not classicism. A classical reaction commonly means the predominance of technique over creativeness, the crushing of creativeness by formalism. And this cannot but evoke a protest from creative subjectivity, a break-through into infinity. Human creativeness is subject to a rhythm which varies the creative direction, classicism is changed for romanticism, romanticism gives place to realism, realism is replaced by a classical reaction, the classical reaction calls forth a revolt of subjectivity and so on. Fullness is achieved by man with difficulty. His life makes its way through winding and negative reactions. Achieved harmony is but relative and temporary, it is replaced by new disharmonies and strife.

Man is constantly exposed to lures and falls into slavery. And he has a capacity for waging a heroic war of liberation. Man loses himself in objectivization and he loses himself in subjectivity which

[245]

leads to no result, that is, he passes over from a pseudo-classicism to a pseudo-romanticism. He is in search of beauty, real beauty and is seduced by false beauty, illusory beauty. From a false objective intellectualism he moves to a false subjective emotionalism. He has invented a mighty technique which may be an instrument for the transfiguration of life, and this mighty technique enslaves him and subjects every side of human life to itself. Art is enslaved by technique, the technique of perfected industry. Beauty agonizes and disappears from an objectivized world. Art is corrupted and replaced by something which is not like art.

Such is the tragedy of human destiny. But the eternal creative spirit rebels against this state of the world and of man. Objectivity arouses the reaction of subjectivity, subjectivity in its refinement passes into new objectivity. Only that spirit liberates which is outside this antithesis of objective and subjective. And the problem of personality is aggravated.

Man has to realize personality. Personality is spirit, free spirit and the link between man and God. It is a link of man with God which is outside objectivization, and outside the false submergence of man in his own closed circle. Through it is revealed infinity and eternity and authentic beauty.

PART IV

1. THE SPIRITUAL LIBERATION OF MAN. VICTORY OVER FEAR AND DEATH

M an is in a state of servitude. He frequently does not notice that he is a slave, and sometimes he loves it. But man also aspires to be set free. It would be a mistake to think that the average man loves freedom. A still greater mistake would be to suppose that freedom is an easy thing. Freedom is a difficult thing. It is easier to remain in slavery. Love of freedom and aspiration towards liberation are an indication that some upward progress has already been achieved by man. They witness to the fact that inwardly man is already ceasing to be a slave. There is a spiritual principle in man which is not dependent upon the world and is not determined by the world. The liberation of man is the demand, not of nature, nor of reason, nor of society, as is often supposed, but of spirit. Man is not only spirit, he is of a complex make-up, he is also an animal, he is also a phenomenon of the material world, but man is spirit as well. Spirit is freedom, and freedom is the victory of spirit.

But it would be a mistake to think that the slavery of man is always the outcome of the power of the animal and material side of man. On the spiritual side of man itself there may be grievous loss of health, division, exteriorization, there may be self-estrangement of spirit, loss of freedom, captivity of spirit. In this lies all the complexity of the problem of freedom and slavery in man. The spirit is exteriorized, thrown out into the external, and acts upon man as necessity, and it returns to itself within, i.e. to freedom. Hegel understood one side of this process of the spirit, but he did not understand it all; he did understand what is perhaps the most important point. A man who is free should feel himself to be not on the circumference of the objectivized world, but at the centre of the spiritual world. Liberation is being present at the centre and not at the circumference, in real subjectivity and not in ideal objectivity.

But spiritual concentration, to which all the precepts of the spiritual life summon us, may be twofold in its results. It gives spiritual strength, and independence of the manifold which is a torment to man. But it may effect a narrowing of consciousness, it may lead to possession by one single idea. In that case spiritual liberation is turned into a new form of seduction and slavery. Those who tread the spiritual path are aware of this. Liberation never provides a simple escape from reality or the rejection of reality. Spiritual liberation is conflict. Spirit is not an abstract idea, it does not belong to the category of universals. Not only every man, but a dog, a cat, or an insect is of greater existential value, than an abstract idea, or than a common universal.

Spiritual liberation is accompanied by transition not to the abstract but to the concrete. The Gospel is evidence of this. In that lies the personalism of the Gospel. Spiritual liberation is victory over the power of what is foreign. In this is the meaning of love. But man easily becomes a slave, without noticing it. He is set free, because there is in him a spiritual principle, a capacity which is not determined from without. But so complex is human nature and so entangled man's existence, that he may fall out of one form of slavery into another, he may fall into abstract spirituality, into the determining power of a common idea. Spirit is unique, integral, and is present in each one of its acts. But man is not spirit, he only possesses spirit and therefore in man's spiritual acts themselves, dismemberment, abstraction and rebirth of the spirit are possible. The final liberation is possible only through a bond between the human spirit and the Spirit of God. Spiritual liberation is always a turning to a profounder depth than the spiritual principle in man, it is a turning to God. But even the turning to God may be impaired by a malady of the spirit and be converted into idolatry. Therefore constant purification is necessary. God can act only upon freedom, in freedom and through freedom. He does not act upon necessity, in necessity and through necessity. He does not act in the laws of nature or in the laws of the state. Therefore, the doctrine of Providence and the doctrine of Grace require revision, the traditional doctrines are not admissible.

The spiritual liberation of man is the realization of personality in man. It is the attainment of wholeness. And at the same time it is unwearied conflict. The fundamental question of the realization of personality is not a question of victory over the determinism of matter, that is one side of the subject only. The fundamental question is the question of an entire victory over slavery. The world is evil, not because matter is in it, but because it is not free, because it is enslaved. The troubles of man's life in the material world are not due to the fact that matter is evil, they have arisen from a wrong tendency of spirit. The fundamental antithesis is not between spirit and matter, but between freedom and slavery. The spiritual victory is not only victory over the elementary dependence of man upon matter. Still more difficult is the victory over deceptive illusions which precipitate man into slavery in its least recognizable form. The evil in human existence appears not only in plain view, but also in deceptive forms of good. Antichrist can seduce through a deceptive likeness to the form of Christ. Thus indeed it happens within the Christian world. Many universal common abstract ideas are evil in an exalted form. I have written about this throughout this whole book.

It is not enough to say that one must be set free from sin. Sin not only wears a primitive aspect and entices us, it is possible to be possessed by the idea of sin, the lure of a false conflict with the sin which is to be seen on all sides in life is also possible. It is not only real sin which enslaves man, but also possession by the idea of sin which corrodes the whole life. This is one of the servile perversions of the spiritual life. The slavery which is felt by man as violence from without is to be hated less passionately than the slavery which seduces man and which he has come to love. A demoniacal character attaches to everything relative which is transformed into the absolute, to everything finite which is transformed into the infinite, to everything profane which is transformed into the sacred, to everything human which is transformed into the divine. Man's relation to the state, to civilization, and even to the church becomes demoniacal. There is a church in the existential sense, which is community and fellowship, and there are churches which are objectivizations and social institutions. When the church, as objectivization and a social institution is regarded as holy and impeccable, then the creation of an idol and the slavery of man begin. This is a perversion of the religious life and a demoniacal element within religious life. Human life is mutilated by imaginary, exaggerated, exalted passions, religious national, social, and by degrading fears. In this soil the enslavement of man springs up. Man possesses the capacity for turning love for God and for the highest ideas, into the most terrible slavery.

The victory of spirit over slavery is in the first place a victory over fear, over the fear of life and the fear of death. In fear-anguish, Kirkegaard sees the fundamental religious phenomenon, and a token of the significance of the inward life. The Bible says that the fear of the Lord is the beginning of wisdom. And at the same time fear is slavery. How are these to be reconciled? In this world man experiences the fear of life and the fear of death. This fear is weakened and dulled in the realm of everyday life. The organization of ordinary day to day life aims at establishing security, although, of course, it cannot completely overcome the dangers of life and death. But submerged in the realm of everyday life, absorbed in its interests, man deserts the deeps, and the disquietude that belongs to the deeps. Heidegger says truly that *Das Mann* takes the edge off the tragic in life. But everything is inconsistent and twofold. Everyday life dulls the fears which are linked with the deeps of life and death, but establishes other fears of its own under the power of which man lives the whole time, fears linked with the affairs of this world. In actual fact, fear determines the greater part of political movements, it determines also the socialized forms of religion. Anxious solicitude which Heidegger regards as belonging to the structure of existence, inevitably passes into fear, into everyday fear, which must be distinguished from transcendental fear.

Fear can be a more exalted condition than heedless submersion in everyday things. But fear, fear of all sorts, is all the same a form of human slavery. Perfect love casteth out fear. Fearlessness is the highest state. Slavish fear hinders the revelation of truth. Fear gives birth to lies. Man thinks to protect himself from danger by falsehood, it is upon lies, and not upon truth that he establishes the realm of everyday life. The world of objectivization is penetrated through and through by useful lies, while truth, on the other hand, is made plain to the fearless. Knowledge of truth demands a victory over fear, it requires the virtue of fearlessness, and courage in the face of danger. The highest degree of fear, which is experienced and overcome, may become a source of knowledge. But the knowledge of truth is bestowed not by fear, but by victory over fear. The fear of death is the limit of fear. It may be a base everyday fear, but it may be a lofty transcendental fear. But the fear of death denotes the slavery of man, a slavery well known to every man. Man is the slave of death and triumph over the fear of death is the greatest triumph over fear in general.

And here there is to be noted an astounding inconsistency in man in relation to the fear of death. Man fears not only his own death, but also the death of other people. And at the same time man fairly easily makes up his mind to murder, and it would appear fears least of all the death which comes to pass as the result of his committing murder. This is the problem of crime, which is always, if not actual, at least potential, murder. Crime is linked with murder, murder is linked with death. Murder is committed not only by gangsters; murder is committed in an organized way and upon a colossal scale by the state, by those who are in possession of power, or by those who have only just seized it. And, mark, in all these murders, the horror of death shews itself dulled and blunted, even almost entirely absent, although the horror of the death ought to be doubled—as being horror of death in general, and horror of the death which is the result of murder having been committed as well. Capital punishment is ceasing to be taken as murder, so is death in war, and especially, it is ceasing to be taken as a death which arouses horror. And this is a consequence of the objectivization of human existence.

In the objectivized world, all values are perverted. Man instead of being a resuscitator, a conqueror of death, has become a murderer, a sower of death. And he kills, in order to create a life in which there will be less fear. Man kills from fear; at the root of every murder, whether committed by an individual person or by the state, lies fear and slavery. Fear and slavery always have fateful results. If man were to succeed in triumphing over slavish fear, he would cease to murder. From fear of death man sows death, as a result of feeling a slave, he desires to dominate. Domination is always constrained to kill. The state is always subject to fear and therefore it is constrained to kill. It has no desire to wrestle against death. Men in authority are very much like gangsters.

I know of no more lofty moral consciousness in its attitude to death than that of Feodorov. Feodorov grieved over the death of every being and demanded that man should become a resuscitator. But grieving over death, since it has become active, is not the fear of death. A resuscitator conquers the fear of death. Personalism does not put the question of death and immortality in exactly the same way as Feodorov. Feodorov is right in saying that the fight against death is not only a personal matter, it is a 'public undertaking'. It is not only my death, but the death of all, which sets me a problem. Victory not only over the fear of death but over death itself, is the realization of personality. The realization of personality is impossible in the finite, it presupposes the infinite, not quantitative infinity but qualitative, i.e. eternity. The individual person dies, since he is born in the generic process, but personality does not die, since it is not born in the generic process. Victory over the fear of death is the victory of spiritual personality over the biological individual. But this does not mean the separation of the immortal spiritual principle, from the mortal human principle, but the transfiguration of the whole man. This is not evolution, or development in the naturalist sense. Development is the result of deficiency, of inability to attain to completeness, and it is subordinate to the power of time, it is a process of becoming within time, and not creativeness which conquers time.

Insufficiency, deficiency, dissatisfaction, aspiration towards something greater have a twofold character; there is a lower and a higher condition of man. Wealth may be a false fulfilment, and a false liberation from slavery. The passing from deficiency to completeness, from poverty to riches, may be evolution and show itself from without as evolution. But behind this there is concealed a deeper process, a process of creativeness, a process of freedom which breaks through determinism. Victory over death cannot be evolution, cannot be a result of necessity. Victory over death is creativeness, the united creativeness of man and God, it is a result of freedom. The tension and passion of life attract to death and are linked with death. In the turning wheel of the world of nature, life and death cannot be torn asunder, 'And may young life play at the entrance of the tomb'. The tension of life's passion in itself attracts to death because it is enclosed

[252]

in the finite, it does not issue forth into the infinite eternal. Eternal life is attained not by mortifying and destroying the passionate tension of life, but by its spiritual transfiguration, by the control of its creative activity of spirit. The rejection of immortality is weariness, a refusal of activity.

Creativeness is liberation from slavery. Man is free when he finds himself in a state of creative activity. Creativeness leads to ecstasy of the moment. The products of creativeness are within time, but the creative act itself lies outside time. Thus also every heroic act leads outside time. It is possible for the heroic act not to be subordinate to any end and to be the ecstasy of the moment. But pure heroism may be a lure arising from pride and self-assertion. It was so that Nietzsche understood heroism. So also does Malraux understand it. Man can experience various forms of liberating ecstasy. There can be the ecstasy of conflict, erotic ecstasy, there can be the ecstasy of wrath, in which man feels himself capable of destroying the world. There is the ecstasy of sacrificial service taken upon oneself—the ecstasy of the Cross. This is the Christian ecstasy. Ecstasy is always an issuing from a state in which man is shackled and enslaved, an emergence into a moment of freedom. But ecstasy can bestow a fictitious liberation and once more lead to a still greater enslavement of man. There are ecstasies which remove the boundaries of personality and plunge personality into the formless cosmic element. Spiritual ecstasy is characterized by this, that in it personality is not destroyed but strengthened. In ecstasy personality must issue from itself, but in issuing from itself, remain itself. There is the same enslavement in being confined within itself and in being dissolved in the formless world element. Here are the temptation of individualism and the opposite temptation of cosmic and social collectivism.

In the spiritual liberation of man there is movement in the direction of freedom, truth and love. Freedom cannot be vain and lead to no result. 'Ye shall know the truth and the truth shall make you free'. But the knowledge of truth presupposes freedom. Knowledge of truth which is not free, is not only valueless, it is also impossible. But freedom also presupposes the existence of truth, of meaning, of God. Truth and meaning liberate, and again liberation leads to truth,

[253]

and meaning. Freedom must be loving and love must be free. It is only the gathering together of freedom, truth and love which realizes personality, free and creative personality. The exclusive affirmation of one of these principles only always introduces distortion, and injures human personality. Each one of the principles can in and by itself be a source of seduction and slavery. Freedom which is given a wrong direction may be a source of slavery. In the objectivization of the spirit the higher is dragged downwards and adjusted; but in creative incarnation of spirit the lower matter of this world is raised, and a change takes place in world data.

Human consciousness is subject to a variety of illusions in understanding the relation between this world in which man feels himself to be in a state of servitude, and the other world in which he awaits his liberation. Man is the point of intersection of two worlds. One of the illusions consists in interpreting the difference between the two worlds as a difference of substance. In actual fact it is a difference in mode of existence. Man passes from slavery to freedom, from a state of disintegration to a condition of completeness, from impersonality to personality, from passivity to creativeness, that is to say he passes over to spirituality. This world is the world of objectivization, of determinism, of alienation, of hostility, of law. While the other world is the world of spirituality, of freedom, love, kinship.

Another illusion of consciousness lies in this that the relations between the two worlds are understood as absolute objectivized transcendence. In this case the transition from one world to the other is passively awaited and the activity of man has no part to play. In actual fact the other world, the world of spirituality, the Kingdom of God, is not only awaited, it is constructed also by the creativeness of man, it is the creative transfiguration of a world which is exposed to the malady of objectivization. It is spiritual revolution. That other world cannot be established by human strength only, but also it cannot be established without the creative activity of man. This brings me to the problem of eschatology, to the problem of the end of history, and it means the liberation of man from his slavery to history.

2. THE LURE AND SLAVERY OF HISTORY. THE THREE KINDS OF TIME. THE TWOFOLD INTERPRETATION OF THE END OF HISTORY. ACTIVE-CREATIVE ESCHATOLOGY

The greatest of all forms of the seduction and slavery of man is connected with history. The solidity of history and the apparent magnificence of the processes which go on in history impose upon man and overawe him to an unusual degree. He is crushed by history and consents to be a tool for the accomplishment of history, to be made use of by the artfulness of reason. (Hegel's *List der Vernünft*.)

Of the tragic conflict between personality and history and of the fact that it finds no decision within the limits of history, I have already spoken. It is now necessary to consider this subject in the light of eschatology. What are called historical personalities enter actively into history, but in actual fact history takes no notice of personality, of its individual unrepeatability, its uniqueness and irreplaceability. It is interested in the 'common' even at such times as it turns its attention to the individual. History is made for the average man and for the masses, but for history the average man is an abstract unit and not a concrete being. Every average man is turned into a means to serve the interests of average humanity. History, so to speak, does not pursue human purposes, although man acts in it, it takes its stand under the banner of the power of the 'common' and universal over the particular and individual. Man is compelled to bear the burden of history, he cannot move out of history and throw it from him, his destiny is realized in it. It is not the case that the history of mankind is part of the history of the natural world, but the history of the natural world is a part of history. The meaning of world life is revealed in history, not in nature. A sharp collision takes place in history between freedom and necessity, between subject and object. In history freedom itself is turned into fate. Christianity is profoundly historical, it is the revelation of God in history. God enters into history and makes known the meaning of its movement. Metahistory breaks through into history and everything significant in history is connected with this break-through of metahistory. But the metahistorical is connected with the historical and is disclosed in it. History is the meeting, the dialogue and the struggle of man with God. And at the same time a large part of history is nothingness and non-being, fictitious greatness, and but rarely does authentic existence break through into it.

Spirit breaks through into history and acts in it but in its historical objectivization it becomes alienated from itself, and exhausted, it passes over into something unlike itself. To human consciousness history is inconsistent and calls forth a twofold relation to itself. Man not only accepts the burden of history, not only carries on a conflict with it, and realizes his destiny, but he has a tendency to deify history, to regard the processes which take place in it as sacred. And here begins the lure and slavery of history. Man is ready to bow the knee before historical necessity, historical fate, and to see in it divine activity. Historical necessity becomes a criterion of values and the consciousness of this necessity is regarded as the only freedom. The lure of history is the lure of objectivization. Hegel was, so to speak, a philosophical incarnation of the spirit of history, of the genius of history. To him history was the conquering march of the spirit towards freedom. And although the category of freedom played an immense rôle with Hegel and he even defined spirit as freedom, his philosophy was a consistent and radical logical determinism (logical determinism is not less enslaving to man than naturalistic determinism). Hegel wanted to instil into man the judgment that slavery to history is freedom. The influence of Hegel's historiolatry was immense, in a notable degree it determined Marxism too, which also has been seduced by historical necessity. To history, Hegel subordinated not only man, but God—God is the creation of history—there is such a thing as a divine becoming. At the same time this means that it is necessary to bow down before the conquerors of history, to acknowledge the rightness of everyone who triumphs.

The above view of history as a philosophical outlook upon the world, leads to a collision with absolute values, it inevitably affirms relativity, the relativity of good and the relativity of truth. The artfulness of historical reason dominates all values. This poisons Marxist ethics too. Man with all the values he holds dear, is turned into the material of history, of historical necessity, which is at the same time the historical logos. Man is fated to live within the historical whole and from it to derive the meaning of his own existence which stands superior to daily routine, even though his own existence should be crushed by this whole. But a higher truth lies in this—that the whole should live in man. The artfulness of reason in history becomes the greatest of lies, and the crucifixion of truth which is in it. There is criminality in history, lying at the base of its 'great events', and this criminality which torments man, points to the fact that there must come an end to history and that only through that end will all truth and right be realized.

There is a meaninglessness in history which points to a meaning which lies beyond the limits of history. This nonsense is often called the reason of history. Belinsky, among us, rebelled against the universal spirit of history, at one moment of his career. Dostoyevsky also rebelled, and so did Kirkegaard and everyone who is on the side of personalism ought so to rebel. Christianity itself was made captive and enslaved by the universal spirit of history, it was adjusted to historical necessity and it announced this adjustment as divine truth. For this reason the eschatology of Christianity was enfeebled and blunted, Christian eschatology appeared to be a 'tactless' and 'indelicate' thing, which affronts reason and demands the impossible. This poses in an acute form the problem of the relation between eschatology and history. But the philosophical problem of history is first of all a problem of time. The deification of history is the deification of historical time.

The problem of time occupies a position at the centre of present day philosophy. It is enough to name Bergson and Heidegger. This problem has a special significance for a philosophy of the existential type. The philosophy of history is to a considerable extent the philosophy of time. History is linked with time. To speak of time, is not always to speak of one and the same thing. Time has a variety of meanings and it is needful to make distinctions. There are three times: cosmic time, historical time; and existential time, and every man lives in these three forms of time. Cosmic time is symbolized by the circle. It is connected with the motion of the earth round the sun, with the reckoning of days, months, and years, with the calendar and the clock. This is a circular movement in which a return is constantly taking place, morning comes and evening, spring and autumn. This is nature's time, and as natural beings we live in this time. The Greeks were primarily concerned with the apprehension of cosmic time; among them the aesthetic contemplation of the cosmos predominated, and they almost failed to apprehend historical time. Time is not by any means a sort of eternal and congealed form into which the existence of the world and of man is placed. Not only does change in time exist, but the change of time itself is possible. A turning back of time is possible, and also an end of time; there will be no more time. Time is a mode of existence, and depends upon the character of existence.

It is not true to say that movement and change take place because time exists; it is true to say that time exists because movement and change take place. The character of change is the origin of the character of time. Cosmic time is one of the effects of change in a world which is natural in an objectivized way. Cosmic time is objectivized time, and it is subject to mathematical calculation; it is subject to number, to division into parts and to aggregation. Hours and days are divided into minutes and seconds and are aggregated into months and years. The second of cosmic time, which is at the same time mathematical time, is the atom of divisible time. Cosmic time is rhythmic time, but at the same time it is the time which is torn apart into present, past and future. The objectivized world is the world to which time belongs, and this imprint of temporality which time has left upon it denotes also a malady of time. Time which is torn apart into past, present and future is time which is diseased, and it does an injury to human existence. Death is connected with the disease of time. Time inevitably leads on to death, it is a mortal disease. Natural life, cosmic life in natural cosmic time rests upon the alternating change of birth and death. It knows a periodic spring of the revival of life but that revival takes place not for those whom death has carried away, but for others. Victory over death is impossible in cosmic time. The present, which cannot be seized because it falls between the past and the future, annihilates the past in order to be itself annihilated by the future. In cosmic time the realm of life is subject to death, although the engendering power of life is

[258]

inexhaustible. Cosmic time is death-dealing not for the race but for personality; it desires no knowledge of personality and takes no interest in its fate.

But man is a being who lives in several dimensions of time, in several spheres of existence. Man is not only a cosmic natural being, subject to cosmic time which moves in cycles. Man is also a historical being. Historical life is actuality of another order than nature. History, of course, is subject to cosmic time also, it knows reckoning by years and centuries, but it knows also its own historical time. Historical time comes into being through movement and change of another sort than that which occurs in the cosmic cycle. Historical time is symbolized not by the circle but by the straight line stretching out forwards. The special property of historical time is precisely this stretching out towards what is coming, this reaching forward to determine. In what is coming it waits for the disclosure of a meaning. Historical time brings novelty with it; in it that which was not becomes that which was. It is true that in historical time also there is return and repetition; resemblances can be established. But every event in historical time is individually particular, every decade and century introduces new life. And the very conflict against historical time, against the lure and slavery of history takes place not in cosmic but in historical time. Historical time has a closer connection with human activity than cosmic time. But personality is wounded and enslaved by historical time in a new way, and at times it even looks to a transition to the cosmic sphere of existence for deliverance from the captivity of history. The Divine figures in the cosmos more than in history, but in the cosmos into which man breaks through objectivized nature and objectivized time. The time of history is also objectivized time, but there is a break-through in it from a deeper stratum of human existence.

Historical time strains forward in determination towards what is coming. That is one region which brings it into being. But there is another region also. Historical time is also connected with the past and with tradition which establishes a link between periods of time. Without that memory and that tradition in the inner sense of the word there is no history. 'The historical' is constituted by memory and tradition. Historical time is at once conservative and revolutionary,

but this fact does not reach down as far as the final deeps of existence, which do not belong to historical time. Historical time gives
birth to illusions; the search in the past for what is better, truer,
more beautiful, more perfect (the illusion of the conservatiye) or
the search in the future for the fullness of achievement and the
perfection of meaning (the illusion of progress). Historical time is
time which is torn to pieces. It does not find completeness in any
kind of present (the past and the future are always a kind of present
at the same time). In the present man does not feel the fullness of time,
and he seeks it in the past or in the future, especially in periods of
history which are transitional and full of suffering. This is the seductive illusion of history. The present in which there is fullness and
perfection is not a part of time, but an emergence from time, not an
atom of time, but an atom of eternity, as Kirkegaard says. That
which is experienced in the depth of this existential moment remains.
The successive moments which enter into the sequence of time and
represent a less profound reality, pass away.

In addition to cosmic time and historical time, which are objectivized and subordinate to number, though in different ways, there is
also existential time, profound time, Existential time must not be
thought of in complete isolation from cosmic and historical time, it
is a break-through of one time into the other. *Kairos*, about which
Tillich is fond of speaking, is, as it were, the irruption of eternity into
time, an interruption in cosmic and historical time, an addition to
and a fulfilment of time. With this is connected the messianic
prophetic consciousness which out of the depth of existential time
speaks about historical time.

Existential time may be best symbolized not by the circle nor by
the line but by the point. That is precisely what is meant by saying
that existential time can least of all be symbolized by extension. This
is inward tme, not exteriorized in extension, not objectivized. It is
the time of the world of subjectivity, not objectivity. It is not com-
puted mathematically, it is not summed up nor divided into parts.
The infinity of existential time is a qualitative infinity, not a quantitative. A moment of existential time is not subject to number, it is
not a fractional part of time in a sequence of moments of objectivized
time. A moment of existential time is an emergence into eternity. It

[260]

would be untrue to say that existential time is identical with eternity, but it may be said that it is a participant in several moments of eternity. Every man knows from his own inward experience that he is a participant in several of his own moments of eternity. The protraction of existential time has nothing in common with the protraction of objectivized time, cosmic or historical. This protraction depends upon the intensity of experience within human existence. Minutes which are short from the objective point of view may be lived through as an infinity, and an infinity in opposite directions, in the direction of suffering and in the direction of joy and triumphant rapture. Every state of ecstasy leads out from the computation of objectivized mathematical time and leads into existential qualitative infinity. One moment may be eternity, another moment may be an evil and repellent endlessness. The fact that those who are happy do not keep a watchful eye upon the clock, indicates an emergence from mathematical time, a forgetfulness of clocks and calendars. The greater part of men's life is unhappy and is, therefore, chained to mathematical time. Suffering is a phenomenon of the existential order, but it is objectivized in mathematical time and appears to be infinite in the quantitative sense of the word.

The monstrous and absurd doctrine of the eternal pains of Hell has its roots in the existential experience of suffering and is the result of confusing existential time with time which is objectivized and mathematically calculable. Man experiences the torments of Hell as infinite, having no end; this is a token of very severe torment. But this illusory endlessness has nothing in common with eternity, in fact it just denotes the experience of being present in time which is evil and repellent, and the impossibility of getting out of it into eternity. Tormenting subjectivity assumes forms of ontological objectivity. Everything which is accomplished in existential time, is accomplished along a vertical line, not a horizontal. In terms of the horizontal line it is only a point, at which the break-through takes place out of the depth on to the surface. Events in existential time appear as a line along a horizontal flat surface as a result of the movement of these points which are connected with the break-through out of the depth. This is the exteriorizing of what is not subject to exteriorization, the objectivization of what is not expressible in an object.

[261]

Every creative act is performed in existential time and is merely projected in historical time. The creative impulse and ecstasy is outside objectivized and mathematical time, it does not take place on a flat surface, on the level of the mediocrity of our life, it happens vertically, not horizontally. But the result of the creative act is exteriorized in the time stream of history. The existential breaks through in the historical and the historical in return acts upon the existential. Everything significant and great in history, everything authentically new is a break-through in the existential plane, in creative subjectivity. The emergence of every notable man in history is a phenomenon of that kind. In history, therefore, there is an interruption due to this break-through, there is no continuous uninterrupted process. Within history there is metahistory, which is not a product of historical evolution. There is the miraculous in history. The miraculous is not explicable by historical evolution and the reign of law in history; it is the break-through of events which belong to existential time into historical time, which does not contain these events to the full. The revelation of God in history also is this irruption of events belonging to existential time. The full significance of an event in the life of Christ moved in existential time; in historical time it only shines through the burdensome environment of objectivization. The metahistorical is never contained in the historical, history always distorts metahistory in adjusting it to itself.

The final victory of metahistory over history, of existential time over historical, would denote the end of history. In the religious scheme of things this would mean the coincidence of the first coming of Christ with the second. Between the first and the second metahistorical appearance of Christ lies the tenseness of historical time in which man passes through all the lures and enslavements. This tense historical time cannot of itself come to an end, it streams out towards an infinity which is never converted into eternity. There are two ways out of historical time, in two opposite directions, towards cosmic time and towards existential time. The submersion of historical time in cosmic time is the way out for naturalism, which may take on a mystical colour. History returns to nature, and enters into the cosmic cycle. The other way is the submersion of historical time in existential time. This is the way out taken by eschatology.

History passes into the realm of the freedom of the spirit. And a philosophy of history is always in the last resort either naturalistic, even though it makes use of the categories of spirit, or it is eschatological.

Historical time with everything that happens in it, has a meaning, but that meaning lies outside the limits of historical time itself, it is to be seen in an eschatological perspective. History is the failure of spirit, the Kingdom of God is not realized or expressed in it. But that very failure itself has a meaning. The great testing trials of man and the experience of the seductive lures through which he lives have a meaning. Without them the freedom of man would not have been fully tested and proved. But an optimistic theory of progress is not to be relied upon and it is in profound conflict with personalism. Progress remains entirely at the mercy of death-dealing time. Philosophy has never seriously faced the problem of the end of history and of the world; even theology has not given enough serious attention to it. The problem consists in the question, is time conquerable? It is conquerable only if it be the case that it is not an objective form, but is only the outcome of existence which is alienated from itself. In that case the break-through from the depth can put an end to time and overcome objectivization. But this break-through from the depth cannot be the work of man alone, it is also the work of God, it is the combined work of man and God, a divine-human action. Here we come face to face with the most difficult problem of the action of God's Providence in the world and upon the world. The whole mystery here lies in the fact that God does not act in the determined arrangement of things which belongs to objectivized nature. He acts only in freedom, only through the freedom of man.

Apocalypse is connected with the paradox of time, and in this lies the extraordinary difficulty of its explanation. And indeed to tell the truth the interpretation of the symbolism of apocalypse is to a large extent a futile occupation. I have not the smallest intention of giving an exposition of apocalypse, I only wish to state the philosophical problem of the end of history. In this connection the paradox of time consists in this, that the end of history is thought of as taking place in time, while at the same time the end of history is the end of time, that

[263]

is to say the end of historical time. The end of history is an event of existential time. And at the same time we must not think of this event as being outside history. The end of history, which is accomplished in existential time, happens both 'in the next world' and 'in this world'. The end of history cannot be objectivized, and that is what makes it difficult to understand and explain. Everything important which occurs in existential time appears in historical time as a paradox.

There are two ways of understanding apocalypse, a passive way and an active. In the history of Christian consciousness the former way has always been predominant. There has been a passive foreboding of and a passive waiting for the end of the world; it is determined exclusively by God, judgment upon the world is divine judgment only. On the other view, the end of the world is actively, creatively prepared by man; it depends upon the activity of man also, that is to say it will be a result of divine-human work. Passive waiting for the end is accompanied by the feeling of terror. On the other hand the active preparation of the end is conflict and may be accompanied by the feeling of triumph. The apocalyptic consciousness may be conservative and reactionary and such it frequently has been; and it may be revolutionary and creative, and that is what it ought to be. Apocalyptic forebodings of the coming end of the world have been terribly misused. Every historical epoch which is drawing to a close, every social class which is coming to an end, readily connects its own demise with the coming of the end of the world. The French Revolution and the Napoleonic wars were accompanied by manifestations of such an apocalyptic frame of mind. The end of Imperial Russia, of which many people had a presentiment, was attended by signs of an apocalyptic state of thought. Solovyev and Leontiev represent the type of passive apocalyptic consciousness. Feodorov represents the active type of apocalyptic consciousness. Feodorov's active interpretation of apocalypse showed the audacity of genius, in spite of the fact that his philosophy was unsatisfactory. The conservative apocalyptic consciousness has a feeling of horror when faced by the ruin of things which present themselves as historical sanctities. The revolutionary apocalyptic consciousness actively and creatively turns to the realization of human personality and to the society which is linked with the principle of personality. An active relation to the end of history presupposes a more or less prolonged period of change in the structure of consciousness, a spiritual and social revolution even in historical time, which cannot be brought about by human efforts only, but also cannot be achieved without human effort or by passive waiting. The outpouring of the Spirit, which changes the world, is the activity of the spirit in man himself. The activity of man to which Feodorov summoned men is an immense step forward in Christian consciousness. But with Feodorov the structure of consciousness is not changed; he does not state the problem of the relation of the subject to objectivization. Spiritual revolution, which prepares the end, will be to a notable degree a victory over the illusions of consciousness. Active eschatology is the justification of the creative power of man. Man is liberated from the sway of the objectivization which had enslaved him. And then the problem of the end of history will present itself in a new aspect. The end of history is the victory of existential time over historical time, of creative subjectivity over objectivization, of personality over the universal-common, of existential society over objectivized society.

Objectivization always places man in subjection to the finite, chains him to the finite, and at the same time precipitates him into the perspective of quantitative, mathematical infinity. The end of history is liberation from the sway of the finite, and the opening out of the perspective of qualitative infinity, i.e. eternity. Active eschatology is directed against objectivization and the false identification of incarnation with objectivization. Christianity is in its very nature eschatological, eschatological in the revolutionary sense, but not ascetic. And the denial of the eschatological character of Christianity has always led to its adaptation to the conditions of the objectivized world, to its capitulation in the face of historical time. Objectivization gives rise to a whole series of illusions of consciousness, sometimes conservative and reactionary, sometimes revolutionary and utopian. Thus the projection of world harmony into the future which we see in the religion of progress, is an illusion of consciousness. That which can only be thought of in existential time (the end of time, of historical time) is thought of in a fragment broken off

[265]

historical time (the future). This was where the dialectical genius of Ivan Karamazov which was so much admired by Belinsky, came from, about the return to God of the ticket of admission to world harmony. It is a protest against objectivization.

The identification of the Church with the Kingdom of God, of the historical idea of the Church with the eschatological idea of the Kingdom of God, which derives from St. Augustine, is also one of the illusions born of the objectivized consciousness. It is as a consequence of this that historical objectivizations, such as the Church considered as a social institution, the theocratic state, and ossified forms of life, have been not only regarded as sacrosanct, but have even been actually deified. True chiliasm, that is to say, the hope of the coming of the Kingdom of God not only in heaven but also on earth, has been rejected, and a false chiliasm, as it were, has triumphed and hallowed something which is too earthly and too human, and which belongs exclusively to historical time. But actively creative events in existential time will have their effects not only in heaven but on earth also; they revolutionize history. The illusions of consciousness upon which the so-called 'objective world' rests can be conquered. The creative power of man as it changes the structure of consciousness, can be not only a consolidation of this world, not only a culture, but also a liberation of the world, and the end of history, that is to say, the establishment of the Kingdom of God, not as a symbolic but as a real kingdom. The Kingdom of God denotes not only redemption from sin and a return to original purity, but the creation of a new world. Every authentic creative act of man enters into it, every real act of liberation. It is not only the other world, it is this world transfigured. It is the liberation of nature from captivity, it is the liberation of the animal world also, for which man is answerable. And it begins now, at this moment. The attainment of spirituality, the will to truth and right, to liberation, is already the beginning of the other world. And with it there is no estrangement between the creative act and the creative product; the creative product is to be found, so to speak, in the creative act itself; it is not exteriorized; the very creative power itself is incarnation.

Personality rebels against its enslavement by the common-universal, and the object world, against false sanctities, created by

[266]

objectivization, against the necessity of nature, against the tyranny of society. But it takes upon itself the responsibility for the destiny of all, of all nature, of all living creatures, of all the suffering and all the humiliated, of the whole people, and of all peoples. Personality lives through the whole history of the world, as its own history. Man ought to rebel against the slavery of history not for the sake of finding isolation within his own self, but in order to take all history into his own infinite subjectivity, in which the world is part of man.

The resultant and consistent demand of personalism, when thought out to the end, is a demand for the end of the world and of history, not a passive waiting for this end in fear and anguish, but an active, creative preparation for it. This is a radical change in the direction of consciousness, it is setting consciousness free from illusions which have taken the form of objective realities. Indeed victory over objectivization is precisely a victory of realism over illusionism, over a symbolism which gives itself out to be realism. It is also liberation from the nightmare illusion of the eternal torments of Hell, which holds man in slavery; it is to overcome the false objectivization of Hell, the false dualism of Hell and Paradise which belongs entirely to objectivized time. The path which man has to tread in this life lies through suffering, the cross and death, but it leads on towards resurrection. Nothing but a universal resurrection of everything that lives and has lived can reconcile us to the world process. Resurrection means victory over time, it means change not only of the future but also of the past. In cosmic and in historical time this is impossible, but it is possible in existential time. In this is to be found the meaning of the coming of a Redeemer and of One Who brings men back from the dead. It does great honour to man that it is impossible for him to be reconciled to corruption and death, to the final disappearance both of himself and of every creature in the past, the present and the future.

Everything which is not eternal is unendurable, everything of value in life if it is not eternal, loses its value. But in cosmic and in historical time, in nature and in history, everything passes away, everything disappears. Therefore, that time must come to an end. There will be no more time. The servitude of man to time, to necessity, to death, to the illusions of consciousness, will disappear. Everything will enter into the authentic reality of subjectivity and spirituality, into the divine, or rather the divine-human life. But a stern conflict lies ahead, and it demands sacrifice and suffering. There is no other way. The Kingdom of God is not reached by contemplation alone. Proust, to whom the problem of the passing away of time was a torturing experience, desired to turn time back, to restore life to the past by way of creative artistic memory, by way of passive aesthetic contemplation. This was an illusion although it has links with something which lies very deep. Feodorov desired to conquer death, to turn time back and change the past by way of the 'public undertaking' of active resurrection. This was a great and a Christian idea; but it was not sufficiently connected with the problem of personality and freedom, with the problem of the victory of consciousness over objectivization. The slavery of man is his Fall, his sin. This Fall has its own structure of consciousness, it is conquered not only by repentance and redemption from sin, but by the activity of all the creative powers of man. When man does that to which he is called, then only will the Second Coming of Christ take place, and then there will be a new heaven and a new earth and the kingdom of freedom will come.